# Boatowner's
# *Legal and Financial*
# Advisor

# Boatowner's
# *Legal and Financial*
# Advisor

| | ✣ | |

## Larry V. Rogers

**International Marine**
*Camden, Maine*

*International Marine/*
**Ragged Mountain Press**
A Division of The **McGraw-Hill** *Companies*

10  9  8  7  6  5  4  3

Copyright © 1994 Larry V. Rogers.
All rights reserved. The publisher takes no responsibility for
the use of any of the materials or methods described in this
book, nor for the products thereof. The name "International
Marine" and the International Marine logo are trademarks of
The McGraw-Hill Companies. Printed in the United States of
America.

*Library of Congress Cataloging-in-Publication Data*
Rogers, Larry V.
    Boatowner's legal and financial advisor / Larry V. Rogers.
        p.   cm.
    Includes index.
    ISBN 0-07-158007-7 (acid-free paper)
    1. Boats and boating--Law and legislation--United States.
2. Inland navigation--Law and legislation--United States. 3.
Maritime law--United States. 4. Boats and boating--United
States--Finance. I. Title.
KF2558.P5R64      1994
343.73'096--dc20
[347.30396]                            93-39286
                                         CIP

Questions regarding the content of this book should be
addressed to:
International Marine
P.O. Box 220; Camden, ME  04843
207-236-4837


Questions regarding the ordering of this book should be
addressed to:
The McGraw-Hill Companies; Customer Service Department
P.O. Box 547; Blacklick, OH  43004
Retail customers: 1-800-262-4729; Bookstores: 1-800-722-4726

*Boatowner's Legal and Financial Advisor* is printed on recycled
paper containing a minimum of 50% total recycled fiber with
10% postconsumer de-inked fiber.

Printed by R.R. Donnelley, Crawfordsville, IN
Design by Joyce C. Weston
Production by Molly Mulhern
Edited by Jonathan Eaton, Patricia Miller, and Pamela Benner

# Contents

# Preface

| | ❖ | |

*Discourage litigation. Persuade your neighbors to compromise whenever you can. Point out to them how the nominal winner is often a real loser—in fees, expenses, and waste of time.*

—Abraham Lincoln

Abraham Lincoln gave good advice. When possible, solve disputes through arbitration or mediation. Unfortunately, the likelihood of a recreational boater being involved in a lawsuit is growing, as our already-litigious society goes to sea; recreational boaters now face rapidly growing numbers of increasingly complex and stringent regulations.

In *Boatowner's Legal and Financial Advisor* I've attempted to present a complex and unappealing subject in a nonthreatening, easy-to-comprehend form, devoid of convoluted legalese. I have neither the qualifications nor the space to give specific legal advice for every situation. Rather, my intent is to provide a broad understanding of boating law—a frame of reference within which your rights and obligations as circumstances unfold will be clearer and, hopefully, more logical. Sample agreements in the appendixes provide more specific advice for several of the most common legal needs of boaters.

My hope is that the issues covered won't undermine the enjoyment we recreational boaters feel out on the water. In fact, a dose of reality and an understanding of how the law affects us may help us all enjoy boating a little more. After reading this book, I hope you'll be better prepared and less uncertain, not only on the water but when you have to approach your lawyer or accountant to discuss buying a boat, chartering your boat, or defending yourself against a lawsuit. You'll know what questions to ask, and what your responsibilities and rights are.

I'd like to thank Gerwin McFarland for his help with the chapter on insurance, and Chief Warrant Officer Wesley R. Orvis of the Maritime Law Enforcement Section of the 13th Coast Guard District in Seattle for educating me about Coast Guard law-enforcement efforts. Any errors of interpretation are mine, however. Thanks also to Patricia Miller for editing the manuscript.

Finally, Susan, thank you for your love, support, and understanding.

Larry V. Rogers
*Olympia, Washington*
*September 1993*

# 1

# An Introduction to
# Admiralty Law

| | ✣ | |

As a recreational boater, your chances of seeing the inside of a federal courtroom in an admiralty lawsuit are relatively small. But every boater should know what admiralty law is and how it affects his or her world on the water.

Suppose you purchased a new boat that proved defective—its hull developed blisters in the first season, or the bulkhead cracked, or the engine was out of alignment, or the engine bed cracked, or the keel fell off—and the dealer or builder refused to offer redress. If you decided to sue, you would more than likely find yourself in state court or working with your state's consumer protection division, not in federal admiralty court. Suppose your 16-year-old boat developed blisters, you hired a yard to do the repairs, the blisters reappeared within a year, and the yard refused to offer redress. Again, if you sued, you would probably find yourself in state court rather than federal admiralty court. Vessel purchase or sales problems are seen in state court, as are violations of state boating laws.

As long as admiralty jurisdiction applies, a personal-injury case has an equal chance of being heard in federal admiralty court as in a state court, whether or not the injured party is declared a seaman (see "Savings-to-Suitors Clause" on page 9). Salvage matters are handled in admiralty court.

Probably the most common situation that draws recreational boaters into admiralty court is the hidden lien on a boat being purchased, although such liens are more common on larger boats than on those smaller than, say, 16 feet in length. Hidden liens are discussed in depth in Chapter 9. Knowing about admiralty law may help recreational boaters avoid rough waters.

## The History and Development of Admiralty and Maritime Law

Admiralty law is one of the oldest bodies of law in the world, yet it provides modern mariners with one of the few codes of law that is applied almost universally today.

Scholars believe admiralty law developed from seagoing trade between countries surrounding the Mediterranean and Arabian seas and the Persian Gulf nearly four thousand years ago. The Code of Hammurapi (Hammurabi), written about 1800 B.C., contains provisions for chartering and for collisions between ships. Early Egyptian paintings show large vessels capable of transporting both goods and passengers. Egyptian ships carrying cedar and other products called at ports in the eastern Mediterranean, and later the Greeks and Phoenicians established trading settlements throughout the Mediterranean basin. The Romans adopted the maritime law of the Greeks.

Maritime commerce forced early lawmakers to develop rules for the resolution of disputes between ships from different countries, while at the same time those laws had to accommodate the transient nature of maritime commerce.

The Rhodian Sea Code is the earliest set of maritime laws of which we have written record. Probably written in the eighth century, this three-part compilation is believed to be Byzantine in origin. It covered many topics that are still pertinent today, such as maritime loans, partnerships, theft of goods, injuries to crew, profit sharing among members of the ship's company, space allotted for passengers, and the captain's liability limit for passengers' loss of valuables.

During the Middle Ages, the Italians played a major role in the development of maritime law. They wrote the Ordinance of Trani and the Tables of Amalfi, both around the year 1000 A.D. Although these laws modified the Rhodian Sea Code to suit the Italians' needs, they also introduced the use of special judges who were trained in maritime matters so they could better decide these special kinds of disputes.

As trade expanded between Aquitaine, England, and Flanders, another early sea code, the Rolls (Rules) of Oleron gained more importance. The Rolls were adopted by the seaports of Normandy and Brittany, and they gave rise to other codes that would be applied throughout Europe. They became the foundation for maritime law in the North Sea and the Atlantic Ocean.

American maritime law has its foundation in British maritime practice, as do other American legal doctrines. In the 17th century, maritime cases in the then British colonies in North America were decided by local courts—usually by the governor and his court assistants. When matters between the colonies and England became strained, local courts refused to respond in the manner deemed appropriate by the Crown, and a series of vice-admiralty courts were established. The court staffs were appointed by the king.

After the American Revolution, each commonwealth or state exercised its own rules and laws. Because the various courts diverged in their treatment of similar matters, their results were inconsistent. The drafters of the United States Constitution realized the necessity of creating a system of national admiralty courts. Article III, section 2 of the Constitution granted the United States, and not the individual states, the power to handle "all cases of admiralty and maritime jurisdiction."

After the Constitution was adopted, a comprehensive body of law eventually developed from Article III, section 2, and early federal judges followed it enthusiastically. They gave the provision a wide reading, and, in their attempt to develop a uniform code for the maritime commerce that was so important to the newly developing United States, these federal judges held that all manner of matters were within their jurisdiction.

Because commerce on rivers, lakes, and canals in the first half of the 19th century was quite extensive, the U.S. Congress extended federal admiralty jurisdiction to include the Great Lakes and their connecting rivers. Around the middle of the 19th century, the remaining rivers and canals of the United States were added to that jurisdiction in decisions made by the U.S. Supreme Court.

A series of Supreme Court cases ruled that the individual state and local regulations must not conflict with federal law or interfere with the harmony and uniformity of admiralty jurisdiction, in regard to interstate commerce and broader issues as well. In accordance with this so-called commerce clause of the Constitution, interstate commerce is controlled by the federal government. The theory behind the Supreme Court's rulings is that state and local ordinances are intended for different purposes than are federal regulations. State and local ordinances are based on the *police power* to regulate conduct and preserve resources as may be necessary for the public welfare, which should not conflict with the federal regulation of commerce. The commerce clause is often used to justify the federal government's control over admiralty matters.

Although the federal umbrella encourages uniformity between state and federal laws, it has not prevented many states from enacting extensive laws, subject to the broad powers of the federal government, regulating vessel numbering and licensing, methods of operation, and equipment requirements.

Under state laws, pleasure boat owners or operators may be subject to criminal penalties while they operate on state waters. State laws also help determine fault in civil suits for damages. Through agencies created to administer boating laws, states may adopt additional regulations so long as they do not conflict with federal laws and do not burden interstate commerce.

Likewise, counties and municipalities may adopt laws or ordinances governing pleasure boating within their boundaries. In turn, these laws are invalid if they conflict with state or federal laws, or with laws that are specifically authorized through state law, or with the federal government's control over interstate commerce. If a state has preempted specific activities, a municipality may not pass laws that would also regulate those activities.

For example, a municipality may not pass a law requiring boats to carry equipment over and above that required by state law. Even if the state has not acted to remedy a particular problem, the state law prevails.

Despite the order of prevalence, some lower-level laws have created problems for boaters. Several California and Florida municipalities have tried to enforce local laws limiting the length of a boat's stay at anchor, but the disputes have escalated to state and federal levels. These attempts to limit anchoring are addressed in Chapter 5, the chapter about Boating Regulations.

It is possible, though exceedingly unlikely, for a boater to simultaneously violate three different laws and thus be subject to prosecution in three different courts. Also, because local variations still exist, judges presiding in different regions may come to differing conclusions when deciding nearly identical cases that concern admiralty law.

Fortunately, in an effort to encourage uniform laws, agreements have been made between various states and the U.S. Coast Guard to ensure cooperation in the enforcement of boating laws. Because court decisions from throughout the U.S. have shaped present-day admiralty law, no single comprehensive source can determine what "the law" is on many admiralty matters. Legal rulings continue to depend on the interplay of federal, state, and local laws and their interpretation by the courts.

## Admiralty Jurisdiction

Since the 1700s, judges have ruled that federal admiralty jurisdiction covers all incidents that involve vessels, both on the high seas and in all navigable waters of the United States, but basic definitions and legal interpretations have changed over time, causing much controversy. The debate over the degree to which admiralty law applies to recreational boating has troubled countless court decisions. Some courts will apply admiralty law to recreational boating, but not all decisions are clear-cut.

In borderline cases, courts first try to determine three criteria of admiralty tort (as opposed to contract) jurisdiction:

1. whether a vessel was involved;
2. whether the incident took place on navigable waters;
3. whether the case has a *maritime flavor.*

Definitions of "vessel" and "navigable waters" that were appropriate in the 1800s may not be appropriate today, and the definition of "maritime flavor" could be as ephemeral as the aroma of savory seafood. Because even the strictest definitions are subject to strenuous interpretation in a court of law, each of these three jurisdictional criteria raises as many questions as it answers.

For example, is an oil-drilling platform a vessel? If it is deemed a vessel when it is towed to a new drilling location, then is it still a vessel when it sits on the bottom of the Gulf of Mexico drilling for oil?

In the courts' effort to determine whether a structure is a "vessel," they developed what is commonly referred to as the "purpose" test. It asks: (a) Is it designed to be mobile and can it move across the water, whether or not under its own power? (b) Is it subject to the perils of the sea? (c) Is it designed to be permanently fixed in position? (d) Is calling it a vessel consistent with the law?

Floating dry docks and platforms, barges, and rafts used to repair piers, docks, bridges, and pipelines may or may not be considered vessels. Several factors, including the cause of the lawsuit, the statute under which the suit is filed, and the specific function of the barge, raft, or dry dock will determine whether it is deemed a vessel. Oil and gas platforms that are permanently fixed to the ocean floor are not vessels, but oil and gas exploration equipment that is designed to be moved on a regular basis falls under the "vessel" definition—for purposes of admiralty law.

In general, a "vessel" is defined by the federal statutes as "every description of watercraft or other artificial contrivance used, or capable of being used, as a means of transportation on water." Unfortunately, this broad definition allows different courts to interpret the term differently, creating inconsistencies between their outcomes.

Even the word "water" stirs up controversy in the context of the second criterion for admiralty jurisdiction. Although British admiralty law limits its own jurisdiction to the high seas or waters that are subject to the ebb and flow of the tide, in the U.S. the definition of "water" has more to do with commerce. To be subject to federal control, a vessel must be on waters—connected to the sea or not—that are used for or are capable of being used for interstate or foreign commerce.

In the U.S., navigable waters are waters that are usable in their natural state or are capable of being made navigable by the expenditure of a reasonable amount of money. When all court decisions have been distilled, the waters must:

• be physically connected to the open sea or the Great Lakes; *and*

• be usable or susceptible to use in marine shipping and commerce;
*or*
• lie between two or more states;
*or*
• be used for travel to or from a foreign nation.

For example, Lake Tahoe and Lake Mead are under federal jurisdiction, because they lie between the states of Nevada and California and Nevada and Arizona respectively, although not connected to the sea. Lake Okeechobee is under federal jurisdiction, because it is connected to the sea by the Caloosahatchee River and the St. Lucie Canal. Lake George is not under federal jurisdiction, because it lies wholly within the state of New York and has no connection to the sea.

The Coast Guard determines federal jurisdiction and publishes its findings in the regularly updated *Code of Federal Regulations*, published by the federal government. Look for a copy of this huge set of books, known as the CFRs, in the reference section of any local library. A scan of the books' indexes will yield the several chapters relevant to boatowners.

In addition to the CFRs list, court decisions have also held the following to be navigable waters: Allegheny River, Androscoggin River, Arkansas River, Bayou Segnette, Cape Fear River, Catahoula Lake, Chippewa River, Colorado River, Columbia River, Connecticut River, Cumberland River, Dale Hollow Lake, Delaware River, Des Moines River, Des Plaines River, Duck Creek, Ellicott Creek, Fox River, Hudson River, James River, Joyce Slough, Kansas River, Lake Champlain, Lake Coeur d'Alene, Lake Ferguson, Lake Gaston, Lake Tahoe, Lake Texoma, Lake Wylie, Maumee River, Miller's River, Mississippi River, Missouri River, Mohawk River, Monongahela River, Moyie River, Muskingum River, Navajo Lake, Niagra River, Norris Lake, Oconto River, Ohio River, Pacific Lake, Pine River, Pond Branch, Potomac River, Presque Isle Stream, Rappahannock River, Rock River, Sacramento River, Saginaw River, Seneca River, Susquehanna River, Suwannee River, Sweetwater Lake, Toledo Bend Lake, Wabash River, and Willow River. Just because a river or lake is not listed here does not mean that federal law does not govern it. The criteria of navigability and interstate commerce are the best guidelines.

Maritime flavor, the third criterion used for determining admiralty jurisdiction, can be found in cases that do not involve a vessel or occur on navigable waters. Maritime flavor is defined as "a significant relationship to traditional maritime activity."

Courts have found maritime flavor in cases involving events and transactions that were significant to the shipping industry, and when there was a need for national uniformity. Courts have even used historical decisions to show evidence of this elusive maritime flavor.

Despite controversial interpretations of the definitions of "vessel," "water," and "maritime flavor," the three broad criteria have been used to establish general guidelines for determining whether or not a particular case falls *in admiralty*, meaning within the jurisdiction of admiralty law. However, some cases in which admiralty law would seem to apply are decided differently by the courts.

For example, admiralty jurisdiction has not been applied to contracts for the purchase or sale of vessels, because the transaction usually takes place on land, not at sea. Nor does admiralty law apply to a boat or ship under construction, because the law historically does not recognize a vessel as a vessel until it is launched.

The line dividing admiralty from the rest of the world of law seems to meander in and out of common situations faced by boaters. Disputes that arise from the navigation of vessels or commerce on the water, including carrying goods and providing services to ships doing business on the water, are covered under admiralty law.

A contract to buy fish from a boatowner is not considered maritime. Although a contract for the repair of a vessel is in admiralty, a contract for rebuilding that same vessel is not. In a 1991 U.S. Supreme Court case, the judges ruled that agency contracts are no longer per se preempted from admiralty jurisdiction. Thus, a contract to place your boat with a yacht-charter brokerage house *might* fall in admiralty, but a charter agreement for the use of a yacht executed between the broker and the chartering party *will* fall in admiralty.

Admiralty jurisdiction also applies to legal wrongs, called *torts*, committed onboard vessels or concerning them. In a case involving the vessel *Plymouth* in 1866, the U.S. Supreme Court said: "Every species of tort, however occurring, and whether on board a vessel or not, if upon the high seas or navigable waters, is of admiralty cognizance."

When a drunken sailor rolled off a dock into the water and drowned, the court held that the case could be brought before an admiralty court. A person falling off a gangway while boarding a boat is also "in admiralty" even if that person never falls into the water, because—as the courts have said—the activity is related to traditional maritime activity.

However, a wrong must also have a maritime flavor before it is considered under admiralty law. When an airplane crashed into navigable waters, the U.S. Supreme Court said that, even though the crash occurred in navigable waters, admiralty jurisdiction did not apply—because the event had no connection to water commerce or traditional maritime activity.

### Savings-to-Suitors Clause

Article III of the U.S. Constitution stipulates that admiralty suits be filed in federal courts, but, thanks to a clause of the Federal Judiciary Act of 1789, the litigants in many admiralty suits may also resolve their disputes in state or local courts, or they may use nonjudicial methods called alternate dispute resolution or ADR.

Known as the *savings-to-suitors clause*, it says that, in all cases, suitors may also have the right to common law remedy where the common law is competent to give it. Therefore, any suitor has the option to bring his or her case into federal court or into a state court that applies admiralty law.

The generally higher cost of going to admiralty court might force you to file your suit in a lower court instead. It may be less expensive to get to a local court than to travel to a federal court some distance from your home. Arranging for witnesses to appear in federal court in another city also will involve more work and expense. Filing fees and other charges incurred during the course of a lawsuit may be less expensive in a local court. Appeals from federal-court decisions are more complex and involve significantly more money to pursue than do appeals from local or state courts.

Court costs are much higher when vessel seizure is involved; the party seizing the vessel must pay for its moorage and for keeping it secured while it is under arrest, and he or she must post a bond with the federal court to secure performance of these duties. Unfortunately, vessel seizure cases can only be heard in federal admiralty court.

Minor disputes may enable you to go to a local small-claims court, but you will likely forfeit your right to a jury trial.

Another option is alternative dispute resolution, discussed below; however, if you resolve a dispute outside the judicial process using arbitration or mediation, you usually have no right to appeal the decision, as you do in court. An admiralty lawyer can advise you on the best course in your case.

## Admiralty Law and Recreational Boating

Every year, thousands of new recreational boaters flock to our already crowded waterways, and our government struggles to control the ever-increasing fleet of recreational boats. In the past, many recreational boaters argued that admiralty law should not be applied to them or their boats. By turning to local attorneys who were not schooled in admiralty law, many resolved their problems without going to admiralty court.

In 1982, however, the Supreme Court ruled that admiralty jurisdiction can apply to recreational boating. The deciding case involved the collision of a 16-foot bassboat and an 18-foot pleasureboat that was towing a skier on the Amite River in Louisiana. The lower court ruled that there was no admiralty jurisdiction, because neither boat had been involved in commercial maritime operations, thus relying on traditional requirements for admiralty jurisdiction. The Supreme Court, however, held that because of the need for consistency in regulations—whether the activity is commercial or recreational—recreational boating should be included under the federal court's admiralty jurisdiction. Note, however, that a recreational boater involved in an incident on a landlocked lake might not be able to claim admiralty jurisdiction because the court tests for two factors: (1) Did the activity take place on navigable waters? and (2) did the activity have a maritime nature.

In a more recent case, however, the U.S. Supreme Court employed stiffer criteria for recreational boats and their inclusion in admiralty jurisdiction. In the case of Sisson versus Ruby (1990), the court again ruled that a recreational boatowner could bring his case into federal admiralty court after the lower courts ruled that he could not. They did so on the basis that the incident took place on navigable waters and involved a *traditional maritime activity*. For more on this case and the possible benefits of filing a suit in admiralty court, see Chapter 11, "Limitation of Liability."

## When to See a Lawyer

The complexity of admiralty law and its involvement in many jurisdictions have inspired lawyers around the country to specialize in it. They often represent shipping companies, ship owners, or insurance companies that write admiralty insurance policies. They may also represent seamen who have been injured while working aboard vessels and are seeking damages.

When to see a lawyer often depends on the size of the problem. Most lawyers are not interested in handling matters that the parties can handle themselves, nor cases that will cost more to handle than the solution warrants.

If your dispute involves less than a few hundred dollars, your lawyer should either recommend that you try to work out the dispute yourself or refer you to a local mediation service (discussed later in this chapter). The increasing availability of such services makes it possible to get inexpensive help without hiring a lawyer.

If your dispute involves more than a few hundred dollars, your lawyer should give you some guidance without charging you for the initial visit and be available to take charge if you feel you're in over your head.

If you are involved in a larger case, particularly involving potential liability, you or your insurance company should retain a lawyer. If you have a family lawyer, inquire about his or her background and experience in admiralty matters. If he or she has no admiralty experience, ask for a referral to a lawyer who has. Do not expect your family lawyer to make a quick study of admiralty law and represent you well, because admiralty lawsuits require specialized knowledge and prior experience. Many local bar associations have referral services, and you can check the Yellow Pages for lawyers who advertise under admiralty law.

When calling to inquire if an admiralty-law specialist is interested in representing you, don't be surprised if he or she is not. Many admiralty lawyers handle cases involving thousands, if not hundreds of thousands, of dollars, so your recreational boating case may seem minor in comparison.

It may take time to find a lawyer you're comfortable with and who will accept your case.

## Alternative Methods
## of Dispute Resolution

Your likelihood of being sued continues to grow. One lawsuit is filed for every 10 people in this country every year, and the figures are growing. Anyone who can pay a filing fee can file a lien or start a lawsuit, thereby tying up time and money that would be better spent elsewhere. It is estimated that Americans spend more than $300 billion annually on attorney services.

People seldom realize the emotional toll of going to court. The judicial system is characterized by delays, antiquated rules and rituals, unfamiliar language, and high emotional costs. Attorneys can inquire about your most private thoughts and actions. In some areas of this country, a case may not come to trial for five years. With appeals and other delays, a court battle can literally last a lifetime.

People concerned with this judicial gridlock are beginning to look for alternatives. For years, the construction industry has made a concerted effort to avoid going to court. Most large construction contracts now specify that any disputes arising during the life of the contract will be handled by arbitration, not litigation. Other areas of business are also turning to alternative dispute resolution techniques. Two of the most popular methods are *arbitration* and *mediation.*

### Arbitration

In arbitration, the parties to a dispute hire a neutral party to act as a private judge, and the case is decided outside the judicial system. The delays inherent in the judicial system can be avoided, and evidence can be presented without regard to the technical rules used in court. Arbitration can be private, without media attention, and can be scheduled for the convenience of the parties involved.

### Mediation

Mediation has been used successfully in the labor-relations field for years, and its use is now spreading to other areas of conflict. Mediation is fast, cheap, and private, and a growing number of mediation services are available around the country.

Mediation is sometimes referred to as "turbo-charged negotiation." The process is simple. The parties to a dispute simply engage an impartial third party to help them negotiate a settlement. Mediation is different from arbitration; in arbitration a neutral "judge" imposes a settlement on the parties, but in mediation the parties themselves, rather than the mediator, are responsible for the terms of the settlement.

In mediation, the parties to the dispute present their positions, and the mediator asks questions that help define the dispute. After a joint session, the parties meet individually with the mediator and explore settlement options, and the mediator plays devil's advocate. Since everyone agrees before mediation begins that all disclosures are confidential, parties can communicate matters to the mediator that have not been disclosed to the opposition. The mediator then talks alternately with all parties, testing ideas and exploring settlement options in order to reconcile their competing interests.

In a boating case, for example, if your mediator has experience in boating, less mediation time will probably be required. Because mediation is voluntary, it can be stopped at any time by any party. A mediation can last a few hours or several days, depending on the complexity of the dispute. Even multimillion-dollar construction disputes are often settled in less than a day.

Mediation is inexpensive when compared with the cost of lawyers and lawsuits. The charge for mediating a dispute concerning a few hundred dollars may be nominal—$5 to $25. Or the mediator may not charge at all. In more complex disputes involving a number of parties with thousands of dollars at issue, the mediator's fees are generally comparable to what a lawyer charges on an hourly or daily basis. Yet, while the mediation of a complex dispute may cost the parties a few thousand dollars, it is decidedly cheaper than paying lawyers to prepare interrogatories, attend depositions, argue motions, and hold conferences. Such tasks can amount to hundreds of hours of work, which is billed at rates exceeding $100 an hour—often much higher.

One of the amazing things about mediation is its success rate. Up to 90 percent of all mediations are successful. Even parties who don't settle can gain a better understanding of their chances of winning through arbitration or in a court of law. Compliance with mediated settlements is also higher than with judgments won in court.

### Arbitration and Mediation Services

A wide variety of mediation services is available in most parts of the country. They range from nonprofit community-based dispute resolution centers (DRCs) to specialized for-profit mediation services that employ mediators specially trained to handle all kinds of disputes, including landlord versus tenant, neighbor versus neighbor, consumer versus merchant, employer versus employee, family disputes, small commercial disputes, and community matters. Mediation services accept referrals from small claims courts and law-enforcement agencies. DRCs usually charge no, or very low, fees for mediation services—ranging up to $25 per party. Volunteers, who have typically taken part in an extensive training program, act as the mediators.

United States Arbitration & Mediation, which has offices in 40 cities throughout the country, arbitrates and mediates in all areas of the law except domestic matters, and all of its arbitrators and mediators are attorneys.

Judicial Arbitration & Mediation Services, Inc. (JAMS) uses only retired justices or judges. It handles a wide variety of disputes and can provide other types of alternate dispute resolution (ADR) services in addition to mediation. The organization was founded in 1979 and has offices throughout the West Coast.

The American Arbitration Association is the oldest and perhaps best known of the ADR organizations. Founded in 1926, this nonprofit organization offers arbitration and mediation services for all types of disputes. It provides administrative services to set up mediations using a national panel of qualified arbitrators and mediators. The panel includes retired judges, attorneys, and other professionals. AAA has 35 offices throughout the country.

Many firms and governmental organizations are looking to mediation as the primary means of resolving disputes. More than 350 of the country's largest corporations, from American Telephone & Telegraph to General Motors to Zenith, have signed a pledge to try using ADR before going to court.

The courts are also looking at mediation as a means of relieving court congestion. The Western District of Washington Federal Court, which sits on matters of admiralty, requires its cases to go through mediation before coming to trial.

Companies have begun to insert clauses into their contracts requiring that parties try mediation before moving on to arbitration or litigation. If an experienced mediator is named within large contracts, he or she becomes part of the project team and can be called on to mediate minor disputes as they arise. If the mediation fails, its attempt will not prejudice a party's right to other methods of dispute resolution.

More than 95 percent of all lawsuits never make it to the courtroom. As the court date approaches, litigants feel the tremendous pressure to settle out of court. If their dispute is going to settle anyway, they can decide to settle it before they spend a lot of money on legal fees. Mediation allows litigants to take control of their dispute and forge settlements perhaps more to their liking than what a judge and jury might impose.

Mediation provides an alternative to the expensive, frustrating, time-consuming litigation process, in which lawyers are the only real winners. If you get into a dispute, try mediation—it just might work, and it will definitely save you time and money.

## Conclusion

This book was written to help you avoid problems before they develop. The more you understand the responsibilities and obligations of boat ownership, and the more correctly you operate your vessel and deal with people who work on your boat, the less likely you are to encounter disagreements. And the more fun you'll have with your boat.

If you find yourself in trouble, avoid lawyers and courtrooms if you can. Admiralty law is complex, so consult an attorney who has that knowledge. Consider alternative dispute resolution techniques for smaller matters, but if you do need an attorney, shop for one you are comfortable with and have confidence in. Remember, in the long run, it is far cheaper to consult an attorney before a transaction takes place, before problems arise, than it is to get out of hot water.

# 2

# Law
# Enforcement

| | ✛ | |

## Myths and Realities

Two common myths should be put to rest. The fact that your vessel is documented by the Coast Guard does not mean that a state, county, or municipal law-enforcement officer cannot cite or arrest you for violation of a nonfederal law. Nor is a state-registered vessel immune from federal laws.

Such myths arise from the confusion over the many legal jurisdictions that oversee boating regulations, as we've seen in Chapter 1. The fact is that many jurisdictions have maritime-law enforcement powers. Commercial and recreational boating are both on the increase, but unfortunately, so too is the use of boats in drug smuggling. These realities, among others, have increased the likelihood that you—as an honest, law-abiding boatowner—will have to deal with law enforcement personnel.

Any or all of the following agencies could enforce laws that pertain to you and your boat, depending on where you keep it and where you take it:

- U.S. Coast Guard
- U.S. Customs Service
- Immigration and Naturalization Service
- Drug Enforcement Administration
- State boating or marine officers

• Wildlife or fisheries officers
• Sheriff's officers
• City police
• County marine patrols
• Municipal marine patrols

For example, the state of Florida authorizes any of these agencies to enforce its maritime laws by inspecting vessels, investigating incidents, making arrests, and removing vessels. (See also Chapter 5, "Boating Regulations.") California boaters encounter special Harbor Patrols and municipal lifeguard services with enforcement powers.

When dealing with any law enforcement officer, remember that most are trained professionals with extensive experience. They have more important things to do than harass boaters. If you treat them in a professional manner, their response is likely to be the same.

## The United States
## Coast Guard

When people think of boating-law enforcement, they usually think of the U.S. Coast Guard. Its jurisdiction and range of tasks in boating matters are broader than any other law-enforcement agency, and it has a long and diverse history.

### *History*

The Coast Guard grew out of the federal Revenue Cutter Service, which was created by an act of Congress passed in August of 1790. The act authorized President George Washington to have up to 10 cutters built for the collection of customs revenue, but it did not provide for personnel. During the early history of the Service, periodic attempts were made to merge it with other military branches or to eliminate it all together.

From 1790 until 1915, this forerunner to the Coast Guard not only collected revenue, it also served in the War of 1812, the first Seminole War, the Mexican War, the Union's side of the Civil War, and the Spanish-American War. It helped prevent foreign slave trade, protected herds of fur seals and sea otters from poachers in the Bering Sea, and even fought cholera and yellow fever by blockading and quarantining certain U.S. ports.

The Revenue Cutter Service did not become involved in rescue operations until 1832, when the Secretary of the Treasury ordered it to do so during winter months. Prior to that time, the Service helped those in trouble only when it happened upon them. Congress formally authorized rescue operations in 1837. That action led eventually to the creation of the U.S. Life-Saving Service.

The U.S. Life-Saving Service cooperated with private rescue organizations such as the Massachusetts Humane Society and the Life-Saving Benevolent Association of New York, and others. From their cooperation evolved a reasonably efficient system for rescuing vessels and passengers in distress. The shore-based half, usually consisting of a boathouse and some surf boats, worked in conjunction with the Service afloat.

After the Civil War, the United States acquired territory that would soon be known as Alaska, so the Revenue Cutter Service expanded its operations into the Gulf of Alaska and the Bering Sea. Arctic Ocean cruises that began in 1879 helped whalers who were stranded by the ice and provided medical and other assistance to remote settlements.

Early on, the administration of the Service was removed from the collectors of customs and given to the Treasury Department as its Division of Marine Revenue. Accounts seem to indicate that, at times, no one really had an interest in its operations. The Service had no formal means of manning its ships or commissioning its officers, but men joined from the state navies, the Continental Navy, and the ranks of the privateers.

Personnel training was carried out aboard an assortment of vessels over the years, and a school for training was authorized in 1910 in New London, Connecticut. In 1913, the Treasury Department proposed a merger of the Life-Saving Service and the Revenue Cutter Service, and in January, 1915, President Woodrow Wilson signed into law a bill forming the United States Coast Guard.

The bill established that, during times of peace, the Coast Guard would be part of the military forces of the United States under control of the Treasury Department. In times of war or when so ordered by the President, however, it would be under command of the Navy. Construction of the present Coast Guard Academy in New London began in 1932. The Coast Guard's peacetime administration was transferred on April 1, 1967 to the newly created Department of Transportation.

## Basic Functions

The Coast Guard's pervasive presence in boating is the result of federal laws that set out the five basic functions and responsibilities of the service: (1) law enforcement, (2) administration of boating regulations, (3) maintenance of aids to navigation and rescue, (4) oceanographic research, (5) military functions with the Navy. The Coast Guard operates not only on waters along our national boundaries but also on all navigable waters of the U.S. and its territories and on other waters around the world.

The Coast Guard has full and complete law-enforcement authority including the right to inquire, inspect, search, seize, and arrest anyone for any violation of U.S. law on the high seas or U.S. jurisdictional waters. That authority is carried by any commissioned, warrant, or petty officer and applies to any vessel found operating in U.S. waters. When a U.S. Coast Guard officer is enforcing a law, he or she is acting as an agent of the agency that enforces that particular law and is subject to that agency's rules.

Specifically, the Coast Guard may board any vessel and make inquiries of anyone aboard, may examine the ship's documents and papers, inspect and, as in examples discussed later in this chapter, search the vessel and use any necessary force in order to do so. It may arrest anyone who has committed an offense and may seize any vessel or cargo illegally brought into the U.S.

As the administrator of federal boating regulations, the Coast Guard regulates vessel documentation, vessel and personnel licensing, safety, and performs marine inspections and casualty investigations.

Vessel documentation provides a means for identifying vessels and their ownership and for licensing vessels involved in commercial fishing, "coastwise trade," "Great Lakes trade," and some "recreational" activities. A boat may be used only in the trade or business for which it is licensed, although a dual license may be available in some cases. As of this writing in 1993, a vessel built outside the U.S. may not be documented for "coastwise trade" or fishing. The North American Free Trade Agreement, if adopted, may treat Canadian- and Mexican-built vessels the same as U.S.-built. A documented vessel may not be sold to a non-U.S. citizen without approval of the Secretary of Transportation. U.S. vessels may not be mortgaged to foreign mortgage holders. This is not true of registered but undocumented vessels.

If you are a U.S. citizen and own a pleasure vessel in excess of five net tons, you could ask the Coast Guard to document it. Obtaining documented-vessel status is not difficult. For more on vessel documentation, see Chapter 4.

Some veteran cruisers believe documentation is an advantage when visiting foreign countries or even passing through their waters. Nearly every nation participates in the vessel documentation system, each receiving a block of numbers to issue to vessels of its citizens. So when you sail your U.S.-documented vessel into another country's waters, your documentation number signifies to that government that you are a U.S. citizen and your vessel must be respected as U.S. territory. This can be a political advantage near strife-torn countries of Latin America and the eastern Mediterranean, where drug smuggling and gun running are prevalent even well offshore. You may still be boarded by foreign navies but are likely to be treated with more courtesy than if your boat were not documented.

If you radio a "May Day" off a foreign country, the U.S. Coast Guard's Search and Rescue planes and ships will be able to come to your assistance more quickly, since your documentation numbers prove to both countries that a U.S. citizen is in distress. That number will immediately allow both countries to cut the diplomatic red tape that otherwise prohibits trespass by foreign militaries.

Once your boat is documented, you must keep the original version, not a copy, of its Coast Guard document onboard for inspection by the Coast Guard. If you have a preferred mortgage on your boat, keep a copy onboard, not the original.

Many pleasure boats are not documented, but are simply registered and numbered in whichever state they are most often used. If you use your boat primarily in Oregon but keep it and its trailer in California, the boat and trailer should be registered in Oregon, the state in which they are primarily used. For more about registration, see Chapter 4.

The Coast Guard classifies all vessels into two categories: *uninspected* and *inspected.* The term uninspected vessel refers to boats that never carry more than six paying passengers. Most private pleasure boats fall into this large category. Because inspected vessels can carry anywhere from seven to many hundreds of paying passengers and can be offered for hire, they must comply with strict requirements concerning their construction materials, structure, navigation equipment, methods of operation, manning, and gear carried for firefighting and lifesaving.

Specific requirements vary widely, however, depending on where the boat is used, what it is used for, what kind of engine and fuel it uses, what its size is, how many passengers and crew it carries, and many other factors. A 90-foot inspected vessel operating year round, 24 hours a day more than 100 miles offshore of Alaska is required, for example, to be of stronger construction and have better communication and survival gear onboard than would a 40-foot inspected vessel taking 10 passengers for two-hour harbor excursions through the inland waterways of Florida. The same distinctions of location, purpose, size, capacity, and kind of vessel hold true for uninspected vessels. Many items such as propane stoves frequently used on uninspected pleasure boats are prohibited on inspected vessels. Specific requirements are determined by the local Coast Guard Office of Marine Safety.

An inspected vessel must be reinspected after any structural modifications are done, so, as a matter of expedience, these boatowners usually arrange for a Coast Guard inspection while the modifications are being done. If the owner of an inspected vessel begins modifications before gaining Coast Guard approval, the Coast Guard has the statutory authority to reject the modification.

The licensing of captains and crewmembers falls under Coast Guard jurisdiction. The Coast Guard writes and administers tests for the various levels of Master and Ocean Operator licenses. Many vessel insurers offer discounts to boatowners who earn Coast Guard licenses, and a yacht that is used for crewed charters must be operated by either a Master or Ocean Operator. Commercial fishing boats must obey Coast Guard manning requirements and abide by its operational standards for safety. The Coast Guard also administers tests for Merchant Marine licenses, such as Mate, Able Bodied Seaman, Ordinary Seaman, etc.

The Coast Guard investigates marine casualties in order to determine their causes and prevent recurrence. A Coast Guard investigation does not affix civil liability, but its conclusions can certainly influence civil lawsuits. A Coast Guard investigation can lead to suspension or revocation of seamen's documents and captains' licenses, or, worse yet, to criminal charges. During an investigation, the Coast Guard has full authority to subpoena witnesses and documents and to inspect, examine, search and seize anything it feels is relevant.

To insure safety on the water, the Coast Guard performs random drug and alcohol tests of licensed captains and crewmembers aboard inspected vessels, such as group sportfishing boats and harbor excursion vessels. Even some unlicensed crewmembers are subject to random testing for drugs and alcohol if their jobs have anything to do with safety onboard.

Several sportfishing captains in the Los Angeles area were discovered to have amphetamines in their systems during random, unannounced testing. The Coast Guard revoked their licenses and they faced state and federal criminal charges. During the investigations, the captains admitted they had relied on drugs to keep them awake, but that they did so only after the vessels' owners had expected them to work long hours on the bridge without sleep.

Commercial operations are now required to inform their employees of these random drug and alcohol tests.

Recreational boaters are subject to drug and alcohol testing by the Coast Guard when they are involved in boating-related incidents. Under the Coast Guard's campaign to end BWI (Boating While Intoxicated) accidents and casualties, recreational boaters can be asked to pass the Coast Guard's field sobriety test or drug-detection test if their behavior shows evidence of intoxication. The Coast Guard's definition of intoxication is a blood-alcohol level of .10 percent, but if the state has a tougher standard, the state's definition is used.

In the past, the Coast Guard was probably most recognized for its rescue operations, and every Coast Guard history extols the heroics of Coast Guard personnel in their efforts to save floundering vessels and rescue victims from watery demise. Recently, however, the Coast Guard's mandate to perform rescue operations has been subject to debate, in part because the statute addressing rescue says "may," not "must" or "shall." Some argue that the Coast Guard's policy to get involved in rescue operations has been too permissive. Most boaters urge the Coast Guard to make search and rescue a higher priority.

In any case, recent pressure from federal budget slashing has forced the Coast Guard to encourage boaters to become more self-reliant. Except when life or property is at risk, the Coast Guard now asks boaters to first request nonemergency assistance from commercial towing or salvage operators.

In many boating and fishing centers, this gap has been filled by volunteer members of local Coast Guard Auxiliary groups who monitor VHF channel 16. With private boats already on the water, these Coast Guard Auxiliarists frequently come to the rescue with a few gallons of fuel, a battery jump, a ¾-inch socket wrench, or a neighborly tow into port. They've even been known to return seasick guests to dry land.

The Coast Guard's role in emergency situations is unchanged, however. If you find yourself in serious trouble on, or even under, any U.S. waters, you can still count on the Coast Guard to do whatever is necessary. It may furnish you with necessary food, shelter, and clothing; it may also destroy or take in tow any vessel, derelict, or other hazard to navigation; and it may take possession of property until its rightful owner appears to reclaim it.

Even though the Coast Guard is no longer in the business of casual assistance, more than a few boaters have gratefully accepted mechanical help with sputtering engines, given "unofficially," while they were being boarded officially. Hundreds of boaters have looked up to the welcome sight of an orange-and-white Coast Guard rescue helicopter, as it airlifted an emergency bilge pump to their sinking vessel.

The Coast Guard is also responsible for the installation, operation and maintenance of the thousands of aids to navigation—from lighthouses to radio beacons, Loran-C navigation systems and unlighted buoys that boaters use whenever they leave the dock.

It also participates in oceanographic research, iceberg patrols, National Oceanographic and Atmospheric Administration (NOAA) charting, and environmental cleanup. In cooperation with the Navy, some boardings on the high seas are done from naval vessels.

Finally, the Coast Guard is charged with providing effective marine communications through monitoring VHF channel 16, SSB-22A, radio weather broadcasts, EPIRBs, and SAR/SAT.

### Coast Guard Cooperation

The Coast Guard's unique mandate authorizes it to cooperate with federal agencies such as the Departments of State, Treasury, and Commerce, as well as state and local political subdivisions.

Through the State Department, the Coast Guard exchanges information and cooperation with foreign governments in cases that involve international treaties, the International Rules of the Road, communications at sea, aids to navigation, and life-saving equipment. As indicated earlier, Coast Guard officers act as the Treasury Department's customs officers in order to enforce customs laws.

On behalf of the Commerce Department, Coast Guard stations broadcast maritime weather information of vital importance to pleasure boaters and commercial fishermen over VHF and HF marine radio bands. The Coast Guard helps regulate fishing in U.S. waters, also under the Commerce Department auspices.

The National Transportation Safety Board depends on Coast Guard cooperation in the investigation of some marine accidents, and the Coast Guard implements the many requirements of the Occupational Safety and Health Act (OSHA).

States, counties and municipalities call on the Coast Guard's valuable experience with maritime matters.

## Customs and Immigration Services

Recreational boaters are increasingly apt to encounter someone from the U.S. Customs Service and the Immigration and Naturalization Service. Although early in its history the Coast Guard was in charge of customs matters, they are now separate operations of the Treasury Department.

The primary duties of the U.S. Customs Service are to prevent smuggling and to enforce regulations. When goods are brought into this country without the payment of their legal duty, they have been smuggled. Some goods are directly prohibited. The Immigration and Naturalization Service makes sure that people, rather than goods, do not enter the country illegally. Everyone who has traveled outside the U.S. and returned has probably dealt with officers from both these services. One inspected your passport, and the other inspected your luggage or possessions.

Boaters entering this country are especially likely to encounter these two services. Their extensive authority to enforce their respective laws includes the right to board and search your boat, to seize any goods believed to be in violation of the law, and to arrest anyone believed to be entering the country in violation of federal law.

## The Drug Enforcement
## Administration

The other federal agency you may come in contact with is the Drug Enforcement Administration or DEA. The DEA was formed in 1973 to take over functions formerly performed by the Bureau of Narcotics and Dangerous Drugs, which was part of the Department of the Treasury. The DEA is currently under the control of the United States Attorney General. As such, it has full law-enforcement authority and can gather intelligence and conduct investigations of illegal drug trafficking.

## What to Expect
## When You're Boarded

Being boarded is not a pleasurable experience, but it is one of the realities of pleasure boating. The more you know about the procedure, the easier it will be. It should go something like this:

First you will be hailed on VHF radio channel 16 by a passing Coast Guard vessel and asked to identify yourself. If the Coast Guard radio operator advises you to stand by to be boarded, he or she may order you to stop dead in the water or to idle ahead, depending on the sea conditions, so that their boarding skiff can come alongside you safely. All boarding parties carry drug-testing and alcohol-detection devices. They also carry listening devices, so they can hear conversations on board your boat prior to their boarding.

The boarding team will be made up of at least two people armed with holstered 9mm handguns. After identifying themselves, they will ask you, as the skipper of the vessel, if any weapons are on board. If you say yes, they will take possession of the weapons as soon as they board and will keep them until the boarding is completed. During the boarding, everyone but the skipper may be asked to stand near the bow or somewhere in plain view of the larger Coast Guard vessel, which will be standing off nearby.

During the boarding, the Coast Guard officers will look for violations of applicable federal and state laws. These laws concern equipment, drugs, aliens, and the operation of a vessel while under the influence of drugs or alcohol. They will run a check for outstanding arrest warrants for anyone onboard, using the National Crime Information Computer.

The boarding party will confirm the boat's identity by inspecting its documentation or registration numbers. Documentation numbers are usually inscribed on a bulkhead deep within the hull. As a safety precaution, boarding officers will check all spaces large enough to hide a person. Being familiar with the standard layouts of most boats, they will look for false bottoms and misplaced bulkheads.

Boarding officers will not search for drugs unless something causes them to suspect drugs are hidden aboard the boat. If warranted, they can proceed with a more comprehensive search. If destructive techniques are to be used in a search, the boat will first be moved to a secured area.

If your boat's paint is scratched during a boarding or if its toe rail gets dented, the Coast Guard's policy is to investigate and to reimburse you for any damages. If damage is sustained during a search that turns up no drugs, you are supposed to be reimbursed for that damage. Ask the boarding party for a damage claim form, or get one from the Coast Guard's nearest district office. There have been complaints about the insufficiency and tardiness of damage awards; your best hope is to avoid a thorough search through the completeness and consistency of your answers to questions, and a general attitude of cooperation.

Fifty-eight percent of all boardings find some violation. The skipper is given a Boarding Report—similar to a traffic ticket—describing the violations found. The Boarding Report is later checked by other Coast Guard personnel to make sure correct citations are included, before it is forwarded to the appropriate Coast Guard Area Command for processing.

You are notified by mail of the amount due and asked to pay it. Penalties range from $500 to $25,000. If warranted, the Coast Guard has the authority to terminate the voyage and take the boat in tow to the nearest U.S. port.

If you're issued a Boarding Report that you disagree with, you can appeal to the Coast Guard Area Command for a hearing by a commissioned officer. If you're still dissatisfied, you may then appeal to the Coast Guard Commandant. Unless a death was involved, there are no further provisions for appeal, because a Boarding Report is a civil, administrative citation, not a criminal one. As such, it is similar to violation of a municipal code where the only punishment is the assessment of monetary damages.

If you don't pay the fine, it may be given to a collection agency, and the IRS may be notified to hold your tax return until the charges are paid. The Coast Guard takes Visa or MasterCard but not American Express. If you are on your way to Tahiti for two years, you can't pay the fine during the boarding with cash or credit card. Someone minding your business back home will have to pay the bill when it arrives in the mail.

If your violations are "warnable," you may escape with a nonmonetary warning. Warnable violations include numbering, personal flotation devices (PFDs), horns and bells, fire extinguishers, flame arrestors, marine sanitation devices (MSDs), visual distress equipment and not carrying a current copy of the appropriate Rules of the Road. All other violations carry fines, but since fines go into the U.S. government's general fund, the Coast Guard does not benefit directly.

A courtesy Coast Guard Auxiliary inspection sticker may significantly speed the boarding process, because Coast Guard officers will know you have had a recent inspection.

### *Boardings Gone Wrong*

The case of Bolling versus the U.S. Coast Guard is a prime example of the emotions aroused by repeat boardings by various law enforcement agencies—and of the Coast Guard's ultimate authority. The issue was reported extensively by *Soundings* nautical news magazine.

While on a four-month trip from Nova Scotia to Florida, the 120-foot yacht *Albert* was boarded repeatedly. The Coast Guard attempted to board *Albert* again off Wilmington, North Carolina, but this time the boat's owner, Florida boater William Bolling III, refused to allow the officers to come aboard. Instead he brandished a rifle and pistol, weighed anchor, and held the Coast Guard at bay for six hours while he motored to a dock in Cape Fear, 22 miles away. When the boarding finally took place, Bolling's son assaulted one of the boarding officers by jamming him against a bulkhead with a deck chair.

Though the search yielded only a few minor technical violations, Bolling, 59, and his son were charged with felonies and jailed without bail. Bolling faced 10 years in prison for arming himself against the Coast Guard. The two were later indicted on charges that they forcibly assaulted, resisted, opposed, impeded, intimidated, and interfered with Coast Guardsmen performing their duties.

Bolling said he resisted because he believed he and his family were being harassed with repeated boardings that had begun soon after he purchased *Albert*, a 29-year-old Icelandic Coast Guard vessel that had been converted to a yacht. The searches were apparently prompted by the vessel's previous inclusion on the "watch list" maintained by the El Paso Intelligence Center (EPIC), an intelligence-gathering network serving nine federal agencies. The prosecutor, Assistant U.S. Attorney Kieran Shanahan, said that each time the vessel, which looked like a drug boat, was spotted in a different Coast Guard jurisdiction, a boarding was made by a different person.

Bolling said he was boarded 17 times by the Coast Guard and searched 11 times in five months. The Coast Guard said it recorded three boardings, but that U.S. Customs or other agencies may also have boarded *Albert*.

At the time of the incident, federal agencies tapping into EPIC had not been updating the records if no significant violations were found, so when *Albert* was spotted, nothing in EPIC indicated that the vessel had been boarded recently, searched, and given a clean bill.

"Prior to coming into Cape Fear," Shanahan told *Soundings*, "they may have been the victims of a computer-generated problem. Bolling III became a criminal when he refused to allow the Coast Guard to board . . ."

The Bolling boarding issue drew headlines for months, pitting the

Coast Guard's authority to board and search without a warrant against pleasure boaters' right to privacy and free passage. Meanwhile, Bolling's legal fees rose to $90,000, and sympathetic boating groups raised funds to help pay the bills. Just before the trial, the Bollings pleaded guilty to the lesser charges of misdemeanor assault, which carried the possible sentence of six months in prison and $125,000 in fines. In the end, a U.S. District Court judge fined Bolling $250, his son $500, and suspended the son's jail sentence.

The sad incident occurred in October, 1986. It may have been responsible for the Coast Guard's softened policy on boarding recreational boats, particularly in waters not known for drug trafficking, which went into effect in early 1987.

The following incident is reprinted with permission from *Cruising World* magazine, June 1992:

In 1989 a sailboat under way from St. Petersburg to Jacksonville, Florida, was stopped, boarded and ultimately destroyed by customs officers (not Coast Guard) who had found simple inconsistencies in the boat's documentation and a conflict in the information from its captain and mate. What's worse, an exemption in the Tort Claims Act prevented the Customs Service from reimbursing the boat owner for the damage it had unjustly caused—leaving him no legal recourse short of a Congressional private relief bill to recover his investment. Craig Klein's story is rich with lessons on how to deal with boarding officials.

Upon purchasing *Peggotty* in St. Petersburg, Klein changed the boat's title from a Florida registration to a federal documentation and then hired a professional captain and a mate to deliver the boat to his home in Jacksonville. While it was under way a local marine policeman near Stuart noticed *Peggotty*'s faded registration numbers and contacted the Customs Service. Klein had chosen not to remove the bow number until his federal documentation papers came through. Based on the unclear registration, 11 customs officers boarded *Peggotty* and questioned the captain and mate about when they had passed through the Okeechobee Waterway; the captain gave one date, the mate another. Klein noted in his testimony before the U.S. House Of Representatives that both had been correct, as it had been a two-day trip, and a record of their passage was available from the Okeechobee lock operators.

But the customs officers considered these inconsistencies probable cause to search the boat thoroughly and bring a drug-sniffing dog aboard. The dog mistakenly barked positive and the captain and mate were arrested. The officers hauled *Peggotty* out and conducted their search with the aid of a fire ax and a power drill. When they were finished, more than 15 ½-inch holes pierced *Peggotty*'s hull and fuel tank. No contraband was found. Only with a Congressman's help was Klein able to recover his losses.

*Peggotty*'s fate demonstrates that clear, accurate responses to a boarding party's simple questions are the key to a successful boarding. Know where to find the ship's papers and be ready to explain circumstances that an officer might find confusing. If asked about the nature and details of the voyage, describe it thoroughly and accurately enough to avoid planting suspicion. When possible, have only one person speak for the crew. If an officer wants to inspect an out-of-the-way space, show him how to gain access without causing damage.

Above all, during an official boarding, don't fail the Attitude Test. Most boarding officers know that skippers don't relish the intrusion of the government into their private lives and they are taught to do their jobs as quickly, professionally and painlessly as possible. But they also know that the full weight of all three government branches is squarely on their side.

## Zero Tolerance

The term *Zero Tolerance* came into popular use during the Reagan administration's push to increase enforcement of the country's drug laws. It simply means that there will be no tolerance of any drugs found on boats. If even a very small amount of drugs were found on a boat, the boat would be seized under federal law. In an early case, one butt of a marijuana cigarette found in the stateroom of a crew member caused the seizure of a private yacht valued at more than a million dollars.

Zero Tolerance has been modified in recent years. The Coast Guard's criteria for seizing a vessel include the owner's knowledge or involvement with the drugs found. If drugs are found on someone other than the boat's owner and without the owner's knowledge, that individual will be given a summons to appear before a U.S. Customs Magistrate, and the boatowner need not worry about his or her boat being seized.

The boat will be seized if (a) the owner, master, or person in charge is in possession of the controlled substance; (b) the owner, master, or person in charge appears to be impaired by drugs; (c) the owner, master, or person in charge refuses to sign the summons form; (d) the same boat has been involved in two previous drug violations; or (e) the owner has failed to pay prior penalties assessed by the Coast Guard.

If the boat is seized, it will be moved to an adequate dock or anchorage, and its custody will be transferred to U.S. Customs or state officials. Federal forfeiture statutes are stiff, so getting your boat back can be difficult.

Here are a few steps that boatowners and operators can take to protect themselves from Zero Tolerance problems, according to the Coast Guard:

• Employment contracts should state that possession of drugs will be grounds for immediate termination, and that drug testing and periodic inspections can be made a condition of employment.

• Vessel charter agreements should contain a clause prohibiting the use or possession of drugs.

• Periodic inspections should be made throughout the boat. Drug-sniffing dogs can be brought onboard upon the owner or operator's request.

• Zero Tolerance notices should be posted onboard, and if you use your boat for business, a similar notice should appear in your advertising.

• Compartments that could be used to hide drugs should be secured, so guests or employees cannot stash drugs without your knowledge.

• When drugs are discovered—in use or in possession—the discovery should be reported to the Coast Guard or local enforcement officials.

## A Word About
## Search and Seizure

Boaters have a right to be upset with the increased suspicion and surveillance that are byproducts of the war on drugs. Some boaters feel harassed, but while the war on drugs continues to involve just about every law enforcement agency in this country, the uncomfortable suspicion and surveillance are still going to be the good guys' best weapons.

The increasing number of search-and-seizure cases being litigated might make one think that Americans' rights are being eroded for the sake of the war on drugs, but the law remains fundamentally the same as it was before this war was declared.

The search-and-seizure issue involves the Fourth Amendment " . . . right of the people to be secure in their persons, houses, papers and effects, against unreasonable searches and seizures . . . . " The issue is reasonableness, and the courts have held for many years prior to the war on drugs that just because a search happens to be inconvenient does not mean it is unreasonable.

Although the search-and-seizure law is too complex to analyze here, boaters should be aware of some general rules. The Coast Guard may board any vessel subject to the jurisdiction of the laws of the United States, address inquiries to anyone on board, examine the vessel's documents, and search the vessel in order to look at its registration or documentation papers and numbers. The documentation number is carved or welded into its main bulkhead or may be glued onto its main beam. There is no limit to the frequency of inspections.

If no warrant authorizes the search, and if the Coast Guard has no reasonable suspicion of illegal activity, then the search may not extend to "private areas" of the boat, but it can extend to wherever the identification numbers are located. Because documented vessels often have their number carved, welded or glued below decks, the search may lead the officers well into or past the private areas. Such an "administrative" search may also be conducted at night, but under stricter requirements.

If an administrative search uncovers facts that suggest that further investigation is warranted, then the boarding party is said to have "probable cause" to proceed with a full-scale search of the vessel. Such facts include the smell of marijuana, traces of drugs or drug paraphernalia, or an indication from someone onboard that drugs were present.

The Coast Guard's authority to search and seize vessels extends to U.S. territorial waters and the high seas. It may search any vessel that is registered in the U.S. or in any state or territory, foreign vessels, and those carrying no designation. Search-and-seizure authority extends to the waters of another country only if the vessel is of American registration.

State law enforcement officers generally limit their searches and seizures to their states or jurisdictions. Probable cause still applies, as do a citizen's Constitutional protections. Thus, if a state marine-patrol officer stopped a vessel in state territorial waters in order to check on illegal shrimping, he or she would be authorized to seize the vessel and make arrests if bales of marijuana were seen in plain view on the deck.

In addition to the large number of federal rules and regulations administered by the Coast Guard, a boatowner is likely to deal with an equally bewildering array of state, county and municipal regulations that overlay and supplement the federal ones. Every state has its own laws governing boating and boat operations that may be enforced by any number of law enforcement personnel—from sheriffs, constables and police officers to specialized law-enforcement such as state boating or marine officers, wildlife and fisheries officers and specially designated boat patrols.

The only requirement that all of these laws, rules, and regulations must meet is that they not conflict with federal law. They may supplement and enlarge upon federal law. So if you are stopped by a state, county, or local marine patrol, and if they have probable cause to believe you are carrying drugs on board, they can search the boat without a warrant, just as the Coast Guard can. Some jurisdictions have seen fit to establish where you can anchor, how long you can stay, and when you should leave. If you break a harbor or waterway speed limit or leave a wake in a no-wake area, and you are apprehended, you will be prosecuted by the authority that employed the apprehending officer. We will return to the subject of boating regulations in Chapter 5.

# 3

# Taxes

| | ❖ | |

Although the Internal Revenue Service has gradually eliminated many tax shelters over the last few years, boat ownership still offers a surprising variety of tax benefits. You can reap those benefits if you can claim your boat as a primary residence or second home. You can also benefit from putting your boat in a charter operation, running an active charter service, or operating your boat in conjunction with other business ventures. You are entitled to claim deductions on your tax return if you have paid certain taxes on your boat or have donated it to certain charities.

## Tax Benefits for Owners of Pleasure Boats

The federal government has gradually eliminated write-offs for most Americans, and among them are deductions for some state and local taxes and for interest paid on credit cards and auto loans. Although you can't deduct the sales tax that you paid when you bought your boat, you can still claim personal-property and excise tax that your state may require you to pay on your boat annually.

### Personal-Property Tax

If you pay a regular excise or personal-property tax on your boat, you can still deduct it from your income. This deduction is becoming increasingly valuable as state and local jurisdictions increase their taxes to offset the loss of federal funding. However, the federal "luxury tax" on the purchase price of vessels over $100,000 was not deductible, even before it was repealed in President Clinton's Budget Bill.

If you're not sure whether you pay these taxes, here are two examples. The State of Washington requires you to pay one-half of one percent of the value of your boat in annual excise tax when you renew your boat's state registration. California requires that you provide proof of payment of personal-property tax to the county in which you keep your boat before it will allow you to renew your California boat registration each year.

To take this deduction, look on line 7 of Schedule A of Form 1040 of your tax return under "Taxes You Paid."

### Boat Loan Deductions

While the interest paid on auto loans and credit cards is no longer deductible, interest paid on certain boat loans is. You still can deduct the interest if you took out a home-equity loan to finance your boat, or if your boat qualifies as your primary residence or second home.

To take this deduction, look on line 9b of Schedule A of your Form 1040.

*Home-equity loans.* If you have taken out a home-equity loan to buy a boat, the interest is deductible as long as the amount of the loan does not exceed the fair market value of your home or what you paid for your house, subsequent home improvements and any debt incurred for certain qualifying medical and educational expenses.

*Primary residence.* If your boat is your primary residence, you can deduct the interest on your loan just as land dwellers do. The deduction goes on line 9a or 9b of Schedule A—Itemized Deductions of your tax return.

*Second home.* In general, the tax code allows you to claim interest paid on a loan for second home as a tax deduction. So if your boat qualifies as a second home, you may deduct that interest. Because many people's second homes are mobile homes or RVs, the code includes a variety of stipulations, including one that the boat be large enough to be lived on and large enough to provide sleeping accommodations and cooking facilities.

Keeping in mind that one man's home is another man's castle, the IRS has not set minimum standards for what qualifies as a "home" or residence. It has said:

> Whether property is a residence shall be determined based on all the facts and circumstances, including the good faith of the taxpayer. A residence generally includes a house, condominium, mobile home, boat, or house trailer, that contains sleeping space and toilet and cooking facilities.

The IRS has not defined what it means by "sleeping space" or "toilet and cooking facilities." Some people can be happy living on a 20-foot sailboat cooking on a one-burner stove and using a porta-pottie, while others wouldn't be able to live on a 50-foot luxury cruiser with air conditioning, sound systems, microwave, and dishwasher. The IRS is likely to accept the 20-foot sailboat as a "residence," but it isn't likely to go along when you try to claim your 16-foot open runabout. Don't forget that the definition includes "good faith of the taxpayer."

You may want to substantiate this deduction when you file. Some IRS offices have said they are disallowing this deduction when boatowners fail to submit Form 1098, or a mortgage interest statement from their banks, with their tax returns. The problem is that some banks will not give a Form 1098 for a boat loan, claiming that the form is only for interest paid on real-estate mortgages and does not apply to boat loans.

It is up to you, the taxpayer, to substantiate your deductions, so if your bank won't give you a Form 1098, get a written statement from your bank showing the interest paid on your boat loan and include a copy with your tax return.

### Charitable-Donation Deductions

Two types of charitable donations may qualify as deductions: expenses incurred when you donate your time to qualified boating organizations, and direct donations of the use of your boat to qualified organizations, not necessarily boating groups. Let's look at them separately.

If you are a member of the U.S. Coast Guard Auxiliary and use your boat in its activities, you can deduct 12 cents per mile traveled, and you can claim the cost of buying and maintaining uniforms worn during Auxiliary activities.

So if you donate Saturday to your local Auxiliary group and take your boat 25 miles out to help rescue another boater in distress and 25 miles back in to port, you will have earned yourself a $6.00 deduction for the day, even if you weren't wearing a uniform. This is why they are called charitable donations.

To make this type of deduction, look on line 14 of Schedule A of your tax return.

The second type of donation that may be tax deductible is the direct donation of your boat to a qualifying organization. For example, if a chapter of the Sea Scouts is looking for boats to restore and use as trainers for the young sailors, you can donate your boat and be entitled to a tax deduction.

How much of a deduction could this be? The type of organization to which you donate determines the size of the deduction you can take. To establish the value of this donation for tax purposes, it is a good idea to obtain a yacht survey at the time of the donation. If you are audited, your yacht survey can verify the value of the boat when it was donated. For more information about obtaining this yacht survey, see Chapter 6.

Which organizations qualify as receivers of this type of tax-deductible donation? Generally, they are nonprofit, charitable organizations, but only the IRS is responsible for recognizing and qualifying groups for this status. Even though you may be a member of a local environmental group that is registered with your state as a nonprofit corporation, if it isn't registered with the IRS under Section 501C or related section of the Internal Revenue Code, your donation will not be tax deductible on your federal tax return.

If you are considering donating your boat to an organization and expecting to take a deduction, ask for a copy of the group's letter of qualification from the IRS, which will identify it as a nonprofit charitable organization for the purpose of tax-deductible donations. This letter will also state under which section of the Internal Revenue Code the group qualifies. Include a copy of this group's IRS letter with your tax return, and look for the deduction on line 14 of Schedule A of your Form 1040.

## When Your
## Boat Is Your Business

Two obvious advantages to using your boat in a business are that you can claim most, if not all, related costs as deductible expenses on your income-tax return, and in some cases any losses you incur can be deducted from your other reported income.

The disadvantages, which may not be so obvious, are these: You must show a profit during at least three out of five years of operations, and you must operate your business in a businesslike manner. When the IRS tries to establish the legitimacy of your business, it will ask several questions:

• How much time do you spend on the business?
• Does your livelihood depend on the income generated by the business?
• Were reported losses incurred due to circumstances beyond your control?
• Do you have the knowledge to operate the business?
• Do you act as though you're running a business, or are you simply trying to avoid paying taxes?

Running a small business is not as complex as some people fear, but filing your tax returns becomes more involved. You'll probably need to secure a local business license and file additional state or local tax returns.

If you set up your business as a sole proprietorship, which means operating it yourself without employees, then you should fill out and include the Schedule C form with your tax returns. The Schedule C allows you to list all the income and expenses incurred in your small business. Since a boat is a hole in the water that you throw money into, most boatowners welcome the opportunity to list their staggering expenses and have someone notice.

If, after talking with your accountant and lawyer, you decide to operate your business through a partnership or corporation, additional tax returns will have to be filed. Remember, partnerships and corporations are separate taxable entities in the eyes of the IRS. If you chose to incorporate, you'll find that the laws governing your federal and state tax liability are complex.

Liability for state corporate taxes varies greatly from state to state. For example, in the state of Washington, in addition to facing federal taxes you are required to:

- pay an annual registration fee to the Secretary of State to maintain your corporation in good standing;
- register with the Washington State Department of Licensing to obtain its appropriate licenses;
- register with and be licensed by the municipality in which you operate;
- pay annual personal property tax on any equipment used in your business;
- collect sales tax on any charter income, if you are chartering your boat;
- pay Washington Business and Occupational Tax on any income generated by your business, whether it is a corporation, partnership or sole proprietorship.

Because tax laws vary widely, you should ask your tax accountant about which avenue is best for you in your location.

The Internal Revenue Service's *Tax Guide for Small Business* (Publication #334) is a good guide to basic information. It is free from any IRS office, and because it is updated annually, it contains the most current facts about income tax as well as business taxes such as excise and employment tax. It also offers advice about sole proprietorships, partnerships, and corporations. Other IRS publications that may be of value are:

#1 Your Rights as a Taxpayer
#17 Your Federal Income Tax (Digest of IRS publications)
#463 Travel, Entertainment, and Gift Expenses
#502 Medical and Dental Expenses
#505 Tax Withholding and Estimated Tax

#533 Self-employment Tax
#534 Depreciation
#544 Sales and Other Disposition of Assets
#551 Basis of Assets
#552 Record Keeping for Individuals
#560 Self-employed Retirement Plans
#587 Business Use of Your Home
#589 Tax Information on Subchapter S Corporations
#590 Individual Retirement Arrangements
#910 Guide to Free Tax Services
#917 Business Use of a Car

More than 140 tax topics are covered by the IRS in prerecorded phone messages that you can listen to by calling this toll-free number: (800) 829-4477. If you still have questions or are having a particular problem with your return, talk to an IRS representative.

Be aware, however, that the information you get over the phone may not be correct and you should try to verify it from another source. Reliance on advice given over the phone by the IRS will not excuse you from paying penalties or interest if the advice is wrong.

If—after all of this—you still want to start a business involving your boat, you will be able to deduct all legitimate business expenses in calculating your taxable income as long as those expenses meet the IRS's three basic rules:

1. They must relate to your business. No personal, nonbusiness expenses can be deducted in your business.
2. They must be "ordinary and necessary." They must be expenses that are normally incurred in your type of business, and they must be appropriate for your type of business.
3. The amount of the expenses must be reasonable.

Business expenses can range from fuel for your boat to educational courses that help you pass tests for required U.S. Coast Guard licenses, from bait and tackle used in sportfishing expeditions to professional fees paid to your lawyer or accountant. Expenses can include:

• use of your automobile
• business cards and stationary
• yacht and business insurance
• consultant fees
• commissions to people who find your clients
• depreciation of major equipment
• dues to business associations and professional societies
• education expense, such as Coast Guard licensing exam courses
• equipment, including half of the items in the nearest chandlery
• entertainment
• interest on business debt
• license fees, including business license, captain's license, and vessel certification fees
• minor repairs, which keep large communities of boat workers happy in most harbors
• office equipment, including shore-based radio and weather fax machine
• office rental, including part of your home as an office
• slip rental
• postage, such as mailings of brochures to prospective clients
• salaries to employees
• wages to hourly employees
• tools, including the other half of the items in the nearest chandlery
• telephone expenses
• utilities, including dock power

Do not attempt to deduct expenses that are unrelated to your business, such as mileage for a car you don't use in the business or entertainment if your business isn't the purpose of the particular expense. Likewise, you can't claim the full amount of rent you pay on your house if you are only using a portion of it for an office.

If you question whether a specific expense will qualify as a business deduction, talk to your accountant or call the IRS's toll-free number listed under "Federal Government—IRS" in the front of most telephone directories.

## *Chartering*

Chartering is the broadest category of business commonly related to boat ownership. Just as there is an infinite variety of boats in the world, so too can you find an almost unlimited range of boat-chartering operations for both pleasure boats and commercial craft. Will you use your boat year-round to take marlin fishermen into fertile waters, or will happy couples come onboard during June weekends to get married?

Chartering your boat may afford you a tax savings, but since the tax laws changed in 1987, the type of tax treatment your chartering activity warrants depends on whether you skipper the boat yourself (*nonpassive activity*), manage your own boat in a bareboat operation (*passive rental activity*), or simply let someone else run your boat in a bareboat charter operation for you (*passive activity*).

Prior to 1987, losses incurred by most yacht-rental businesses could be used to offset your salary income and reduce the amount of tax you paid each year. For example, if you had an income of $15,000 from a salaried job plus income of $6,000 from chartering your boat, and if your expenses for chartering the boat were $8,000, you could have offset all of the $6,000 charter income as well as $2,000 of your salary income. You could have paid tax only on the remaining $13,000 of your salary income.

After the 1987 change, the IRS defined most rental activity, including the rental of vessels, as "passive." It set a $25,000 limit on the amount of losses from passive activity you can claim against your salary income (*nonpassive*), and then only if you manage a bareboat operation yourself but don't actually skipper the boat. You might run the operation out of a spare room, doing the advertising, answering the phone, etc. This qualifies as *passive rental activity*. If, on the other hand, you place your boat with a charter manager and are essentially uninvolved with the operation (*passive activity*), you cannot offset any active income with passive losses: you can only offset passive income from the charter operation with passive losses.

In the latter case, you might be better off if your boat qualifies as a second home, in which case you can deduct the interest you pay on the boat.

If your charter business does qualify as nonpassive, you must weigh the deduction advantages against other factors that may be even more important to you. For example, if you'd like to continue using your boat for pleasure, be aware that the IRS restricts owners of active charter boats to 15 days of personal use in a given year. This stiff law may put a crimp in your plans.

After you listen to all the old charter captains spin their tales, read Chapter 13 for factual details on running a charter business.

### Other Business-Related Deductions

If you operate your boat as a business, you can claim the usual deduction for its use, just as you would any other piece of business equipment. And within each of the many varieties of boating businesses will be a hundred different yet equally legitimate expenses, depending on the nature of the business.

For example, a luxury charter yacht might deduct food and drink, but a tugboat, aboard which drink might be forbidden, would be deducting a very different quality of food and perhaps twice as much for giant-size fenders and massive hawsers. A 365-passenger vessel used for harbor excursions might have a healthy deduction for printing admission tickets. A trawler converted for sport-diving expeditions may have thousands of dollars of deductions involved in compressors and scuba gear, while the little Whaler that zooms around your marina cleaning slimy bottoms may deduct only one little hookah compressor.

Commercial fishing businesses qualify for additional tax advantages not usually available to other boating-related businesses. One of these is a credit or refund for excise tax paid on fuel used while fishing commercially. They may also qualify for the Capital Construction Fund (CCF), administered through the National Marine Fisheries Service. The fund finances the purchase and reconstruction of fishing vessels. You can obtain more information by contacting the CCF at: National Marine Fisheries Service, Capital Construction Fund Program, 1335 East-West Highway, Silver Spring, Maryland 20910; (302) 427-2393.

If you own a nonboating business and use your boat to entertain clients, can you claim some boating expenses as deductions? No, those days are gone. Merely having a boat owned by your business does not make it deductible, unless it meets the three basic criteria discussed earlier in this chapter. If the IRS accepts the boat as a legitimate business expense, you will be subject to the limitation on personal use discussed in Chapter 13 on chartering.

### Other Taxes

If you own a business, you'll encounter a few other taxes. There is a federal excise tax on some fishing equipment and outboard motors as well as on fuel used on some inland waters.

You may also be required by your state to charge and collect sales tax on your boating related business, so ask your state and local tax offices.

Fortunately, we no longer have the unloved "Luxury Tax," which was repealed in President Clinton's Budget Bill, but while it was in effect it amounted to 10 percent of any new boat's price tag that exceeded $100,000.

Another tax on pleasure boating, the controversial "user fee," will be discussed in Chapter 4.

## Keeping Good
## Tax Records

You have at least two reasons for keeping good tax records, especially if you are a boatowner. The first is that it is easier for you and your tax preparer to do your taxes at the end of each year if you have kept adequate records. The second and more important reason is that if and when you are audited by the IRS, you will be asked for proof of certain information on your tax return. Good tax records will make your audit easier.

If you also own or manage a boat-related business, keeping accurate records will help you run it more effectively.

Although the law does not require that you keep your records in any specific way, your records should be accurate and complete enough to show specific information about two things: your income and your expenses. This is true whether you keep tax records in the traditional way—in paper account books, diaries, and logs—or electronically in a computer program. No matter which method you prefer, it's always best to record your income at the time you receive it and your expenses at the time you incur them, or as promptly afterward as possible, rather than attempt to re-create this information later from memory.

The easiest way to keep track of business expenses is to maintain a business checking account separate from your personal checking account. Arrange to pay all business expenses by check from your business account, but also get receipts. For those times when you must pay cash, as sometimes happens when you hire part-time help on the waterfront, have your own book of Cash Receipts and get the receivers to sign them. Record on your check register whether the expense was deductible. Also, all assets that you purchase for use in your business should be written down or entered into your computer, including amount and date, so that you can calculate any depreciation deductions.

Under the income side of your bookkeeping, you should identify specific sources of income when you deposit them, so that eventually you can determine whether that income was taxable or not.

All of this information will allow you to calculate your total income, from which you subtract your total deductions and end up with either a net profit or loss. This will help you decide whether you must pay self-employment tax.

Your records must be as complete as possible, because they are subject to inspection by the IRS at any time. Records should be kept for at least three years after the return was filed. If you have employees, you must keep your employment tax records for four years.

# 4

# Registration and Documentation

❘ ❘ ❖ ❘ ❘

Every boater looks forward to the day the new boat is finally delivered. During the excitement of selecting, purchasing and perhaps commissioning the dream machine, very little thought is given to what numbers it will carry for identification.

Of the more than 15 million boats in the United States, only about 70,000 are documented with the U.S. Coast Guard. That's fewer than one percent. Most boats, about nine million of them, are either registered or titled with the various states, and the remaining six million are either exempt from registration because they have no inboard engine or outboard motor, or are simply (and unlawfully) not registered.

## The Federal Umbrella

Although all states have laws that govern the operation and registration of boats within their borders, all such laws trace their origins to the Federal Motorboat Act of 1910, which allowed the federal government to regulate recreational boating in the United States. The Coast Guard, the Customs Service, and the Bureau of Marine Inspection and Navigation, which was part of the Department of Commerce, all were authorized to enforce equipment regulations and requirements for boats.

The Federal Numbering Act of 1918 instituted a numbering system for all undocumented vessels, and the Federal Boating Act of 1958 shifted the burden of numbering undocumented boats from the federal government to the various states and territories. From that time on, owners of undocumented boats carrying a motor of any kind have had to apply for a certificate of number from the state or territory in which the boat is principally used, which is not necessarily where the owner resides or the boat is stored.

The 1958 act also authorized the states to collect fees for their issuance of these numbers, but it set no maximum or minimum limits to the fees. Some states charge only a small fee to cover their cost of issuing the certificate, but other states consider the fees a potentially significant source of revenue—in some cases for nonboating activities—so they charge much higher fees for the same numbering certificate. In some states the class of your boat (which is determined by its length, see Chapter 5 on regulations) determines the fee you will pay.

Both the 1940 and 1958 acts were superseded by the Federal Boating Safety Act of 1971, which in effect rewrote recreational boating regulations. Its basic thrust was to set minimum standards for boats and equipment, to organize the numbering of all boats not documented with the Coast Guard, to establish the Boating Safety Advisory Council, and to help the states and territories with money for boating-safety programs.

In 1983 Congress amended the federal shipping statutes in an effort to streamline and clarify recreational boating regulations. The result is that today each state or territory must meet minimum registration requirements set by the federal government. These include:

- vessel numbering
- safety equipment onboard
- navigation rules
- lights and day shapes
- pollution rules
- boating accident reports
- distress assistance

Many of these regulations are discussed at length in Chapter 5. To learn about the state boating laws that you are subject to, contact your local boating-law enforcement office. See Appendix F for a list of those addresses.

Both registered and titled boats must carry large, easily readable identification numbers. Some authorities argue that when these boats are stolen, it is easier to trace them than it would be if they were documented and carried no easily identifiable numbers. But we know of no statistics to support this.

Recreational boaters are often unsure whether boats of about 28 feet and longer should be (a) registered with state authorities, (b) documented with the Coast Guard, or (c) both. It's hard for recreational boaters to know who is in charge—the federal government or the authorities in their home state. This chapter should help clarify these things.

## State Registration and Titling Systems

Federal law requires the states to assign numbers to all vessels with propulsion machinery that are used in waters under federal jurisdiction. Each state has adopted a system of either registration or titling, except in Alaska where the Coast Guard handles the numbering of all vessels. Even though federal law exempts documented vessels and certain other boats (foreign-flagged vessels temporarily in this country, lifeboats carried aboard ships, and government-owned boats not used for recreation) from being registered, it does permit any state to go beyond federal law and require the numbering of documented vessels, sailboats, and rowboats, if that state sees fit to do so. (For a free copy of the U.S. Coast Guard's "Federal Requirements" pamphlet for recreational boats, call the Boating Safety Hotline at 1-800-368-5647.)

So if your undocumented boat—no matter what size—has a motor, it must be either registered or titled in the state of its principal use. And, depending on that state's laws, your sailboat or documented vessel may have to be registered or titled as well.

Registration and titling help states regulate boating activities within their borders and provide a source of revenue from fees and taxes. Identification numbers can also help authorities locate a boat after it is stolen.

What is the principal difference between registration and titling? In a state that uses the registration method, you may only be required to pay a fee to be given a number to put on your boat. In a titling state, you have to show proof that you own the boat before you are issued the identification numbers and a title that names you as the owner. You can sign over this title to someone buying your boat, just as you can with your car's title.

Even though titled and registered boats carry large identification numbers, boat thieves can alter the numbers. For example, there's the case of the *Queen Bee*, a 44-foot motorsailer that was stolen from a yard in Galesville, Maryland in 1972. Even though a description of the boat was provided to the Coast Guard and other authorities, it was allowed to proceed through the Intracoastal Waterway, because its numbers had been altered. *Queen Bee* was not recovered until she was finally run aground at Beaufort, South Carolina.

### State Registration

About half the states have a registration system as opposed to a titling system. The registration systems used by many states simply require that you pay an annual fee to secure a number and a sticker to put on your boat. Registered vessels are not required to display their home ports on their bows or transoms.

Because you get no title to prove you are the owner of the boat, and because no *chain of title* is established, these registration systems do not protect good-faith purchasers from buying boats that are stolen or burdened with liens or mortgages. No such tracking is possible in a registration state, but authorities there can determine who holds the current registration of a particular boat.

Some boaters argue that the real objective of state registration is to tax boats, and that their only motivation for getting the registration sticker is to show authorities at a glance that they have paid their registration fees. Failure to register a boat can subject its owner to fines and other criminal charges that vary from state to state.

The numbers issued to the owner must appear on both sides of the bow or forward portion of the boat. They must be at least three inches high, of plain block design of a solid color that contrasts with the background, and read from left to right. Plastic, wooden or adhesive numbers manufactured for this purpose can be purchased at marine chandlers and then secured in place, or the numbers can be painted onto the hull or superstructure. Only one set of numbers may be displayed, and the only other thing that may be shown nearby is the state or Coast Guard validation stickers showing that current fees have been paid.

### State Titling

Those states that do not require registration instead have a titling system, but titled boats must carry identifying numbers identical to those of registered boats, as described in the paragraph above.

Titled boats, like registered boats, are not required to display their home ports on the bows or transoms.

The boat titling method is similar to that used for titling automobiles. A new boat title is issued whenever a boat is purchased or sold, and it names the legal owner and in some cases any lender who is still owed money. When the boat is resold, the title must be signed by the seller and taken to the state authority by the new owner for issuance of a new title. In this way, a chain of title is established.

Some would argue that the titling system helps authorities track stolen boats more easily, and presumably it warns prospective buyers of liens against a boat. This often works, but no system is foolproof. For example, no titling system can protect against unrecorded liens incurred when work was done to a boat or when it created debts outside the U.S. Under admiralty law, a lien need not be filed to be effective. See the discussion of liens in Chapter 9.

## The Federal Documentation System

The federal documentation system operated by the U.S. Coast Guard was originally designed for the registration of large commercial vessels. But as the numbers of boaters increased, new problems arose for the people who make loans for recreational boats. Lenders eventually found that they could, and should, protect themselves from foreclosures of boat loans by using the federal government and its system of courts. Lenders began insisting on federal documentation of the boats for which they made big loans. This phenomenon led to a dramatic increase in the number of boats documented with the Coast Guard.

Originally, documentation provided a central location for keeping track of boats registered with the federal government and a means to trace the title of a boat. Someone buying a documented vessel could readily tell who the seller was, whether the seller actually owned it free and clear, or whether any mortgages or recorded liens encumbered the boat.

Because boats can be transported so easily, lenders still feel that requiring boats to be documented with the Coast Guard gives them greater protection if the boat is moved out of the lenders' region. Lenders can check with the Coast Guard office where the boat is documented to see who the owner is and if any liens are outstanding.

Unfortunately, this protection is somewhat limited if the boat is moved from the Coast Guard district in which it is documented and the documentation is changed. The tracking system doesn't work as planned for documented vessels, because vessels might also be registered or titled.

You might check for encumbrances with the Coast Guard and then buy a boat that you believe is free of mortgages and liens, only to learn later that someone had filed a lien with the state filing authority. You might buy a boat that was properly registered with a state authority, but later find out it had been financed in another jurisdiction and moved.

A documented vessel need not carry its official identification number on its bow, unless it is also either registered or titled. However, the number must be permanently affixed on some structural part of the hull, usually on a main bulkhead. This tradition of placing documentation numbers inside dates back to the age of sail, when wooden shipwrecks were fairly common. One of the last structural timbers to decompose on the sea floor was the main bulkhead, so salvors could identify the ship decades later.

Documentation numbers must be preceded by the abbreviation "No." in Arabic letters not less than three inches high. Don't confuse the official documentation number with the manufacturer's serial number.

Because the documentation numbers might be visible only from inside the boat, thieves may initially find documented boats easier to move and disguise. But amateur pirates find that tampering with numbers is more difficult when they are carved, welded or embossed into a main bulkhead.

Documented vessels used exclusively for pleasure must also carry both the boat name and its hailing or home port in clearly legible letters not less than four inches in height on the exterior of the hull. The hailing port is where the owner resides. The home port is where the vessel's documentation office is located, which may or may not be where the owner resides.

For boat names and ports, most big chandlers sell individual letters of the proper size in wood, adhesive vinyl, or plastic. But if you're looking for a chance to add some personality to your boat, let a professional boat painter get creative—so long as the graphics of the name and port are still clearly legible.

Commercial documented vessels must have their full name on both bows and the name and the hailing or home port on the stern.

The biggest advantage to documenting a vessel is that it helps when you're trying to secure a loan. In fact, if the boat can be documented, the bank financing your purchase may require it. Banks believe that it is easier to protect their loans with documented vessels. If aesthetics are important to you, consider that only documented vessels may legally fly the U.S. ensign, and documented boats that aren't registered or titled don't need to carry official numbers on their bows.

If you buy a previously documented boat, the Coast Guard district headquarters will issue you a new certificate when you apply.

Documentation does not always mean that you need not register with your state authority. Federal law allows—and some states require—that documented vessels also be registered or titled. California, Alaska, and Hawaii do not require registration of documented pleasure boats. In Washington state, documented pleasure boats are not exempt from registration, but documented commercial boats are. Oregon and Florida require all documented vessels used primarily in state waters to be registered.

Nor can you avoid paying taxes levied by state or local authorities by documenting your boat. State and local laws have closed these loopholes in recent years.

When encountering the U.S. Coast Guard or a foreign navy in foreign waters, it makes little difference whether your boat is registered or titled. A certificate of documentation, however, is conclusive evidence of nationality. A documented vessel may be sold to a foreign citizen, but he or she cannot continue its documentation. In times of war, documented vessels may not be conscripted any more than may undocumented vessels. Nor is immunity from confiscation by foreign governments affected by documentation.

## Documentation
## Procedures

Before you get excited about documenting your boat with the Coast Guard, you need to know if it qualifies. The minimum *net tonnage* is five tons, which has little to do with the weight of the boat—and nothing to do with tons that weigh 2,000 pounds. Derived from commercial shipping, a *net ton* equals 100 cubic feet of interior cargo space. To find a boat's net tonnage, a formula is used. For most pleasure boats, five net tons works out to be an overall length of about 25 to 27 feet.

### *Procedure for Determining Net Tonnage*

This procedure has three parts. First, measure and write down your boat's overall length as *L*, overall breadth as *B*, and overall depth as *D*. You need to use the Coast Guard's definition of these terms.

Overall length L is "the horizontal distance between the foremost part of the stem and the aftermost part of the stern, excluding bowsprits, boomkins, rudders, outboard motor brackets and similar fittings or attachments."

Overall breadth B is "the horizontal distance, excluding rubrails, from the outside of the skin (outside planking or plating) on one side to the outside of the skin on the other, taken at the widest part of the hull."

Overall depth D is "the vertical taken at or near midships from a line drawn horizontally through the uppermost edges of the skin at the sides of the hull (excluding the cap rail and trunks, cabins, or deckhouses) to the outboard face of the bottom skin of the hull. This excludes the keel unless the keel is covered by the skin."

Multiply L times B times D, and your answer is called LBD.

Second, use the LBD and various formulae to find the GT or gross tonnage. The type of boat determines which formula you use.

For most powerboats, GT = ⅔ (LBD/100). For most sailboats, GT = ½ (LBD/100). For most multihulls, GT equals the sum of the tonnage of the hulls.

It's a little more complex for houseboats or other boats on which "the volume of a deckhouse is disproportionate to the volume of the hull." In these cases, the volume of the deck is calculated in cubic feet and the answer is divided by 100 to get the GT of the deckhouse. The deckhouse GT is added to the GT of the hull to get the whole houseboat's GT.

Third, use the GT to determine the NT or net tonnage. Again, the type of boat determines the formula.

For inboard-powered sailboats, NT = 0.9 x GT. For powerboats not designed for sailing, NT = 0.8 x GT. For boats with no propulsion machinery, NT = GT.

If you decide to document your boat, you may obtain the application appropriate for your type of vessel from your local Coast Guard district headquarters. Return the completed application with the appropriate fee, which is currently about $100.

You might prefer to hire a documentation service to handle this paperwork, or your bank or finance company may require it. To find a vessel documentation service, look in the phone book of most large cities and boating communities. Depending on what part of the country you live in, the service fee for documenting a vessel runs from $150 to $500, or more for vessels over 40 feet.

One problem with the documentation process is that, due to staff cutbacks in the Coast Guard, the paperwork process can take from 30 days to as long as a year. In the meantime, your state authority will insist on registration or titling.

## Reciprocity

One of the cornerstones of the federal regulatory scheme is the assurance of coordination and cooperation between all states and territories in their efforts to develop uniformity in boating laws and regulations. This concept is known as *reciprocity*.

As a result, federal law requires that each state and territory recognize the numbers awarded to a boat by any other state or territory for at least 90 days. You may take your boat, registered in your state of residence, to another state and operate it there for up to 90 days without registering there. If you stay longer than 90 days, you will have to meet the registration requirements of the new state.

Some states, such as Florida, recognize that hundreds of boaters from colder states often cruise down and visit longer than 90 days but do not wish to become permanent residents, so the state allows them to maintain their out-of-state vessel registration indefinitely.

If you plan a cruise to another state or territory that will keep you there for more than 90 days, you should find out what their vessel registration requirements expect of you.

## User Fees

One of the most controversial registration requirements facing boaters in recent history was the federally mandated user fee, which is currently being phased out.

Attempting to balance the federal budget, Congress passed a very unpopular law that required boatowners to pay an annual user fee that was based on boat length. The structure has been as follows:

- $25 for boats 16 feet but less than 20 feet
- $35 for boats 20 feet but less than 27 feet
- $50 for boats 27 feet but less than 40 feet
- $100 for boats over 40 feet

The fees do not apply to boats under 16 feet in length, public vessels such as rescue boats or fireboats, lifeboats, yacht tenders, rowboats, canoes, kayaks, rowing sculls, unpowered houseboats, some Coast Guard auxiliary vessels, or foreign vessels temporarily in the U.S. Vessels owned by some nonprofit charitable organizations and used for training purposes were exempted.

If your boat is one of those not yet phased out, your remaining fees may be paid with Visa or MasterCard by calling (800) 848-2100, or by obtaining a decal request form from the Coast Guard and mailing it to U.S. RVF, P.O. Box 740169, Atlanta, Georgia 30321-0169.

The decal should be affixed on the bow within six inches of the state-issued registration numbers. Don't cover the state decal showing payment of their fees.

The irony of the user fee is that none of the moneys collected will be used to fund Coast Guard or boating activities. Instead, they'll go into the U.S. Treasury to offset our budget deficits.

# 5

# Boating Regulations

| | ✛ | |

Traditionally, boating laws have tended to focus more on the safety equipment carried on board than on how boaters were boating, but that has begun to change. Every year, more jurisdictions are jumping into the abyss of regulating boating operations. Where you can anchor and for how long are volatile issues, as are environmental pollution and boating while intoxicated.

Whether you sail only on weekends or plan to retire aboard your power cruiser at the dock, these issues are inescapable. The best way to stay out of trouble with the law is to know it. Call your state or local boating-law authority to learn about boating laws specific to your favorite waters. But regardless of where you live or how often you use your boat, the following are the basic boating laws that everyone should know.

## Equipment Regulation

Federal law specifies the minimum equipment required aboard vessels at all times, although the actual law may have been passed by the state in which you operate your boat. Generally, the law deals with personal flotation devices, firefighting and ventilation equipment, and distress signaling gear, all in relation to the size of your boat. We will discuss only the minimum equipment required to be aboard your boat before it leaves the dock;

you could always upgrade it or add more. As you load a shopping cart with this gear at your local chandlery, remember that it may save someone's life someday, maybe yours.

All boats with motors (including outboard motors) are organized for purposes of these regulations by classes. Presently the classes are:

- Class A—less than 16 feet in length
- Class 1—16 feet up to 26 feet
- Class 2—26 feet up to 40 feet
- Class 3—40 feet up to 65 feet

### Personal Flotation Devices

The law requires that you carry one approved personal flotation device or PFD for each person on board. They must be kept where they are readily available when needed. PFDs are categorized into five types, and they are clearly labeled with the number of their type:

- Type I PFD: This vest-type life preserver is designed to turn an unconscious person face up in the water and is required to offer more than 20 pounds of buoyancy.
- Type II PFD: Similar to Type I but offering only 15½ pounds of buoyancy, this vest-type life preserver is usually more comfortable to wear.
- Type III PFD: Also a vest-type life preserver, this type offers the same 15½ pounds of buoyancy as Type II, but it does not have to be designed to turn an unconscious person face up in the water.
- Type IV PFD: This throw-type device is not meant to be worn. It is specifically designed to be thrown to someone in the water who can grasp it and hang on. It offers 16½ pounds of buoyancy. Some life rings and buoyant cushions qualify.
- Type V PFD: Designed for specific or restricted use, this so-called *float coat* provides the wearer with buoyancy while in the water. Some sports vests and water skiing vests are also recognized as Type V PFDs.

Which type you must carry on board depends on the size of your boat.

If your boat is under 16 feet, you need one Type I, II, III, or IV for each person onboard. That means your throwing ring can suffice for one person instead of a vest-type life preserver. If your boat is over 16 feet in length, each person onboard needs one Type I, II, or III, and you must additionally carry a Type IV, the throwing ring. Remember, you can't put a child in an adult PFD nor an adult in a child's. The PFDs must be in serviceable condition and "immediately available."

### Fire Extinguishers

Fire is one of the most deadly accidents that occur aboard a boat, so seasoned mariners pay close attention to firefighting equipment. The kinds and sizes of equipment you select depend on what is burning and where, but as always, the size of your boat determines how much gear you must carry.

Of the four types of acceptable equipment that you may carry on board, dry chemical extinguishers are probably the most convenient and low cost and can be quickly recharged. However, when expended on a fire, the fine powder tends to dust everything nearby and is messy to clean up. The chemicals are often corrosive, so they must be removed immediately.

Carbon dioxide extinguishers are cleaner than dry chemical types and leave no residue to be cleaned up after the fire is out. $CO_2$ is not a harmful chemical to humans, but recharging and checking $CO_2$ extinguishers is more difficult than dry chemical ones.

Halon 1211 and Halon 1301 are colorless, odorless gases used to fight fires on board. Halon is heavier than air and in light concentrations can be breathed by humans. Unfortunately, Halon affects the earth's ozone layer, and if drawn into your boat's engine, it turns into a toxic gas.

Foam, the final approved type, is seldom chosen for pleasure boats, because it must be kept from freezing. It must be recharged annually, and once used, the harmful chemicals in the foam are difficult to clean up.

All firefighting systems must be approved by the Coast Guard and carry a plate indicating that fact. They may be hand-held, semiportable, or fixed, installed systems. As with PFDs, the equipment you are required to carry depends on the size of your boat.

Many large yachts, for example, have automatic firefighting systems installed so that several nozzles mounted overhead in the engine room spray predirected streams of Halon as soon as a sensor indicates a fire has begun. Automatic shut-downs turn off the flow of diesel, halt ventilation fans and seal off air intake vents to smother the fire. Such systems have extinguished fires before anyone onboard knew a fire had begun.

Fires are classified into three types according to the combustible material involved. Class A fires consume wood, paper, cloth, and other material that is extinguishable with water. Class B fires involve flammable products such as diesel fuel, gasoline, fiberglass resin, paint, and solvents used on boats. Depriving such fires of their oxygen is the fastest way to put them out. Class C fires involve electrical equipment.

Fire extinguishers are rated A, B, and C, according to the class of fire they are designed to fight. For example, a Type B extinguisher is designed to fight a Class B fire, one involving diesel, gasoline, resin, paint, solvent, or other flammables. Because Class B fires are the primary concern aboard boats, the law requires that your boat carry at least a Type B extinguisher. Type B-C extinguishers are effective for both classes of fire.

Extinguishers are also rated by size, with I being the smallest and V being the biggest. In general, if your boat is less than 26 feet in length, you are required to carry one Type B-I extinguisher in working condition on board. If your boat is less than 40 feet in length but at least 26 feet in length, you must have two Type B-I (or one Type B-II) extinguishers. If it is less than 65 feet in length but at least 40 feet, you must have three Type B-I extinguishers (or one Type B-I and one Type B-II).

If your boat is less than 26 feet and has a fixed firefighting system installed in the engine compartment, you need not have any other extinguishers aboard. If it is between 26 and 40 feet in length and has a fixed firefighting system installed, then you must also have one Type B-I extinguisher. If the boat is between 40 feet and 65 feet you will have to have two Type B-I (or one Type B-II) extinguishers in addition to the fixed system.

It's a very good idea to show each guest where all the fire extinguishers are located and how to use them. You can make it part of the tour, and while you're at it, remember that all portable extinguishers and fixed systems must have periodic inspections and recharging.

## Special Rules for Gasoline Engines

If you have a gasoline-powered inboard engine, it must be equipped with a flame arrestor approved by the Coast Guard. The purpose of the flame arrestor is to prevent—as the name implies—flames in the event that your engine backfires.

If your boat has an inboard gasoline engine or internal gasoline fuel tanks, it must have at least two ventilation ducts for every engine or fuel-tank compartment, no matter how many tanks are in a compartment. Older boats built before July 31, 1980, need only have natural ventilation using cowls or other designs, but boats built since that date must have mechanically powered exhaust blowers.

## Signals and Other Equipment Regulations

In many lakes and coastal areas, fog can form quickly and blind boaters trying to return to port or to a safe dock. Rain, snow, and smog can also impair visibility, so even in this age of inexpensive radar, boats are required to carry bells and horns. These seemingly insignificant items can become important in a sudden fog—or when the boarding officer asks to see your bell. Also, a copy of the appropriate *Rules of the Road* must be on board every vessel of 39 feet (12 meters) or longer.

If your boat is at least 16 feet in length, it must be equipped with a whistle or horn—operated either by mouth, hand, or power—loud enough to be heard for at least a half mile. A compressed-air canister-type horn is considered power-operated.

If your boat is 26 feet or longer, you must also have an adequate bell for use in fog.

If your boat is 26 feet in length but less than 40 feet, the whistle or horn must be hand- or power-operated and audible for one mile.

If your boat is longer than 40 feet but less than 65 feet, the whistle or horn must be power-operated and audible for one mile.

All boats 16 feet in length or longer must also carry Coast Guard–approved visual distress signals for both day and night operation. They must be marked with a Coast Guard approval number or certifications and must be in date. Expired flares are a common justification for a citation.

What the Coast Guard requires are actually minimum equipment needs, especially when compared to the real-life hazards boaters can find themselves in. The mere fact that something isn't required shouldn't stop you from carrying it.

Ask yourself if you have an adequate anchoring system including chain and rode. Are your bilge pumps sufficient if, say, you lose all electric power? Are your safety harnesses practical? Should you add a few more fire extinguishers? Could those musty old PFDs really support you if you were unconscious? Would that antique life ring crumble if you grabbed it?

How would someone get back aboard after they fell over the side? Are your tiny marina fenders adequate for a strange dock? Where is that boathook when you need it? Don't substitute a dangerous fishing gaff. Does your built-in searchlight still point where you aim it? Do your hand-held lanterns have fresh batteries?

Boats can end up in unexpected places quite easily, so do you have charts covering the entire region? Where's that navigational publication when you need it? Do you have a real leadline or could you fashion one in a hurry? What's really in that store-bought first-aid kit? Does your tool cabinet have an ax? How much gasket material and underwater epoxy are in your spare-parts kit? Maybe you should even keep a copy of this book on board.

## Regulating the Operator

No matter how much safety gear your boat carries, there's no substitute for intelligent operation. Unfortunately, in the increasing number of boating accidents reported each year, "operator error" is at the heart of the problem. Therefore, more boating safety laws are focusing on regulating the operators.

Boating While Intoxicated (BWI) citations are more common since the Coast Guard initiated its BWI campaign to curtail accidents caused by drunken boaters. Recreational boaters can get a citation if they have a blood-alcohol concentration (BAC) of at least 0.10 percent by weight while operating a boat, according to federal law. States may set more stringent limits for recreational boaters and for licensed skippers and their crewmembers. In Oregon, for example, the state's BAC of 0.08 will be enforced for recreational operators. In California, anyone running a boat that is carrying one or more passengers for hire can be cited if he or she has a BAC of 0.04.

Boarding officers have eight hours of special BWI training, so they know how to recognize a boat being operated in a suspicious manner, observe the behavior of a suspected drunken boater, and administer the field sobriety test to determine a boater's BAC.

If you refuse to submit to the BAC sobriety test, you will be presumed intoxicated, and in any legal proceedings your refusal will be admissible as evidence of your intoxication. Also, the voyage will immediately be terminated, your boat will be escorted to a safe mooring, and an authorized law-enforcement agency may be called to the scene. If no local authority is involved, you'll be held by the Coast Guard until you're able to operate your boat safely. You could also be arrested for violation of other federal laws.

No blockades, random sobriety tests, or special patrols are being used to enforce BWI laws. The Coast Guard's normal operations have just been expanded to keep boaters from causing accidents while intoxicated.

Some states set a minimum age for operating various types of power-driven water craft. If you take your boat into another state and allow your children to drive, be sure you aren't breaking local laws.

The issue of whether to require a U.S. Coast Guard or other license for recreational boaters touches all boaters, and everyone seems to have an opinion.

Some yacht insurance companies already offer discounts for recreational boatowners who pass the U.S. Coast Guard license test. The National Transportation Safety Board has recommended that every operator of a recreational boat be licensed, and the Florida legislature has repeatedly tried to pass such a law—unsuccessfully. The National Association of State Boating Law Administrators is looking at a model for licensing legislation to be passed by various states.

People proposing the licensing argue that most boating accidents can be avoided and that requiring proficiency tests and offering safety courses would lower the number of recreational boating fatalities. If licenses could be revoked when operators were convicted of boating while intoxicated, the license would serve as a powerful lever to reduce BWI accidents. Some proponents have even urged the revocation of an operator's automobile driving license if he or she is found guilty of boating while intoxicated.

People opposed to licensing of recreational boaters point out that the number of accidents and fatalities are relatively low compared to the number of boaters out there. They also argue that licensing would create another expensive bureaucracy that costs more in taxes for everyone. In Ohio, for example, a licensing system was estimated to cost $13 million to operate, which is the state's total budget for boating enforcement and education. Opponents argue that tax money would be better spent on education and law enforcement than on licensing.

## Anchoring Restrictions

Beyond safety issues, a growing number of jurisdictions are trying to restrict anchoring and to limit or ban liveaboards. Environmental groups are concerned about what boaters leave behind in the water and air.

In recent years, some jurisdictions through which navigable waters flow have moved to restrict public use of that water by limiting the length of time a boat can stay—and exactly where a boat may anchor. These restrictions arise out of real or imagined fear that allowing someone on a boat to stay in a particular location for more than a day or two—or three—would threaten the civic tranquillity. As a result, many boaters have found themselves shunted from one area to another, due to restrictions on how long they could stay in a particular anchorage, cove, or open roadstead.

This issue is of particular concern to liveaboards who are cruising or those who simply want to stay in a place for more than three or four days. *Gently with the Tides*, edited by Michael L. Frankel (International Marine, 1993), discusses the increasing shortage of areas that allow boats to moor for more than a few days.

Reasons voiced by nonboaters for this need to restrict anchoring and living aboard include: that visiting boaters don't pay their fair share of taxes; that liveaboard families contribute to the crowding in schools.

As a result, boaters have found themselves hauled before local magistrates and judges to answer citations for violations of local laws, not unlike homeless people who often find themselves in violation of local loitering ordinances.

The legal basis for this conflict is that federal jurisdiction extends to all navigable waters, and the question asked is whether local or state jurisdictions can do anything that interferes with federal waters.

The legal battles go as follows: (1) the cities argue that they have an interest in keeping the waterways within their boundaries safe and clean for their residents and have an interest in limiting the stay of vessels that seek to visit; (2) the boaters argue that the laws passed by the local governing bodies interfere with the use of federal waters and tend to place a burden on interstate commerce—an argument that has been used successfully to overturn other local and state laws in the past. Such an argument may be difficult to use for recreational boating, since the courts have not been willing to recognize recreational boating as commerce.

While boaters hope that the local, county, and state laws restricting use of navigable waters might violate federal law, the Supreme Court of the United States has not yet addressed the issue. Unless boating organizations unite and support a test case all the way through the court system, the Supreme Court is not likely to settle this issue for quite some time.

Meanwhile, some municipal-court skirmishes over anchoring restrictions have raised public awareness, but there are no major decisions that boaters can look to for support. On the contrary, some federal courts have approved local laws that impose fees for use of municipally installed moorings. Many of those moorings have been installed in the coves and bays previously used as anchorages.

When BOAT/U.S. formally requested a response from the Commandant of the Coast Guard concerning this issue, the Coast Guard said it did not have authority to prevent states and local governments from restricting anchoring, but that the courts must validate the restrictions. It said the Supreme Court has not yet specifically determined whether such restrictions infringe on the rights of navigation.

Unless you are prepared to set yourself up as a test case and have the money and determination to go all the way to the Supreme Court, it is probably better to go along with the local laws even if you don't subscribe to them.

At least one organization has formed to combat the increasing regulations and restrictions being placed on boaters. Concerned Boaters: The National Water Rights Association (P.O. Box 2117, Stuart, FL 34995; tel.: 405-288-0952) works to alert boatowners of restrictive state and local laws and rulings, advises local groups, publishes an informational newsletter, and sponsors annual conferences on these issues. Here is a sampling of issues tracked in the May 1993 newsletter:

• Hawaiian law requires boats entering state waters to pay a fee ($1.15 per foot) within 72 hours of arrival in order just to anchor, with a maximum stay of 90 days. Failure to comply carries a potential fine of $10,000 per day.

• New Jersey limits anchoring to 10 days; San Diego Bay, to 72 hours.

• Municipal anchoring restrictions are proliferating in New York and Florida.

• Since 1990 in Edgartown Harbor, on Martha's Vinyard, Massachusetts, two private companies control nearly all the available moorings and charge $40 to $50 per night for rental. Anchoring is permitted only outside the harbor or in an area of poor holding ground far from docks and services. A similar situation exists in Nantucket Harbor.

Concerned Boaters' opposition of environmental regulations may seem overly strident to some (they do not want airboats or jet skis restricted from marine sanctuaries, for example), but they are performing a useful service for all boaters in highlighting the often confusing and arbitrary web of municipal, county, and state regulations that restrict boaters' rights.

## Liveaboard Restrictions

Many states, counties and municipalities try to regulate where liveaboards can live, whether anchored out, moored to a buoy, or slipped in a marina. As one example, Georgia, Key West, and Sausalito are all outlawing houseboats, according to Concerned Boaters.

Some marinas welcome liveaboards, feeling that they improve security. Thieves are less likely to come in by land or by water if they know they could be spotted by someone living aboard.

Other marinas prohibit liveaboards altogether under the belief that they add to the costs of the marina's operation. Full-time residents use more electricity and water than do slip holders who visit their boats only on occasional weekends. Leases in these marinas will spell out their live-aboard policy. At one marina in Seattle, liveaboards must pay 50 percent more for a mooring than other boaters.

But the vast majority of marinas hold the middle ground; they limit the number of liveaboards to a percentage of the total number of boats in the marina. For example, the California Coastal Commission has an unwritten limit of 10 percent, so most marinas in that state hesitate to accept in writing any more than that amount of liveaboards.

In some areas of the country, living aboard is a serious issue. Because of a significant lack of moorage space in these areas, the competition for a good slip in a good marina is great. As a result, the incentive to accommodate liveaboards is not so great.

What can be done? Most marinas are private businesses. The marina owners are free to establish liveaboard policies any way they wish. Publicly owned facilities may do the same. Marinas that restrict liveaboards are similar to cities that pass zoning laws restricting the kinds of businesses and buildings that may be built in a given area. So there's nothing the live-aboard can do.

If you find a marina that accepts your liveaboard status, the best thing you can do is be a good tenant. Prove that liveaboards are good to have around.

## Discharge Regulations

The number of federal laws covering pollution and boaters is almost staggering:

- The Federal Water Pollution Prevention and Control Act
- The Oil Pollution Act of 1990
- The Trans-Alaska Pipeline Authorization Act
- The Refuse Act
- The Ocean Dumping Act
- Act to Prevent Pollution from Ships

• The Comprehensive Environmental Response, Compensation and Liability Act
• The Deepwater Ports Act

Besides these federal laws, 35 states have passed laws restricting or prohibiting the discharge of pollution from boats. These laws carry a wide variety of standards for imposing damages and have extensive requirements for cleanup.

As this country moves further down the road toward righting past environmental damage, boaters are going to have to pay a greater share of the price. Whether the share is fair or not is subject to extensive and ongoing debate. Notwithstanding the debate, boat owners will be increasingly pressured to contribute to the cost of cleanup and to keep the water and air cleaner.

Recreational boats are being eyed suspiciously as a source of water pollution and air pollution as well. A study made by the federal Environmental Protection Agency showed that two-cycle engines (such as most outboard motors) can contribute in one hour of operation as much air pollution as a car driven 2,500 miles. So the EPA required the manufacturers of marine engines to meet its first set of emission standards by 1995. Of course, manufacturers warn that significant engineering challenges will result in price increases of already expensive marine equipment.

All of this means boaters are going to have to be more aware of the effects of their activities on the environment. Nothing can be thrown over the side anymore, and the demand for pumpout facilities for marine toilet systems will increase.

The recreational boater should be concerned with anything that goes into the water from his boat—both over the side or through the marine sanitation device, known affectionately as the MSD. Discharge of raw sewage from a vessel in U.S. territorial waters (inside the three-mile limit) is illegal.

Agencies in some coastal and inland areas are even putting a pill containing dye in your holding tank when you tie up, to assure that you don't pump sewage over the side.

Boats are not required to be equipped with toilets or heads, but if one is installed, it must include an MSD that meets Coast Guard standards. Remember that self-contained portable toilets or "Porta-Potties" are not considered to be "installed toilets" according to the Coast Guard, so they are not subject to regulation. You don't need an MSD if you have one of these portable toilets on board.

It's surprising to what lengths boaters will go to avoid dealing with the complex installation and maintenance of an MSD. Two couples spent two years restoring a beautiful old schooner in preparation for a cruise to Hawaii. But the graceful ship offered no likely bilge space for the installation of an MSD, so the project never got completed before the bon voyage party, which was held in a posh downtown marina. Instead, a huge red bucket was placed beneath the varnished oak toilet seat, which was to suffice for the offshore passage.

Friends and family trooped through the old schooner, toasting with champagne and, unfortunately, electing to use the charming little onboard head rather than walk up the dock to the marina facilities. When one of the sailors finally noticed that the bucket was almost overflowing, it was too late to do anything but get it out of there. On the way up the steep companionway ladder that led out into the cool night air, he slipped.

The cleanup operation set the departure date back only two days, but the captain bought each crewmember his or her own bucket, much smaller than the red one, to be emptied immediately upon use.

For more than a decade, any vessel with a toilet or head installed has been required to also be equipped with an operable MSD. A vessel under 65 feet in length may have installed a Type I, II, or III MSD. Vessels over 65 feet in length are limited to Type II or III MSDs.

A Type I MSD is any device that treats the sewage with disinfectant chemicals before it is discharged into the water. The discharge must meet certain standards for bacteria content and must not show any visible floating solids.

Type II MSDs are similar to Type I devices but meet higher levels of sewage treatment. Because of their higher power requirements, Type II MSDs are usually installed on large vessels.

Type III MSDs are the ones most used on recreational boats. Type IIIs include heads that recirculate or incinerate and those with holding tanks.

Keep in mind that if your boat has a Y-valve so that your head will either pump over the side or into the holding tank, if you are boarded by the Coast Guard when the valve is in the "over-the-side" position, you can be cited. You are also required to secure the valve while in territorial waters by the use of a padlock, a wire-tie, or a removable handle. The only acceptable place to pump out your holding tank is either at a pumpout station—sometimes called a reception facility—or at sea beyond the territorial limit of the United States.

All MSDs except those using holding tanks must be certified and must carry a label showing the name of the manufacturer, the MSD type, a certification number and a certification statement.

Boats operating in No-Discharge Zones may not discharge any sewage over the side even though they have Type I or Type II systems. The systems must also be secured so that they cannot be used in these areas. The Coast Guard considers all freshwater lakes and similar bodies of water as well as rivers not capable of interstate vessel traffic to be No-Discharge areas.

In addition, the states of California, Michigan, Minnesota, Mississippi, New Hampshire, New Mexico, New York, Texas, Vermont, and Wisconsin have established No Discharge Zones. You should check with your local boating authority to get specific information about state-established No Discharge Zones.

The Refuse Act passed in 1989 prohibits throwing or discharging any refuse into the water. The Federal Water Pollution Prevention and Control Act prohibits the discharge of oil or any hazardous material into the water. It also requires that any vessel with "machinery propulsion" must have a system to retain oil mixtures on board. You may not allow oil into the bilge of your vessel.

You must carry two placards on your boat. One explains the prohibition of oil discharge and the other does the same regarding dumping other refuse.

Governments are very serious in their commitments to cleaning up the environment, as evidenced by the increased potential for liability placed on polluters. Boatowners who are seen contributing to the problem must accept an increasing burden as well. And we can expect more laws to be placed on boaters. The days of flushing your head over the side are gone. The only solution to this increasing burden is to do your part to help.

## Noise Regulations

City ordinances restricting noise have been around since Philadelphia adopted the first one in 1830, which prohibited street vendors from using trumpets to tout their wares. The Supreme Court of the United States has upheld laws restricting the operation of internal combustion engines without mufflers.

As early as 1913, a Rhode Island statute prohibited the use of motorboats unless their engines were "provided with an underwater exhaust or a muffler," and the statute was upheld as constitutional. In 1923, a New York law prohibiting "a boat, barge, vessel or other floating structure" from operating without a muffler was also upheld as constitutional.

Other state and local laws regulating amplified music and other loud sounds have been found valid and enforceable. So it is likely that with the continuing growth in the number of people enjoying boating, more complaints will be made and more enforcement actions taken to keep peace on the waters of recreational boating.

# 6
# Buying and Selling Boats

| | ✛ | |

According to a wise old saying, "The two happiest days of a boat-owner's life are the day he or she buys his boat and the day he sells it."

The saying doesn't mention that even on these two happy days, many minor calamities can arise to ruin things for the unsuspecting buyer or seller. Fortunately, if you know the ropes about buying and selling boats before you get started, you can minimize your problems and enjoy both occasions.

Admiralty law does not usually apply to the purchase and sale of boats. Since boats are considered personal property under the law, the Uniform Commercial Code applies. The UCC, as it is called, has been adopted in every state and sets out the respective obligations and requirements for the transfer of personal property, including boats.

## Before Buying

Before you go very far down the path toward purchasing any boat, consider what happened to an unsuspecting boat buyer, Mr. Jones (not his real name), the Smith Boat Dealership (not its real name), and Mr. Allan Vaitses, who is a real marine surveyor in New England. Mr. Vaitses tells the story of the Melting Fuel Tank:

> Mr. Jones told me that he grew up in a cruising family, so later in life he wanted to buy a boat that he and his widowed father could take on

some coastwise trips—a chance to be on the water together again. He talked to Smith's Boat Dealership and ordered a twin-screw trawler-type design with a comfortable layout, nice lines, and, like many imported yachts, a fiberglass hull and deck heavily finished off with teak joinerywork inside and out. Best of all, she would have the potential for long-range cruising.

Unfortunately, Mr. Jones and his father hadn't been able to enjoy any long trips in the boat for the first two seasons he owned her. It seemed that each time they started out, the engine would quit, sometimes before they cleared the harbor mouth. Each time, the fuel filters would be clogged. At first they thought the builder had carelessly left debris in the tank. Finally, Jones had the tank drained and inspected—revealing that the interior surfaces were actually dissolving due to uncured laminates.

Jones hired a freelance fiberglass boatbuilder to make the repairs. The repairman attacked the problem by steam cleaning the interior of the tank and then coating it with a sealant. These two jobs were further complicated by the fact that the only access to the tank's interior was through the 18-inch inspection plates located under flush hatches in the polished teak parquet-on-plywood cabin sole. The 600-gallon tank consisted of four fore-and-aft integral compartments of various depths due to the V-shaped bottom from the centerline outboard. These compartments ran the full fore-to-aft length of the aft cabin. The starboard outboard compartment was under the sleeping berths, the port outboard one was under the hanging locker, and all the tank compartments projected to some degree under the head and galley.

The four compartments were properly baffled, but they were interconnected. This had been done no doubt to save the cost of four separate fill pipes, vents, and supply lines, but I pointed out that when the boat took on a heel, the fuel rushing to one side could dangerously increase the heel. This cost-saving arrangement also meant that any contamination or leak in one compartment would involve the entire fuel supply.

To abbreviate a long story, drastic measures were the only solution.

Since there were no other spaces onboard to install even a fraction of this 600-gallon fuel capacity without ruining her layout, most of the beautiful teak parquet sole had to be cut away to allow new tank surfaces to be laid up within the original tank compartments. What a mess!

Smith's Boat Dealership was sympathetic in all this, but he quite naturally thought the boatbuilder ought to pay for the repairs. Unfortunately, the foreign builder's company said it had done nothing wrong, that any problems were the owner's doing. When Mr. Jones' lawyers searched for the builder's assets to attach, they discovered that the builder owned nothing in the U.S. Further, the builder never shipped out a boat until 100 percent of payment was received. The lawsuit was brought against Smith's Boat Dealership, and the $20,000 cost put Smith out of the boat dealer business.

The lesson is that there are many things to consider about the boat you are going to own. Next to the purchase of your home, a boat may be the largest investment you ever make. Think things through thoroughly before you begin your search for the right boat.

Finding the boat that suits your needs, desires, and wallet is a subject for an entire book, and indeed several good books are available to help you. In particular, Steve Henkel's *Boating for Less: How to Save Money When Buying, Owning, or Selling Your Power or Sail Boat* (International Marine, 1992) contains three chapters under a heading called "Thinking About Buying a Boat" which you should read before even beginning to look for a boat. Henkel takes you through a process leading to the type and price range of boat that suits your needs.

## The Cost

Remember that the use, size, and kind of boat you have in mind must be balanced with how much you can afford. The initial purchase is only the beginning; you must factor moorage, insurance, operation, and maintenance into the cost equation. Anything with "marine" written on it will probably be three times as expensive.

Many people don't recognize the true costs of buying and keeping a boat. If you finance the purchase instead of paying cash, the interest you pay on your loan can be more than the principal you borrow. The costs of mooring and operating your boat can be more than the monthly loan payments. Are you ready to pay all that for an occasional weekend outing?

# Buying
## Without a Broker

Recent figures indicate that the average price of a boat sold in the U.S. is between $8,000 and $9,000. Thus, on average, most used-boat deals are transacted without the benefit of a broker, since most boat brokers are not interested in sales that won't generate a large commission. It's a buyer's market these days, and there are some wonderful deals on used boats out there. It's probably safe to say that the best deals *and* some of the worst are those conducted without broker participation. When you operate solo, you climb out near the end of the risk-reward branch.

If you're on your own, without a broker, there is much to keep in mind. First, make sure the person selling the boat really owns it. Boat theft is a growing problem, and law books are full of cases where someone bought a boat from a seller who didn't own it.

There is no foolproof way to guarantee that the person selling a boat actually owns it. People intent upon larceny are likely to do just about anything to succeed. But by making a few pertinent inquiries, you can do as much as possible to avoid trouble.

Ask to see the state registration or Coast Guard documentation papers. If the seller's name doesn't appear somewhere on those documents, beware.

Ask to see the previous Bill of Sale for the same reason.

Ask to see the boat's insurance policy, since it isn't likely that a thief would insure a stolen boat.

You might also try to contact the previous owner of the boat, a step that might answer your questions about ownership but won't help when it comes to liens. Having the seller sign an affidavit certifying his or her ownership and that there are no liens, claims, or encumbrances is probably of little value unless the seller is honest. Neither is having him or her sign under oath. After all, a crook is a crook.

### Hidden Liens

It is possible that somewhere a hidden lien exists for work that was done on the boat, so ask the seller if all repairmen and suppliers have been paid, or if any liens are still outstanding. Despite what was said above, it doesn't hurt to ask. For more information on liens, see Chapter 9.

To track down hidden liens yourself, you can also go to the courthouse of the county where the boat is registered. This should be where it was principally used, not necessarily where the seller lives. The county clerk of the court should be able to help you, or you can ask for the office responsible for filing personal-property titles, liens, and mortgages. Ask for information about outstanding chattel mortgages, Bills of Sale, or liens on the boat you're considering buying.

If the boat is documented, the Coast Guard Office of Marine Inspection at the boat's home or hailing port (required to be mounted on the stern of the boat) can provide you with a report showing liens or mortgages outstanding against the boat if they are filed with that office.

Under the UCC, a thief selling you a boat cannot give you what is called *good title* to the boat. When you buy a stolen boat, you buy nothing but problems. If the real owner shows up after you have purchased the boat, he or she can reclaim the boat, and your only recourse is against the thief.

A Florida case involved the buyer of a boat suing the seller, who was a dealer. Unless otherwise agreed, a dealer warrants title to the thing he or she sells. It turned out that the boat was stolen and the buyer sued under the warranty of title given by the dealer. After finding evidence that the dealer knew the boat was stolen, the jury awarded the buyer damages for breach of the warranty of title and for fraud and misrepresentation. Warranties are discussed in more depth later in this chapter.

Healthy skepticism is justified when dealing with a private owner. If the seller can't provide you with any of the above documentation to show ownership of the boat in question, walk away.

## Care and Feeding
## of Yacht Brokers

While most states require real-estate salespeople to be trained and licensed, there is little if any licensing of boat brokers in most jurisdictions. That is not to imply that boat brokers are crooks. A reputable, established boat broker can steer you through the complicated process of buying or selling your boat with a minimum of problems. After all, that's why he or she is paid a commission.

Most large-boat purchases are done through boat dealers or brokers trained to handle the often complex transactions. If you're selling a boat, the broker is your agent, and it is his or her job to represent your interests in any transaction involving your boat. If you're buying a boat, remember that the broker is representing the seller, unless you've made an agreement with a broker for the specific purpose of helping you buy a boat.

If you're selling a boat through a broker, you and the broker have what is called a *fiduciary relationship* arising out of the special confidence you place in him. As a fiduciary, the broker is legally required to exercise fidelity and good faith in his dealings with you, and to account for all funds that he or she may receive on your behalf. The broker may not do anything that is adverse to your interests.

In a fiduciary relationship, the broker must abide by certain standards, which include following all instructions you may give and transmitting all offers to you no matter what he or she thinks of them. Also included is the duty not to use for his or her own purposes any money owed to the owner that may come into the broker's hands. Most brokers maintain an escrow or trust account in which they deposit money received on behalf of customers. Generally, your broker may do nothing that is not in your best interest without your full knowledge and consent.

You may encounter three varieties of brokerage agreements: an open listing, an exclusive listing, or a central listing.

In an open listing, the seller lists his boat with many brokers while retaining the right to sell it himself (commission-free) as well. An exclusive listing is one given to a single broker; often under an exclusive listing, the broker will get a commission even if the owner sells the boat himself. A central listing is split between the broker who first receives the listing from the owner—usually known as the listing broker—and the broker who sells the boat—known as the selling broker. The listing and selling brokers can be from the same or different offices.

Most brokerage agreements will be for a specified time. It is of course in the interest of the broker to make the contract as long as possible. On the other hand, it may be in your best interest to keep the contract short, so that if the current broker is not successful in selling your boat, you may go to another.

Brokers are likely to insist upon an exclusive contract, of which some are worded such that even if you sell the boat on your own, you must pay the broker a commission. You may be able to negotiate an open-listing contract, but brokers will argue that an exclusive contract is an incentive to work harder to sell the boat, but that a nonexclusive contract will be looked upon with less enthusiasm.

## Get It in Writing

The first rule in buying *or* selling a boat is to get it in writing. In spite of the best intentions of parties on both sides, things can go wrong, and the best protection you can have in a subsequent court dispute is a written document signed by both parties setting out the terms and conditions of the sale. You may encounter several different documents when buying or selling a boat—a letter of intent, a sales contract, a purchase order, and a bill of sale.

A letter of intent is a document expressing your intention to buy the boat. It can be used to "hold" the boat while you arrange for a survey and financing. Although letters of intent are seldom used, they are handy in situations where a contract isn't likely to be used.

For example, if you find a boat you are interested in buying, you could write a letter of intent and give it to the owner along with a deposit to hold the boat while you have a survey done and arrange financing. The letter of intent should state that if the boat does not pass the survey to your satisfaction or if your financing falls through, you get your deposit back. If the boat surveys well and your financing goes through, you give the owner a check for the balance of purchase price, and he or she gives you the boat and a bill of sale transferring ownership to you.

A sales contract, which is more formal than a letter of intent, is commonly used in more complex purchases of larger vessels, boats purchased on contract, or owner-financed purchases. In these cases, the contract should set out the terms and conditions of the transaction and specify the particular steps to be taken by which parties, including survey and financing. It could also set times or dates by which certain things will be accomplished. A sales contract is usually drafted during the course of the negotiations.

What terms, conditions, and provisions should a legally sufficient contract contain? It should state:

- general description of the boat
- documentation and/or registration numbers
- hull identification number
- complete inventory of equipment that goes with the boat
- where and when it will be delivered
- liability for loss before and after delivery
- purchase price
- terms of payment
- acknowledgment of earnest money/deposit, if given
- a listing of liens or claims and who will pay them
- whether the sale is subject to a survey and a reasonable length of time for the survey to be completed
- a provision for negotiations if the survey finds problems

If all these items are included in your contract, it will go a long way toward eliminating problems.

Many people confuse a sales contract with a bill of sale, but there is a big difference. See the sample in Appendix A.

A bill of sale (see accompanying sample on pages 80–83) is a document that actually transfers ownership and title of the boat from the seller to the buyer. It is executed and handed over to the buyer only when the deal is closed, pursuant to the terms of the contract.

A purchase order is a specialized sales contract that boat manufacturers and dealers routinely offer. It usually includes language limiting their liability in the event of problems, including their liability or breach of warranties that would otherwise be implied under the UCC, as discussed later in this chapter. Nevertheless a purchase order is a binding contract when signed. It may offer some protection to the buyer, but a formal, carefully drafted contract will give you more protection in the event of a problem.

Get a written inventory of what will be included with the boat. This eliminates disputes later when something you thought was included turns

| DEPARTMENT OF TRANSPORTATION<br>U.S. Coast Guard<br>CG-1340 (Rev. 12-83) | **BILL OF SALE** | OMB APPROVED<br>2115-0110 |
|---|---|---|
| 1. VESSEL NAME | | 2. OFFICIAL NUMBER[1] |

3. NAMES(S) OF SELLER(S) AND INTEREST OWNED BY EACH

3a. TOTAL INTEREST OWNED _____

4. NAME(S) OF BUYER(S) AND INTEREST TRANSFERRED TO EACH

4a. TOTAL INTEREST TRANSFERRED _____

5. CONSIDERATION RECEIVED

6. I (we) do hereby sell to the buyer(s) named above, my (our) right, title, and interest in the vessel together with the following necessaries and appurtenances:

This sale is made to the buyers in the proportion specified, subject to the following warranties and conditions:

| 7. SIGNATURE(S) OF SELLER(S) OR PERSON(S) SIGNING ON BEHALF OF SELLER | 8. DATE SIGNED |
|---|---|
| | |

9. NAME(S) OF PERSON(S) SIGNING ABOVE AND LEGAL CAPACITY IN WHICH SIGNED

10. ACKNOWLEDGMENT *(Insert such acknowledgement language as is required by state law.)*

The acknowledgement may not be taken by an officer or employee of the Coast Guard.

[1]If vessel has never been awarded an official number, complete those items of vessel data on reverse of form as are known.

*Previous Editions May Be Used*

SN 7530-00-F01-1020

Reverse of CG-1340 (Rev. 12-83)

*(Complete only if Vessel Does Not Have An Official Number)*

## VESSEL DATA

a. Builder _____

b. Builder's hull number _____

c. Hull identification number _____

d. Former names _____

e. Former motorboat numbers _____

f. Former alien registrations _____

g. Person from whom seller obtained vessel _____

h. Dimensions _____

_____
SIGNATURE OF SELLER

## INSTRUCTIONS

1. Indicate current documented name. (If vessel has never been documented complete data section on reverse of form.)

2. Indicate official number awarded to vessel. (If vessel has never been documented leave blank; complete data section on reverse of form.)

3. Show names of all sellers, individual interest owned by each and type of ownership (e.g., Tenants by Entireties, Joint Tenants, etc.), if applicable.

3a. Self-explanatory.

4. Show names of all buyers, individual interest transferred to each and type of ownership (e.g., Tenants by Entireties, etc.), if applicable.

4a. Self-explanatory.

5. Self-explanatory.

6. Self-explanatory.

7. Self-explanatory.

8. Show date on which instrument is signed.

9. Self-explanatory.

10. Insert acknowledgment as required by state where acknowledgment is taken. (ATTESTATION AND/OR WITNESSING OF SIGNATURE(S) ARE NOT SUFFICIENT FOR RECORDATION.)

NOTE: This instrument cannot be altered after execution and acknowledgment. Alterations made prior to execution must be noted within acknowledgment.

_____ COAST GUARD DISTRICT

Port of _____

Received for record on the _____ day of _____ , 19 ____

at _____ M., and recorded in Book _____ , Page _____ .

_____
DOCUMENTATION OFFICER

953-408

up missing—for example, the storm anchor or some custom-made bedding.

A written document serves several important functions. First, it is recognized by courts as the expression of the parties' intentions at the time it was signed. It is the best evidence you can present spelling out who was supposed to do what. In the absence of a written document, the court only has your word against the other party's.

A written document will also serve to reduce legal costs in the event of a dispute. Because the legal process involves both a determination of the facts and the application of the law to those facts, if the facts are already set out in a written, signed document, the only job left for a judge is the application of the law.

The bill of sale or other documents need not be drafted by a lawyer. In fact, most stationery stores sell preprinted legal forms that conform to the law of that state. All you have to do is fill in the blanks. It can also be handwritten by any of the parties or someone else. The important thing is that it is signed by all parties to the transaction. The signing does not even have to be done in front of a notary, although doing so will eliminate later problems, since a notary ensures that the person or persons signing a document are in fact who they say they are.

Much as we'd like to change it, our world has become a very litigious one. The simple act of getting an agreement in writing will help to minimize problems and costs if the deal goes bad.

## The Importance of a Marine Survey

One of the cheapest ways to protect yourself when buying a used boat is to hire a marine survey. A survey should provide two things: an extensive evaluation of the condition of the boat and an estimated market value. Although the seller may show you a recent survey of his used boat, you'll do well to have your own survey performed.

A marine survey shouldn't be needed on a new boat, because the selling dealer should make sure everything works properly. If the boat is new, you may choose to rely on the dealer or builder's warranties, including warranty of title, with the caveats already mentioned in this chapter. Warranties are discussed later in this chapter.

But when buying any used boat that costs more than a few thousand dollars, make your offer subject to a marine survey. The money accompanying the offer should be held in an escrow or trust account by the broker until after you have hired a surveyor and he or she has done the survey.

This arrangement allows you to find any hidden problems with the boat and to reduce your offer to reflect the needed repairs. If too many problems are uncovered or if one or two problems are too big, you can withdraw your offer. If no broker is involved, you should still make your offer subject to survey and arrange for the seller to hold your deposit. Since the seller will have to take the boat off the market for two or three weeks, he or she has the right to expect a sign of your seriousness.

Marine surveys may also be required for boat loans, new yacht-insurance policies, and damage claims. The survey will give the lender a valuation for loan purposes.

If you're in the market for a larger boat that costs considerable money, it is a good idea to contact a surveyor before choosing a boat. The surveyor can give you guidance about the best value and the weaknesses and strengths of a particular make and model. The surveyor may also give you guidance on the suitability of a boat for particular uses or locales.

More importantly, the survey will give you a current assessment of the condition and seaworthiness of the boat you intend to buy.

There is no mandatory licensing for marine surveyors. Anyone can hang up a sign or get a listing in the Yellow Pages under "Surveyors, Marine." People calling themselves marine surveyors have little or no regulation. As a result, finding a qualified surveyor can be difficult. Never hire the same surveyor who performed the seller's survey. Don't ask that surveyor or the seller for recommendations. Here's why not:

A West Coast buyer named Gene found an ad for a used oil-field crew boat in Louisiana, and it sounded like just what he was looking for to convert into a yacht for his world cruise. Without local knowledge, Gene asked the seller for a recommendation for a surveyor. That surveyor recommended a local boatyard where the 80-footer could be hauled out, and the yard recommended a mechanic to test the engines and transmissions.

Gene flew down and gave the go-ahead for the survey but had to return to his job before the yard had time to haul the vessel. Two weeks later he got the bills. They seemed rather high, but the survey included an audio-gauge test of the thickness of the steel hull. The surveyor's diagrams showed the hull to be sound, and the mechanic's evaluations said that all systems were shipshape. Since the asking price was too good to pass up, Gene bought the boat and hired a delivery skipper to bring it to San Francisco.

When the delivery team arrived, however, they found that the boat had never been moved, let alone hauled out at a yard. Nor had the engines been turned over in years. They couldn't even tow it away from the dock, because the hull had literally grown to the bottom, 10 feet below the keel. Worst of all, its steel hull was so thin below the waterline that light showed through seeping pinholes everywhere.

The list of people who blatantly lied to the new owner includes the surveyor, the listing broker, the yard owner, the mechanic, the previous boat owner, and the dock master where the boat had been kept for years. Gene's bitter legal battles rage on, but the surveyor is still in business.

Because word-of-mouth is about the only real regulation in the marine surveying industry, the best way to begin your search is by talking with someone at your lending institution or at a major marine-insurance agency. They carry lists of qualified surveyors, and it is in their best interest to make sure the survey is an honest one.

Boatyard owners and brokers who have nothing to gain also can recommend a few qualified marine surveyors. Ask any friends who have recently bought boats and had surveys.

Another source of qualified surveyors is the National Association of Marine Surveyors. The association was formed in 1961 in an effort to establish professional qualifications for marine surveyors. Since 1980, NAMS has maintained a certification process for members. To become a Certified Marine Surveyor (CMS), one must have a minimum of five years of experience as a full-time surveyor, pass a written exam, and be elected to membership in NAMS. A CMS must be recertified every five years. NAMS maintains a toll-free number, (800) 822-NAMS, that you can call to get a list of their certified marine surveyors in your area.

When searching for your surveyor, keep in mind that they tend to specialize. If you're considering a wooden boat, look for a surveyor with considerable experience in that area. The same applies to steel, aluminum, or ferrocement hulls, sail rigs, fishing rigs, high-tech, or traditional vessels.

Be aware that all a surveyor has to offer is his or her own judgment based on experience. You should therefore inquire into your surveyor's considered area of expertise, how many surveys he or she has done in the last year, and what he did before becoming a surveyor. Find out if marine surveying is his or her full-time occupation, or if it is merely a sideline or way to pick up extra cash.

A good surveyor should take your needs and plans into consideration as well as the boat itself. Go along when the survey is performed. It will serve as an educational process and allow you to get to know your boat from an expert's viewpoint.

A qualified diver can give you information about the propeller shaft, bearing, etc., but a boat should be hauled out of the water in order for the surveyor to perform a complete inspection below the waterline. However, other aspects of a survey can be done before or after the haulout, so you don't need to pay for excessive haulout time.

Your surveyor should examine the hull, machinery, and all accessories on the boat. He should check the bottom, seacocks, zincs, rudder, hull surface, and paint condition. He should be looking for dry rot on a wooden boat, and for blistering, gelcoat cracking, and stress cracks on a fiberglass boat. He should check all seawater connections, hoses, the exhaust system, and the electrical system. This should all be done with the idea of locating specific trouble areas for a particular type and brand of boat.

Your surveyor should also inventory all equipment in order to determine its value and find out which safety equipment is missing and will have to be purchased.

If the engine or engines have an unknown number of hours of use, you also may want to bring a qualified mechanic into the picture to run compression tests and to take oil samples from inside the engines. Oil-sample tests can determine excessive internal engine wear.

Surveyors usually charge by the length of the boat or by the hour. Be sure to get a firm price before the survey. You also may have to pay for the surveyor's travel time as well as the cost of the haulout. You should check around for the best rate for the haulout. Some surveyors are competent to evaluate engines and other machinery, but some aren't. If you have to hire a mechanic to evaluate the engines, your total cost will be higher.

As with everything else, beware of bargains. Keep in mind that the real value of your survey is based on the experience, objective view, and personal integrity of the surveyor. While you can try to negotiate a lower price, remember at all times that you get what you pay for.

What happens if your surveyor misses a major flaw in the boat? Most surveyors' agreements carry a disclaimer that excuses them from liability for missed items. If you sign an agreement containing such a clause, you are not likely to be successful in any attempt to sue the surveyor later. If the missed item is one that should have been found by any competent surveyor, you may be able to get around the disclaimer language. The process will involve the services of a lawyer and his or her fees. Unless the missed flaw is a major one, it is not going to be worth your time and money to try to get the surveyor to pay.

## Sea Trials

Another ritual that should be performed whether you're buying a new or a used boat is a sea trial. Too often the real purpose of the trial is overshadowed by the anticipation of ownership—and the thrill of knowing that, "Wow, this baby is almost MINE!"

With both new and used boats, always reserve the right to sea trial your exact vessel before the deal is closed. Be sure that the sea trial is designed to put the boat through realistic conditions under which you will be operating. A quick turn around the harbor is not enough.

Here are some drills you should put the boat through before and during a sea trial. They can uncover problems that may have been missed by the surveyor. Take a notebook and make notes.

If the boat has a diesel engine, make sure the engine is cold before starting it. A warm engine can cover up starting and smoking problems. Check for oil leakage into the bilge before starting the engine. If the bilge is clean, remember to check it at the end of the trial.

Have someone else start the engine while you position yourself on the stern with a view of the exhaust. Black smoke for more than a few seconds can mean problems. If the boat is a sailboat, be sure to raise all sails so you can check for chafe or tears that need repair.

Check maneuverability around the dock. If you can't operate the boat around the dock, at least try some maneuvers in sheltered water. Check how quickly the boat answers the helm and how well it tracks in reverse.

Take the boat to wherever you will encounter a wide range of sea conditions. Even though you only intend to operate the boat on calm days, you will someday get stuck out in a blow, so the time to find out how this boat handles is before you buy it. Operate the boat with the seas head-on, astern, abeam, and off the forward and stern quarters. Spend time on the flying bridge to check the rolling. If the boat has an autopilot, see how it guides the boat under various sea conditions, especially with a heavy following sea.

Be sure that all engine gauges and instruments are working. If you have questions, insist that they be checked by a technician. Check for engine noise and vibration on the main deck level at various speeds or RPMs. Go below and do it again. If the boat has a gen-set, make sure it is operating properly. Check the ride below.

Operate every mechanical system of the boat from the head to the stove. The sea trial is the last opportunity to make sure the boat and everything on it are in operating condition. It is much easier to get the broker or dealer to live up to his or her obligations if you have a written list of the items that need to be fixed and a firm date by which the work will be done.

Listen carefully to the salesman's responses to questions you may have about required repairs. If the boat isn't in top operating condition for a sea trial, be sure to get a firm commitment from the broker or dealer as to when it will be.

## Buying at
## Government Auctions

One of the results of the war on drugs has been the seizure of boats by various law-enforcement agencies—and the subsequent auction of those boats. Millions of dollars worth of property is now being sold to the highest bidder at auctions all over the country. We've all seen the ads extolling the advantages of buying boats for next to nothing at government auctions. These auctions are conducted by the Navy, the Drug Enforcement Administration, the Coast Guard, the Customs Service, and the U.S. Marshal's Service.

The ads you see are usually from mail-order companies in the business of selling information for a fee. The catch is that they are providing guidance and information that is readily available from the government for free. Most of the information is available for the price of a phone call to the General Services Administration, which handles information for the U.S. Marshal's Service, the Drug Enforcement Administration, the FBI, IRS, and government surplus property.

Information about Department of Defense auctions of surplus property can be secured from the Defense Reutilization and Marketing Service. The U.S. Customs contracts with private companies to handle their seized property and can be called for information about their sales. If you would rather pay someone to get the information for you than get it yourself, go ahead and pay for it.

As for the auctions, remember that good deals are the exception. If you attend an auction, you are likely to find yourself bidding against brokers who are looking for a good deal, too. The only problem is that they are more likely to know what a boat is worth than you are. Even worse, you may be bidding against others who have little or no knowledge about the true value of the vessel being sold.

You also get what you pay for. You have no recourse if you are not happy after the sale. All sales are final, no representations or warranties are made concerning the condition of the boat, and there are no refunds. Many auction boats will require considerable work to eliminate hidden compartments and repair damage done by law-enforcement officials in their search for drugs.

At best, you can probably expect to buy a boat at one of these auctions at or near wholesale. At worst, you will buy a boat worth significantly less than you paid for it.

## Warranties
## and Representations

The UCC (Uniform Commercial Code) governs the terms of the deal you make in buying or selling a boat. Whether or not stated in the bill of sale or any agreement you may draft and sign, the UCC imposes warranties, or conditions, upon the sale. In this context, conditions are identical to warranties. These warranties provide you with a certain degree of protection if the deal goes bad. Warranties are either *expressed* or *implied*. (Although the UCC governs the sale of personal property, including boats, it may be interpreted differently by different state courts, resulting in somewhat different legal requirements for purchases and sales of boats.)

Implied warranties are imposed on every transaction involving personal property unless specifically waived in writing. Implied warranties are present in every boat sale whether written, stated, or not. They include the warranty that the seller has a good title to the boat and has a right to sell it. This warranty is helpful with good-faith sellers but of little comfort when dealing with a crook who disappears after getting your money.

Other implied warranties include that of *quiet possession*, which means that the seller is presumed to promise that no existing legal claims will interfere with the buyer's use and possession of the boat. The seller also promises that the boat is free of liens or other obligations that the buyer is not aware of.

The implied warranty of *merchantability* provides that the boat is of average quality and will be resalable by the new owner.

The warranty of *fitness for a particular purpose* provides that when you buy a boat and make known to the seller what you intend to do with it, and you rely on the seller's skill and judgment, the boat should be reasonably fit for that particular use. For example, if you are planning to sail around the world and tell the seller of your plans, and the seller indicates to you that the boat will be perfect for the voyage, the seller is giving you a warranty that the boat is in fact capable of sailing around the world.

Express warranties are those promises or representations made by the seller to the buyer and on which the buyer relies in deciding to buy a boat. These express warranties need not include the terms *warranty* or *guarantee*. They are simply statements made or implied by the seller that the buyer believes and are part of the reason he or she ultimately buys.

For example, a boatbuilder recently designed and built a custom boat for an individual. During the course of design and discussion with the owner, the builder indicated that the boat when built would easily maintain speeds of 15 knots. After the boat was completed, it could only cruise at about 7 to 9 knots. The owner complained and several modifications were made in an unsuccessful effort to increase boat speed. Finally the builder bought the boat back from the owner.

Most contracts or purchase orders prepared by boatbuilders, dealers, or equipment manufacturers contain limited warranty provisions. The UCC, federal law, and some state laws set forth the requirements for limiting the warranties expressed or implied in transactions. Generally, a builder, dealer, or manufacturer may exclude any warranty not expressly provided in the agreement or included with the product—so long as the exclusion meets certain requirements. One of those requirements is that the exclusion must usually be in print different from the rest of the document, so that the buyer will be more likely to notice the exclusion.

Although implied and express warranties serve to protect you as a buyer, nothing should keep you from seeking appropriate expert advice and from doing an inspection and having a survey done on the boat. If there is a breach and you are damaged, your recourse is a lawsuit. And a lawsuit is not an alternative to seek with any hope of emerging unscathed. The law is designed to protect you from unscrupulous sellers, not from your own stupidity or laziness.

## Buying and Selling on Contract

There is an alternative to buying a boat with cash or bank financing. The seller may be willing to sell the boat and carry the financing him or herself. This is often called *selling on contract* or owner financing.

Here's how it works. The seller will sell you his or her boat, and instead of making your payments to the bank or other lender, you will make monthly payments to the seller. You give the seller a down payment, and the balance of the purchase price is paid to the seller on a monthly basis for a specified length of time.

Buying a boat on contract offers you, the buyer, some advantages. You avoid the hassle of applying for a loan through a lender. The loan will not show up on your credit reports, although if you go to a lender for another loan, you should mention that you have the existing boat loan. Sellers who carry the financing are more likely to be somewhat flexible in the amount you pay down and the size of the monthly payments. Some sellers are also willing to give you an interest rate that is lower than the going rate.

If you find one of these deals, here are some things you should be aware of. You will likely be required to sign a contract setting out the terms of the deal. The seller will also be likely to retain the boat's title or other ownership documents until you make the final payment. Some may require you to sign a *financing statement* showing that you owe the seller money, just as the bank files a mortgage when you buy a house or borrow money to buy a boat. The seller will file this statement at the county courthouse where you maintain permanent residence and possibly also in the state and county where the boat will be kept, if different.

The seller will also probably require you to carry him or her as an *additional insured* on your insurance policy. If something happens to the boat, they will be paid by the insurance company. They may also require you to keep the boat insured for at least what is owed.

All this is done to protect the seller if you default on the loan or try to sell the boat without paying off the loan to the seller.

Some people don't like the idea of buying a boat and having the seller carry the financing. They may think that making payments to an individual is somehow different from making monthly payments to a bank. The differences are negligible. In fact, an individual may be more understanding than a bank.

One way to make you more comfortable in these situations is to establish an escrow or collection account at a bank. The parties to the agreement go to a bank and set up an account to which you will make your payments. Some banks will give you a book of coupons to make your payments. Once the payment is received, the bank sends it on to the seller or deposits it into his or her account, after subtracting a monthly fee for the service.

You can also arrange with some banks that an executed document transferring ownership and title to you be held by the bank until the final payment is made, at which time all the documents are sent to you. You can then file the documents with the appropriate state or federal authority.

What if you're the seller? If you are selling a boat and don't need the profit right away, selling a boat on contract can bring you not only the profit from the sale but interest on the money you are in effect lending to the buyer. The interest you get from carrying the loan yourself will be significantly more than you can expect to get from putting your profit in a savings account. With careful preparation and good legal advice, problems can be minimized.

Whether buying or selling a boat on contract, it is a good idea to consult a lawyer. If you are buying, have the lawyer review all documents the seller wants you to sign. If you're selling, have a lawyer draft the documents to be sure you're protected. The money paid for a few hours of legal advice will be substantially less than what you would have to pay if the deal were to go bad.

## Trade-in Tax Advantage

Most boatowners change boats every three or four years, usually upgrading from a smaller boat to a bigger one—although it seems growing numbers of boaters in the 1990s are discovering the advantages of "downsizing."

An alternative to the often protracted process of selling, either on your own or through a broker, is trading in the old boat on a new one—or at least a newer one. Not only do you avoid the hassle of selling, you also avoid that uncomfortable feeling of owning two boats when the new one is delivered and you haven't yet sold the old one. You also save on sales tax on the new boat.

Trading in your old boat doesn't come without a price, however. Because a dealership has costs associated with carrying a trade-in on its inventory along with commissions to be paid when the boat is finally sold, you are not likely to get the amount of money out of your boat that you would from selling it on your own or through a broker.

That loss may be offset by money you save in sales tax. When you sell the old boat on your own or through a broker, the new owner pays sales tax on the full amount paid for your old (his new) boat. If you then go out and buy your new boat, you also pay sales tax on the full price. However, if you trade in your old boat on the new one, you will only pay sales tax on the difference between the value of the old boat and the price of the new one.

For example, if your old boat is worth $25,000, the new owner will pay sales tax on the full value. If the sales-tax rate in your state is 5 percent, the new owner will have to pay an additional $1,250 to the state. After selling the old one, you buy a boat for $50,000, paying sales tax of $2,500. On the other hand, if you trade in the old boat on the new one, you will pay tax on the difference in their values, or $25,000. Your tax bill will then only be $1,250, instead of $2,500, or a savings of $1,250.

Although it isn't likely that the savings in sales tax will be more than the reduction in the amount you realize from the old boat, the savings may help you decide that it is easier to trade in the old one than to sell it.

# 7

# Co-ownership

| | ✣ | |

## Why Co-ownership?

The legal term *co-ownership* simply means the shared ownership of, for example, a boat by two or more unrelated people. Co-ownership is a way of sharing expenses, usually on an equal basis. Two or more people may buy a boat together, or the original owner may bring a co-owner aboard.

Many of us don't hesitate to embark on joint ventures on land, such as co-ops and condominiums. Why not on the water? With good planning and a written agreement, most co-ownership problems can be avoided, or at least minimized. Although most of us cringe at the thought of signing a contract, a thoughtfully written agreement is essential in a co-ownership arrangement. It will guide the harmonious use of the boat, and, if a dispute arises, it will serve as the cool-minded arbiter amid the heat of conflict by establishing parameters and setting out steps to be taken.

## The Economics
## of Co-ownership

The first and foremost reason for considering co-ownership is to lighten the financial burden. Many people are shocked when they calculate what their boat actually costs them.

In *Boating for Less*, author Steve Henkel provides an excellent analysis of the real costs of boat ownership. You have the initial capital costs such as the purchase price of the boat, necessary equipment not included in the original purchase, sales tax, duties if the boat is made outside this country, and all the other little things necessary to get a boat ready for use. In addition to the capital costs, you have what Henkel calls ancillary costs, including the cost of finding the boat of your dreams (such as travel to boat shows and other locations to look at boats), brokerage commissions, attorney fees, surveyor fees, service charges, documentation or registration fees, perhaps fees for licensing a boat trailer, first-year insurance costs, finance charges and fees, freight charges or delivery-skipper fees, and costs of equipment and accessories you decide to add to the boat.

Once you actually begin to enjoy your boat, you begin adding up operating expenses and routine maintenance. These include fuel and oil, slip rent or the cost of dropping a mooring, excise tax and annual registration fees, premiums for hull and liability insurance, cost of preparation for winter storage, derigging and decommissioning costs, winter storage costs, spring launching costs, periodic maintenance costs such as bottom-scrubbing and painting, and annual fees, dues, and subscriptions. If you have financed the purchase of your boat, interest will be a big ongoing cost. In addition, no boater ever gets away from the occasional costs associated with wear, tear, and accidents such as corrosion, electrical problems, cracks, chips, scratches, and dings.

Finally, you have *opportunity cost*, which is usually defined as the value of what you have forgone by putting your money into a boat instead of investing it. That is not to say that going out on your boat for a sail on a beautiful weekend isn't worth a lot, but it doesn't match a good mutual fund for long-term financial return. By bringing in one or more partners, you can reduce most of these costs—capital, operating, maintenance, and opportunity costs—by at least one-half, if not more.

Few people spend every weekend on their boats. Do you use yours every other weekend? Once a month? When you aren't using your boat, someone else could be.

Escalating costs and dwindling marina space combined with less leisure time make the cost of going out on your boat more expensive every year. These days, the average annual cost of owning a 28- to 30-foot boat is around $12,000; that amounts to $1,000 a month. If you use your boat only a couple of weekends each month, six months out of each year, you would be paying about $1,000 per weekend for the boat.

## Money Is Not the Only Reason

In addition to the obvious economic benefits, sharing your love for boating with an enthusiastic partner who will help with difficult or time-consuming jobs can make co-ownership an enjoyable alternative. If you've ever painted the bottom of a 28-footer, you'll appreciate having someone else there to share the pain. If you know plenty about brightwork and your partner is a marine diesel mechanic, a natural division of labor will benefit you both, and you may save outside labor bills as well. The collective knowledge of the partners can make co-ownership worthwhile.

With more than one person using and maintaining the boat, vigilance to details will at least be doubled, so potential safety hazards are more likely to be discovered before they reek havoc. Your partner may discover immediately the slow leak you might not have noticed for three or four weeks.

Co-ownership can take many forms. A lawyer and a doctor in Wyoming owned a 26-foot sailboat together. The doctor had originally purchased the boat, and the lawyer bought half interest a couple of years later. They never wrote up an agreement, but they both cooperated equally in maintaining the boat, preparing it for use in the spring, and getting it ready for winter storage. Most bills were paid out of the doctor's personal account, and the lawyer periodically paid the doctor for half the expenses. Their harmonious partnership lasted until the lawyer moved away and the boat was sold.

Ironically, increased use of a boat doesn't necessarily lead to more repairs; in fact, neglect and nonuse can cause greater deterioration (frozen seacock, water damage, etc.) than can regular use and attention. And if you're using your boat, you're more apt to fix the things that need fixing. Running the engine more frequently will demand regular maintenance of other important systems as well. The higher operating costs associated with increased use will be paid by the person creating those costs—your partner—while the *fixed costs*—such as insurance and moorage—are usually shared equally.

Besides helping with maintenance, a partner with specialized knowledge and experience can teach you about an area of seamanship that you're still getting to know. Look for helpful qualities when you begin seeking the right partner.

Finally, although forming a friendship shouldn't be the primary reason for selecting a partner, few pleasant memories remain longer in our minds than those great times we've spent on boats. Lasting friendships can and often do evolve from these experiences.

## Choosing Partners

Your first undertaking is to decide how many partners you need. This largely depends on the length of the boating season in your area and consequently the number of boating weekends available. From that figure, subtract a couple of weekends during which the boat can get its regular maintenance.

Next, decide how often you are likely to want the use of the boat. Include not only the 10 to 20 regular weekends but also that two-week vacation to Chesapeake Bay or the San Juan Islands. So from the total available time, subtract the time you'll be using it, and the remainder is the amount of time available to a partner.

If you're lucky enough to live where you can boat all year, you may arrive at approximately 40 full weekends of use. You and your partner will probably want equal use of the boat, so if you used the boat on 20 weekends, you could handle one additional partner who also could use the boat on 20 weekends.

If you used your boat only around 15 weekends, you could take on two partners who could each use the boat for 15 weekends per year.

All of this implies that you and your partner or partners will have an equal financial investment and equal use of the boat. While it may be possible to bring in a partner or partners for less than an equal share, you may find a reluctance on the part of the prospective partner to come into an arrangement where someone else holds a "majority interest" and therefore has control over what is done.

Of course the advantage of bringing aboard two partners is that you would be reducing your costs by two-thirds rather than one-half.

### The Right Stuff

Once you've decided how many partners to seek, it's time to start looking for someone who will meet your expectations. The most important thing to look for in a partner is his or her outlook on boating. Social compatibility is less important, since you'll seldom be taking the boat out at the same time.

At this point, a little self-analysis probably will help you determine your expectations in a partner. Are you a strict law-and-order person the minute you step aboard? If so, look for someone who shares your views. Are you known to be ultimately responsible when handling expensive equipment? Are you fastidious about personal cleanliness and general order in your surroundings? Or do your friends really think that what you need is a maid and keeper? Here's an example.

In a boating newspaper, a classified ad said the out-of-state owner of a nice 48-foot sportfisher in Los Angeles harbor was seeking a co-owner who was "responsible, orderly, and hygienic." Bob answered the ad, discussed the basics over the phone with the owner who lived in Arizona, and was grilled about his boat-handling ability and his personal habits. Strange, he thought, but he was in the market, so he decided to take a peek at the boat. When he found the slip, the boat turned out to be dinged up, dirty and cluttered.

"What that boat needs is a new owner," chuckled a boatowner in an adjacent slip. "It stinks!" Bob decided that the owner just needed someone to clean up after him and teach him how to drive. He never called back to Arizona.

Two weeks later, Bob heard that his friend Mark had just become the co-owner of a 48-foot sportfisher in that marina. "Uh oh," he thought. It turned out that the Arizona owner was not the culprit; he had suffered disastrous luck with a previous co-owner, a person who crashed the boat into at least two things every time he took it out. And the ex-partner left clogged heads, dirty linens and fish parts on board every weekend.

Mark and the Arizona partner both had the qualities that help co-ownerships work: responsibility, orderliness, and respect for each other's living space.

Ask yourself what your boating weaknesses and strengths are. Are you truly committed to the work and effort required to keep a boat, or are you just in love with the idea of boating? Is your family as excited about boating as you are, or are they just going along with your idea to please you? Try to settle these questions for yourself before you approach potential partners.

When looking at potential partners, find out what their strong points are as well as their weak points. Can he or she handle a boat safely? How much experience does he or she have? Beware of fair-weather sailors and dreamers.

It is wise to look for someone who has expertise in your weak areas. Do you know much less about diesel or gasoline engines than you do about brightwork and waxing? Why not seek a partner who can tinker with the engine while you keep up with the cosmetic work? Having a partner who can change the engine oil or replace a worn out bilge pump can be a plus. Maybe you and your new partner will be able to improve each other's abilities in celestial navigation, kedging off, heavy-weather sailing, or reading navigational instruments, for example.

Once you have decided on a likely prospect, sit down and talk about what you are about to do. Ask for opinions on how things should be handled. Go aboard together to discuss specifics. Take the boat out together to see how he or she handles being underway, but it is up to you to undock and dock the boat the first time. Then discuss the points outlined below, and play "what if . . ."

Once you are satisfied that you've found the right partner, go to a lawyer to have an agreement drafted and signed (see "The Agreement" below for specific guidelines), or use the agreement in Appendix C.

## Budgeting

Money problems can torpedo any partnership, so be sure to establish a boat budget from the outset. The budget should include payments on the purchase price of the boat, fuel, slip fees or moorage, insurance, the cost of the annual haulout, and any work or equipment needed to get the boat in shape for cruising or sailing.

Set aside additional funds for unexpected expenses or increases in such things as moorage rates, insurance, and equipment.

Review your figures annually, comparing budgeted projections to actual expenses. This will give you enough feedback to plan a better budget each year.

Once the budget is set, decide how the money will be handled. A separate checking account that allows all partners to write checks is one option. The partners can then put money into the account on a regular basis or whenever the balance gets low. This system seems to work better than if each partner pays expenses out of his or her own account. Designate one person to take responsibility for making the monthly moorage and loan payments.

If you develop a good budget and follow it, you shouldn't have too many surprises—sudden unexpected bills—or complaints that the boat is costing more than you or your partner planned.

## The Agreement

Although many people share ownership of a boat without a contract, a written agreement is a boon to successful co-ownership.

An agreement requires partners to anticipate and talk about potential problems; it doesn't allow them to indulge a natural tendency to avoid conflict. Creating the wording of the agreement also will help you to better understand your partner's boating philosophy and awareness of what's involved in owning and operating a boat.

No contract can cover every contingency, but it should cover most of them and provide a means of settling those that aren't covered. As illustrated by the sample form in Appendix C, your co-ownership agreement should detail the complete agreement between the parties, leaving nothing unclear.

Among the things that should be covered are:

1. How will the boat be used and where? Are you and your partners going to race your sailboat or is it just for cruising? Are you going to rent or charter the boat to other people? You should be clear on usage since racing and chartering will have an effect on your insurance costs and the boat's availability.

2. How will the boat be financed? Where are you going to get the

loan, and what will the term of the loan be? Will both of you sign the loan papers, or will it be just in one of your names. It is easier to qualify for a loan if you both sign than if just one does.

3. What insurance coverage will be carried? Which insurance carrier are you going to use and at what levels? Do all the parties agree that you should have the highest deductible so as to lower your premiums? If one of you takes the boat out of its normally insured region, does he or she pay for the rider policy?

Note that if one partner carries the insurance as a rider on his homeowner's policy, and if there is a claim, the insurer might pay damages only up to the homeowner's share of the boat—and to add insult to misery, the insurer will probably base claim on the depreciated value of the boat or its gear.

Suppose, for example, that your boat breaks her mooring in a storm, washes ashore, and is declared a constructive total loss. You and your partner bought the new boat for $25,000 three years ago, and you've had it insured on your homeowner's policy. The insurance company tells you that the depreciated value of your boat was $14,000, and that they will pay only your half of the boat, which is $7,000 (minus deductible). Clearly, you'd have been better off with a yacht policy under both names. For more on yacht policies, see Chapter 12.

4. Where will the boat be kept? Are you going to keep it in a marina slip or tied to a mooring buoy? If the boat is meant to be trailered, will one of you keep it in your garage, or will it go into a storage facility? Will it be kept where it is most easily accessible or where you can get the cheapest rates?

5. How and by whom will the boat be maintained? Are you going to do all the maintenance yourselves, or are you going to pay to have it done by professionals? If you are doing it yourselves, what happens if one of you isn't available when it comes time for a new coat of bottom paint?

6. What gear will be added and when? Is everybody in agreement that you should spend the money for that new spinnaker or dodger? Do you buy it this year, or can it wait?

7. Who uses the boat when? Are you going to get together once a year to decide who will have the boat on those long holiday weekends like Memorial Day, the Fourth of July, and Labor Day? Have you thought of scheduling two-week summer trips for all of the partners? Can one of you loan the boat to a nonpartner?

8. Who will pay for gear that is damaged? Will it come out of the boat account or will it be paid by the person operating the boat when the damage occurred? Will the partner who lost the winch handle overboard buy a new one? If the damage is covered by insurance, will the partner causing the claim be responsible for paying the deductible?

9. How will disagreements be resolved? Why not put a provision in the agreement stating that, if you can't resolve your dispute within a given time (say a month), you then agree to go to the local dispute resolution center to have it mediated? If things really go bad, why not agree that you will not go to court but will use the services of the local office of the American Arbitration Association to have the dispute arbitrated?

10. How will the partnership be dissolved and under what conditions? What if your partner stops paying for his or her share of the boat? What if one of the partners dies, becomes unable to use the boat because of physical problems—or simply loses interest? Can that person or his or her estate simply sell his or her interest to a stranger, or must he or she offer it to you first? If so, how long will you have to come up with either another partner or the money to buy out your partner? Will you have the right to veto a prospective sale when the new partner would be unacceptable to you?

11. Must a partner be aboard whenever the boat is in use? Your insurance and its liability considerations might dictate that a partner be on board at all times.

12. What will happen if the boat is unusable for some reason? If a partner loses his usage because the boat is out of commission for repair, should he continue to pay his share of expenses, or should those bills be pro rated? What if the boat is destroyed or damaged to such an extent that it won't be usable for months? Should you just take the insurance proceeds and terminate the partnership, buy another boat, or have the old boat repaired?

Few lawyers in the United States specialize in recreational boating law, and those who practice maritime law might not be interested in dealing with recreational boating disputes because the rewards often aren't sufficient. A lawyer who specializes in time-share condominiums probably couldn't do a good job for you in this case, because there's a difference between real property time-share condominiums and the type of co-ownership involving a boat. To find a lawyer to draft your agreement, look under "Maritime law" or "Admiralty law" headings in the Yellow Pages. Call to explain what you want done. If the lawyer seems willing, ask how many yacht co-ownership agreements he or she has written, and whether he or she has experience in small-boat law.

If you can't find a lawyer in your area who has handled similar agreements, remember that much of any lawyer's library is filled with books of forms for almost every circumstance. If you show your lawyer the form in this book (Appendix C), he or she should be able to draw up an agreement that will serve your needs.

## Additional Rules

Just like a good agreement, a good set of rules is necessary to ensure harmony and avoid problems.

The rules should include issues not already covered by the agreement, and it can supplement some of the items that are covered by it.

The rules should spell out specifics about operation and maintenance procedures, such as:

• where to find the ship's documents—in case you are boarded by the Coast Guard;
• what start-up procedures must be followed before turning the key—

such as checking the oil in the engine, starting the bilge blower to
evacuate fumes;

• what procedures to follow after returning from a trip—like topping
off the fuel and water tanks, emptying the waste holding tank, removing trash, filling heads with cleaner, starting the battery charger,
returning the ship's circuits to the dock power, etc.

The list of rules should also call for: a general inspection of the vessel
(including checking the oil and transmission-fluid levels); keeping the log;
cleaning; leaving or not leaving food and beverages aboard; keeping clean
linen and towels aboard; leaving personal property aboard—essentially,
anything that will allow each partner convenient use of the boat.

# 8

# Financing
# a Boat

| | ✛ | |

According to the National Marine Bankers Association, 80 percent of all boat purchases are financed. That means that the vast majority of boat-owners—and folks who dream of owning a boat—face many questions about how to finance it.

The good news in 1993 is that because interest rates are so low, many options are available for financing a boat. So many, in fact, that you can tailor your financing to fit your financial situation.

The caveat is that, with all those institutions eager to lend you money, you should be as careful in arranging financing of your new boat as you are in selecting the right make, model, size, and so forth.

## Shop Around

As a general rule, interest rates on boat loans are lower than those on other types of consumer loans, and they are only slightly higher than rates on home loans. Boat brokers, dealers, and lenders want your business. Since they make money only if people finance boats, most are more than willing to help you finance your purchase—assuming you have good credit.

There are all kinds of ways to finance your dream boat, so spend some time shopping for the right loan. In most boating areas, lenders offering boat loans can be found in banks, marine financial institutions, credit unions, and yacht dealerships and brokerages.

The wide availability of boat loans is due to the fact that most boats are purchased by people who have better-than-average incomes. Recent statistics reveal that the average boatowner has an annual family income of $72,000, which makes him or her a better-than-average credit risk. As a result, boat loans generally have a lower delinquency rate, which in turn translates into lower interest rates—often one-third lower than those on auto loans.

Many larger banks have loan departments that specialize in boat loans. In addition, many yacht brokers and dealers have arranged loan programs with specific lending institutions and can thus offer financing similar to that offered by automobile dealers. Some lenders specialize exclusively in boat loans and often provide one-stop shopping, including documentation and everything else needed to complete the deal.

Larger boat shows are good places to shop for boat loans. Bankers and specialized yacht lenders often have booths and are glad to talk with you about their boat loans. Some even offer discounts, incentives and special deals during boat shows.

## What to Look For

Shop not just for the lowest rates but also for a lender with experience in boat loans. Unfortunately, many inexperienced lenders treat boat loans as if they were personal loans, for which they set ceilings on the loan amounts. Lenders with experience in boat loans will not. Dealing with an experienced lender will make it easier to get your loan.

In the days of 20 percent interest rates and runaway inflation, dealers, brokers, and lenders came up with all types of gimmicks to lure boat buyers. Low- or no-down-payment loans were common, as were loans in which buyers paid only interest—no principal. Long pay-off periods were given in order to reduce monthly payments. Because their only way to make money was to sell more boats, lenders struggled to come up with ways to keep boat payments low or within the means of the boat-buying public.

Those days are gone. With interest rates low, the people lending money

for boat purchases today have, for the most part, moved away from gimmicks. The loan package today is a fairly straightforward proposition. You
shouldn't assume, however, that it is easier to qualify for a loan. The recent
problems in the savings and loan and banking industry have made lenders
more careful with their lending programs.

Lenders are now requiring 20 percent down on loans for new boats,
and 25 percent for used boats and "higher risks" such as houseboats,
wooden boats, and high-performance vessels. And banks are more likely
these days to require proof from the purchaser that the down payment will
be made.

Depending on the size of the loan and the value of the boat, terms can
extend as long as 15 to 20 years, but longer-term loans have their share of
problems, which will be discussed later.

Fortunately, boat loans can be obtained without all sorts of fees like
those charged on other types of loans—fees that only increase your cost of
borrowing. So you will not be looking at loan origination fees, points,
appraisal fees, filing fees, escrow fees, and other charges associated with
real estate loans.

Remember that it is easier to get a loan for a production boat than a
home-built boat. And what about a custom-built boat? Well, if you can
afford one, you shouldn't have any problem qualifying for a loan. A lender
will not loan more than the fair value of the boat you're buying, less your
down payment. Fair value is usually established by reference to "blue
books" that carry values for most boats, or by a survey performed at the
bank's request but paid for by the buyer. Banks usually require surveys only
on larger, used boats.

Another approach is to prequalify for a certain-size loan and then shop
around for a boat that fits your loan. This can be done at most banks; talk
to your banker.

Financing commercial boats is a more complex process requiring
financial statements and projections of income for the bank to review. The
reason is that the bank usually looks to the income generated by the boat
for the payments on the loan. If the projected income won't suffice to support the business and make the loan payments, you probably won't get the
loan. The bank is also likely to require proof that you have the knowledge

and skill to operate the boat in the commercial venture for which it is designed. For example, if you contemplate buying a 50-foot trawler with two crew cabins, you should be able to show that you are an experienced fisherman and able to operate a vessel of this size and type in the waters where it will fish.

## Long-Term
## Versus Short-Term Loans

The most common choice boat buyers face is between (a) long-term loans with lower payments or (b) short-term loans with higher payments.

Don't assume that the longer-term loan with the lower monthly payments is the better deal. While the lower monthly payments may be easier on your budget, in the long run you will pay more in interest. For example, a $50,000 loan at 11 percent interest with a 10-year term will give you monthly payments of $688.75. The same amount paid over 15 years will mean monthly payments of $568.30. While the monthly savings of around $120 may sound inviting, consider that you will be making the lower payments for five additional years. With the 10-year loan, your total payments would be $82,650.01, or interest of $32,650.01. With the 15-year loan, your total payments would come to $102,293.72, or interest of $52,293.72. So the $120 a month you're saving with the longer term will cost you almost $20,000 more in interest in the long run.

Another problem with longer-term loans is that in the early years of the loan, most of the monthly payment is applied toward interest with very little going toward the payment of the principal. Consequently, you will be slower in building equity in your boat. When the day comes to sell or trade, you will owe more on the loan and therefore keep less of the selling price.

Some people opt for longer-term loans with no prepayment penalties and then try to pay them off early, paying a little extra each month. This way you can limit your long-term interest payments while preserving the feasibility of making smaller payments if you get into a financial bind.

If you're a boatowner who plans on selling or trading up every few years, then the longer-term, lower-payment approach may be the one for you, since you will never pay off the loan in any event. On the other hand, if you plan on keeping your boat more than three years, a shorter-term loan should be seriously considered.

## Adjustable-Rate
## Versus Fixed-Rate Loans

Another loan choice is between an adjustable-rate or a fixed-rate. In an adjustable-rate loan, also known as a variable-rate loan, the rate of interest fluctuates annually—and sometimes monthly—according to a nationally recognized interest rate. As this benchmark (often the prime rate) rate goes up or down, so goes the rate on your loan and therefore the amount of your monthly payments. Payments for a fixed-rate loan stay the same for the life of the loan.

The initial interest rate on an adjustable-rate loan is usually significantly lower than that of a similar fixed-rate loan, and the lower rate is a tempting inducement. But the question is, if your rate goes up, will you be able to handle the higher monthly payments?

Take a look at the history of interest rates on boat loans in your area. As of mid-1993, interest rates are low, so the obvious risk is that they may go up. When interest rates are low for both fixed and adjustable types, it is better to lock in a lower fixed-rate loan.

When interest rates on boat loans are high, the wise shopper will opt for a variable rate, then ride the rates downward to the point where he or she thinks they have bottomed out. Then they can shop around again to refinance with a fixed-rate loan.

Even if you do elect an adjustable-rate loan and interest rates go up, you still have some degree of protection by making sure that your loan has a cap or ceiling on the interest rate or payments. Most adjustable-rate loans state how high the rate will go, no matter how much the benchmark rate goes up. If the adjustable-rate loan you're about to sign doesn't have a cap, go elsewhere.

## Interest-Only Loans

If low boat payments are your only goal, interest-only loans may be for you. You may still be able to find some lenders offering interest-only loans, but they are not very popular for several reasons.

With an interest-only loan on your dream boat, your monthly payments, which will be relatively low, will be applied only toward the interest on your loan; the principal will not be reduced. The obvious disadvantage is that at the end of the loan period you will still owe the full amount you have borrowed. An interest-only loan is closer to a lease than a purchase.

There aren't many situations in which an interest-only loan will be of benefit to a boat buyer. But if you are expecting to inherit $50,000 from your Great Aunt Millie in the next couple of years, you might opt for an interest-only loan with the intention of paying it off as soon as you receive the inheritance. Or perhaps you are just waiting for the closing of the sale of your previous boat, and you need a bridge loan for the interim.

## Balloon
## Payments

Some boat loans carry what is commonly referred to as a balloon payment, so be cautious. With a balloon-payment loan, your monthly payments are calculated on a long-term basis, say for 10, 15, or 20 years, which makes them lower than on a short-term loan, but the loan comes due in a shorter term, say in three to five years. At the end of the shorter term, you will either have to pay off the remaining amount due on the loan or refinance it with your lender or someone else. If your financial situation is not as good when the balloon payment comes due, you may have difficulty finding a willing lender. If interest rates have gone up, even if your financial condition has stayed the same, you may not qualify for a new loan. It may be a good idea to stay away from loans carrying balloon payments.

## Prepayment
## Penalties

Prepayment penalties are fees that a lender may assess you when you pay off your loan early. Avoid any boat loan that includes such a penalty.

The first problem with prepayment penalties is that they allow you no flexibility. For example, if interest rates were to go down and you wanted to take advantage of the drop by refinancing your boat loan at the lower rate, you would have to pay a penalty before you could refinance. Also, if you want to pay off some additional principal on your boat loan, you won't be able to do so without paying the penalty as well. Most lenders in today's market don't have prepayment penalties. Don't consider a lender who does.

## Home-Equity Loans

Since interest paid on consumer loans and credit cards is no longer tax deductible, lenders have developed another way to entice people to borrow money. The home-equity loan or second mortgage is now being used by many people to pay off credit cards and take out consumer loans for things like boats and vacations. Such loans allow the boat buyer to continue to write off the interest at tax time.

Home-equity loans enable you to borrow using a portion of the equity you have in your home as collateral. Your equity in something means the difference between what you owe and the value of the property, whether it's your home or your boat. Even though the interest paid on a home-equity loan is, as a rule, tax deductible, there are some things to consider.

First, your home equity may be the largest asset you have in this world. Many people need their home equity to finance their retirement years. Do you really want to borrow from your retirement nest egg to buy a boat? Similarly, many of us use our home equity to move up to larger and nicer homes. Before home-equity loans appeared, our access to that equity was limited, and that acted as a forced savings plan. Just because you now have easier access to your home equity, are you sure you want to use it to buy a boat?

Moving can also cause problems with a boat financed through a home-equity loan. If you decide to sell your house and move to a new location, all loans on the house will be paid off from the sale. While that means the boat will be paid off, it also means the loan on the boat can't be carried with you after your move. And the equity that might have been available to buy the new house in the new location will have been used up paying off the boat. If you want to carry the equity to the new location, you will have to sell the boat as well as the house, thus increasing the costs and frustrations.

If you're in a hurry to get your boat, you had better look for something other than a home-equity loan to finance it, because approval for home-equity loans takes longer. Also, there are extra costs involved, including appraisal fees, points, credit reports, filing fees, title insurance, escrow fees, and other expenses.

Think long and carefully before using a home-equity loan to finance a boat.

## Tax-deductible
## Boat Loans

Getting a regular loan and claiming your boat as a second home is an alternative to using home equity to finance a boat, yet one that still allows you to claim the interest paid on the loan as a tax deduction. Though the major tax reforms passed in 1986 eliminated the tax deductibility of interest on credit cards and other consumer loans, Congress did leave the deduction of interest paid on loans for second homes.

Whether planned or not, that means that interest paid on some boat loans is still deductible. If the boat is big enough to have what the IRS considers to be sleeping and cooking accommodations, then the interest might be deductible.

If you live aboard your boat and use it as your primary residence, you can deduct the interest paid on the loan just as you would on a house. See Chapter 3 for a discussion of when a boat may be treated as a second home for tax purposes.

The other way to get maximum tax advantages from your boat is to use it in a business such as chartering. The chapter on chartering will give you some guidance.

Why be concerned with whether interest is deductible? If the interest paid on your boat loan is deductible, it reduces the effective interest rate on your loan. When buying anything on credit, most people ignore the cost of the money that they borrow in calculating the cost of the thing they're buying.

If you buy a boat and the price is $10,000, and you finance the purchase, the actual cost will be much higher. If you pay 20 percent down, or $2,000, and finance the $8,000 balance with a 10 percent loan for 10 years, by the time you make the last payment, you will have paid the $8,000 you borrowed and interest of $4,686.47! With the down payment you made, your boat will cost you a total of $14,686.47, or almost 50 percent more than the purchase price. If you finance it for five years, you will have paid

$8,000 and interest of $2,198.58. With the down payment of $2,000, your total cost will be $12,198.58.

If you are able to deduct the interest on your tax return, that interest serves to reduce the amount of income you must pay tax on. Less income to be taxed means less tax to pay to the IRS.

When you're buying a boat, think about the real cost of financing it, including interest. If you are in a position to deduct the interest on your tax return, it will help lessen the cost of borrowing, but it won't eliminate it.

## The Low
## Down-Payment Myth

Many people confuse investment strategies used for purchasing real estate with those used for buying a boat. When investing in real estate, the experts generally recommend that you buy with the smallest down payment you can negotiate on the theory that as the real estate appreciates in value, you can benefit from what is known as leverage. Leverage means that the return on your investment in the property will be greater, because what appreciates or increases is the value of the property, not just your investment in it.

However, using the same approach to buying a boat can be problematic. While real estate generally appreciates in value, boats generally do not. When a boat buyer makes a small down payment and the boat ultimately depreciates in value, the owner finds himself with a loan balance for more than the value of the boat.

In the old days of high interest rates, lenders often encouraged buyers to buy with no or a low down payment. With the current problems facing the savings and loan and banking industry, such deals are rare. Most lenders today want to see your money before they'll lend you any of theirs.

Assuming you bought a boat with a price tag of $35,000 five years ago and paid only 10 percent down, you financed the purchase with a loan of $31,500. Today you might very well find the boat to be worth only $25,000. If you took a long-term loan of 15 years and had a 12 percent fixed interest rate, you would still owe, after five years of payments, $26,350.40. If you sold the boat today, you would have to come up with 1,350.40 out of your pocket just to pay off the loan.

Someone may tell you that a boat is a good inflation hedge, but though this may be true of the larger and more expensive yachts, the majority of recreational boats do not serve that purpose. An inflation hedge is an investment that increases in value faster than does the inflation rate. For example, say you bought a certain make and model of boat in 1985. If the cumulative inflation since then were 35 percent but the same boat purchased new were to cost 50 percent more than you paid, then your boat would be an inflation hedge.

If you happen to find one of these seagoing hedges against inflation, think carefully before signing up. As a general rule, you should not think of a recreational boat as a good investment. Instead, think of boating as an absorbing hobby, and think of a boat as a vehicle for fun and relaxation.

# 9

# Repairs, Maintenance, and Liens

| | ✢ | |

If you pay strict attention to your regime of routine boat maintenance, you can greatly reduce the number of times you have to take your boat to a work dock or haulout yard for repairs. And when you do have to visit a boatyard for professional maintenance, your history of vigilance to details will pay off in smaller bills.

Many maintenance and boatbuilding professionals will tell you that you should spend 10 percent of the original value of your boat each year to maintain it and replace things that wear out.

Your own conscientious maintenance program is the best preventive medicine; it prevents sticker shock caused by outrageous boatyard bills. Nearly every boatowner has a horror story about a botched repair job or an unfortunate miscommunication with a boatyard. Your knowledge of certain laws and of normal boatyard operation can reduce your legal liability and lower your frustration level next time you visit your favorite boatyard or have to hire a mechanic or maintenance person.

Maritime liens should concern every boatowner and anyone thinking of buying a used boat, because these so-called hidden liens can exist without a written record. They often are the result of unpaid bills for repairs or maintenance.

## Repairs and Maintenance

The relationship between a boatowner and a yard implies certain rights and obligations—your obligations to the yard owner and his or hers to you.

These implicit obligations are known as *bailments.* Each time you entrust something of yours to someone else, you create a bailment. The owner of the property—namely, the boat—is the *bailor;* the party who holds it for safekeeping—such as a boatyard—is the *bailee.* Leaving your clothes with a dry cleaner or your car with a mechanic are examples of other bailments.

### *The Law of Bailments*

In a bailment between a boatowner and a boatyard, the law generally says that the yard must exercise reasonable care in ensuring that nothing bad happens to your boat while it is in the yard. If the yard can show that they were acting in a usual and reasonable manner while protecting your boat but it is damaged anyway, they will not have to pay for the damage—you will. Although boating-related bailment cases are most often heard in common-law courts (due to the relative insignificance of typical cases and the cost of pursuing action in federal court; see "Savings-to-Suitors Clause" in Chapter 2), admiralty law applies because the law recognizes maritime bailments.

The law specifically recognizes three types of bailments:

- bailments that benefit the bailor (you ask someone to watch your boat while you run an errand);
- bailments that benefit the bailee (you loan your boat to a friend);
- bailments that benefit both the bailor and the bailee (you place your boat in the care of a boatyard).

Since the boatyard profits from the work it does on your boat, and you benefit from the work the yard performs, the boatyard situation is a *mutual benefit bailment.* Although the yard will not insure your boat against anything that may happen to it, it must pay when something bad happens that is clearly its fault.

The bailment relationship between yards and boatowners gives rise to all sorts of questions and claims that sometimes lead to lawsuits. Such disputes often involve the physical condition of the boat when it was delivered to the yard, and exactly what happened to the boat while it was in the yard.

Later in this chapter we'll look at what happens when a bailment was found not to exist and therefore the yard was not liable for damages done to the boat.

### Yard Damage

Suppose a boatyard contracts to cover your boat for winter storage. While visiting the yard in late February, you discover a huge hole in the cover that could have admitted snow and rain. You're not surprised that when you launch your boat in the spring, it leaks. After it's hauled out, a split is discovered in the fiberglass keel casing that wasn't there last fall. You suspect that water got in through the defective cover, found its way into the bilge and froze, causing the split. What recourse do you have?

The natural reaction of a yard owner defending against a boatowner's claim is to point the finger of guilt at someone else. Typically, the yard owner will claim that the damage is a result of the boat's condition before it was brought to the yard. Courts have held yards not liable for damage to boats that were in poor condition when they came into the yard and sank after the work was completed.

Often, a yard will attempt to limit its liability by showing that the boat wasn't actually delivered to it, and courts have decided such cases both ways. The claim usually involves a boat tied to the yard's dock while waiting to be hauled or dry-docked for work.

In one case, the *Cape San Juan* sank while waiting to be dry-docked at a yard in Texas. Electrolysis had produced two holes below the waterline, causing the boat to sink. The federal court held that the yard was not responsible because the boatowner could not prove that a bailment existed. No written agreement for the yard work existed, and the owner of the *Cape San Juan* and its crewmembers had access to the vessel while it was tied up.

A similar case that went the other way involved a new boat brought into a yard in the New York area for winter storage. The boat was moored on a buoy with the understanding that the yard would haul the boat the next day. Because of other business, the yard left the boat moored for a week. One night a storm hit, and the boat broke from its mooring and was destroyed. The yard was held liable.

Yard security is responsible for the majority of claims, which mostly involve fire or theft. The number of variables in typical yard-security claims is so great that it is difficult to generalize about liability.

In one case, however, a court held a yard liable for the destruction of a 27-foot sailboat by fire. No one had been working on the boat on the day of the fire, and the cause of the fire was never determined. The court held the yard liable because evidence indicated that gasoline and solvents as well as wood chips, sawdust, and rags had not been properly disposed of.

In a similar case, a boat was destroyed by a fire in an adjoining boat. There was no evidence to show the cause of the fire, but there was some indication that work had been done to the adjoining boat. Covers had been removed from its generators, and engine parts had been removed. The court held the yard not liable, because there was no proof that the fire was caused by the actions of the yard.

These two common-law cases clearly show that similar situations can result in completely different court decisions.

Another common problem at boatyards is equipment theft. In such cases, the courts first ask if a bailment was established and, if so, then what degree of care was taken by the yard to protect the boat. Was it fenced and lighted? Was it patrolled by security guards? Before you take your boat into a yard, it's a good idea to take an inventory of what's on board. In the event of a theft, such a list will eliminate oceans of red tape.

Storm damage cases have gone both ways, too. In another New York example, an owner made an agreement with a yard to store his boat, and the yard agreed to keep the boat tied up to a specific dock and to keep the bilges pumped and, in general, to care for the boat through the winter. At some point, the yard moved the boat to a different moorage to make room for a larger vessel, and a storm caused damage to the moved boat. The court held the yard liable for damages.

Another case held the yard not liable for storm damages, because the yard showed that it had taken extraordinary steps to protect the boat during the storm, even though the boat sank in spite of those efforts.

Just because the boat storage or repair agreement you sign may contain a clause relieving the yard of liability in the event of fire, theft, vandalism or other possible threats, that does not mean the yard won't be found liable if something bad happens. Many yards include disclaimers in their written-estimate forms, and even though your signature is usually required on these and other papers before the yard will start work, the courts in many jurisdictions have ignored such disclaimers.

The operator of a Massachusetts marina was held liable for damages from a fire of unknown origin in spite of a so-called *exculpatory* clause in its agreement, because the yard was proved to be negligent in failing to control the spread of fire, not employing a watchman and not having sufficient water to fight a fire.

If you have a problem with a yard that has such a disclaimer, you might want to check with an attorney to see what your rights are—if the size of the claim warrants the effort.

### *Repair Disputes*

Many disagreements with yards are the result of the uncertainties inherent in the business of boat repair. Until a mechanic opens up the top end of your Perkins 4108, he can't know for sure if he'll have to tear into the bottom and pan as well—or just the head. If he discovers corrosion in the pistons from bad fuel, he could be negligent if he doesn't open up your generator engine as well. Maybe your fuel tanks need draining and cleaning, too, to prevent the problem in the future. Given the unknown factors involved in this case, how can the mechanic give you a specific price for the repair before work begins?

If you have a dispute with a yard, more than likely it will concern the cost of work that was done or work that was supposed to have been done.

Say you motor over to your local yard and get an estimate for some gelcoat repair and a new polyurethane finish on your 35-foot sloop. After some discussion and examination of the boat—still in the water—by the yard manager, he gives you an oral estimate of $4,000. A week later, the yard hauls the boat, and after examining the bottom, it finds some areas that need repair, and you make some minor changes to the work order. When the work is completed, you are presented with a bill for $8,000, and the yard won't release the boat until the bill is paid in full. You'll probably have to pay the bill.

Remember that estimates are called estimates because that's what they are—just estimates. A yard will not guarantee the ultimate charge for a job, because it has no way of knowing what those charges will be. While some jobs are easy to estimate, others are not. Mechanical problems are especially difficult until the yard gets inside the engine or equipment to see what the problem really is. Getting at a problem can also increase the cost when you or the manufacturer has crammed everything into a constricted space, leaving only enough room to look at the equipment—but not enough to get to it to repair it. If the yard has to remove other gear to get to the problem, the cost will go up.

Poor communication can also create problems. If the owner wants all the through hulls on his old, wooden 50-footer checked, he and the yard should be clear on what may be involved in locating, mapping, and checking 30 through hulls—some of which may have been disconnected and equipment installed over them. If the owner thinks it will only take a few hours at $45 per hour, and if the yard actually needs two people working on the job for half a day to complete the task, then there will probably be problems when the bill is presented.

For major work, you may want to consider getting a surveyor in to estimate the work to be done. Insurance companies may insist on one for work they will be paying for. Just make sure you get a competent, experienced surveyor.

One way to save a lot of trouble is to get a written estimate from the yard before they begin to work on your boat. Avoid "time plus materials" arrangements that don't include a maximum charge for the service. Any repair authorization should include an understanding of what the yard should do if it finds unexpected problems. Fix everything? Fix up to an agreed dollar amount? Stop work and ask you for additional authority?

Accidents happen with boatyard tools everyday, even with dangerous machinery like boat lifts and spar cranes. An unskilled worker grinding down a lump of fiberglass on a patch may accidentally sneeze or slip, and his or her high-speed tool could quickly grind a nasty gouge in your hull. Even after the yard repairs the accidental gouge, your hull may never look the same again.

Disputes over the quality of workmanship are also common in boating. Here, the law provides you with some degree of protection, since it includes an implied warranty that the work will be done in a skillful and workmanlike manner. This warranty is modified or eliminated by anything you agree to in writing, such as a written limited warranty on parts and labor.

Threats of suing or taking your business elsewhere aren't usually effective with boatyards or independent boat workers. But, remember, you don't have to go to court to resolve disputes, especially when informal negotiation is cheaper. One resolution method is that you and the boatyard both agree to abide by the opinion of an objective, independent third party. Otherwise, you may want to try your local dispute resolution center or mediation center. If all else fails, as a very last resort, take them to court.

While the law of bailments gives you some protection when a yard has your boat, in many situations you'll still have to pay for any damage incurred. Make sure your insurance covers your boat while it is in a yard. If it does, then at least someone will pay for the replacement or repair of your boat, but if it's your insurance that ends up paying, your premiums may go up.

In any case, be sure that you and the yard both have a firm understanding of the work to be done and its cost. And, get it in writing.

## Federal
## Maritime Liens

A *lien* is a claim for money that can be placed against a boat when its owner doesn't make payments. A lien is created when the owner borrows money to buy a boat, has work done on his or her boat, or secures supplies for the boat. The most common lien is a mortgage. The bank that loans you money to buy your boat has a lien on it. If you don't make your payments as required, the bank has the right to foreclose on the lien or mortgage in order to recover its money.

Most maritime liens had their origin in federal laws, although you may run into liens that are the result of state laws (see below). The most common federal lien was created by the Ship Mortgage Act of 1920. Before that year, the courts had held that ship mortgages were not subject to admiralty law and therefore could not be enforced in federal admiralty court. That position made it difficult for ship owners to secure financing. As long as lenders had no legal method of collecting their debts, they weren't interested in loaning money to owners of ships—dubious property that could slip away from any dock and disappear over the horizon.

### Preferred Ship Mortgages

The Ship Mortgage Act of 1920 changed the law by introducing the maritime *preferred ship mortgage* and providing for its enforcement in federal admiralty court. Now afforded protection under the law, lenders could loan money to ship owners and reasonably expect payment.

As indicated in Chapter 8, if you borrow money to buy a recreational boat that can be USCG-documented, your lender will probably secure a preferred ship mortgage on your boat. Several provisions and requirements of this type of lien are particularly relevant to recreational boatowners: the boat must be large enough to be documented with the Coast Guard, five net tons or about 28 feet and larger; the mortgage can also cover nonmaritime property such as personal equipment kept on the boat; and no limitation is set on the rate of interest that can be charged on the loan.

In addition, in order for a lender to secure a preferred ship mortgage, you, as the owner, must sign the mortgage before a notary public, along with an affidavit stating that you are acting in good faith and not in an effort to defraud anyone. A preferred ship mortgage is called an *express maritime lien*, because it is created by the express actions of the owner in signing the mortgage. The mortgage and affidavit must be recorded with the Coast Guard at your boat's home port. Finally, the existence of the preferred ship mortgage must be noted in your boat's documents, and a copy of the mortgage must be carried on the boat. These papers must be on board so that anyone providing a service, such as a supplier or repairman, can determine whether there is an existing mortgage on the boat.

### Implied Maritime Liens

Suppliers, vessel repairmen and seamen are actually covered under another type of lien—*implied maritime liens*—which are unique to maritime law.

Implied maritime liens take effect from the moment the work is completed, or supplies are delivered, or as soon as the owner fails to pay for services rendered. An implied maritime lien, though not a written and signed document, offers suppliers and repairmen just as much protection from failure to pay as does a preferred ship mortgage. All such liens are ranked according to when they were filed with the Coast Guard, when supplies were provided, or when repair work was done.

The priority of maritime liens depends on two factors: ranking or classification of the liens and determining which liens within a classification have priority. The following rankings are generally recognized: first, costs and expenses associated with the custody of the vessel by the admiralty court; second, seamen's claims for wages, maintenance, and cure; third, salvage claims; fourth, maritime tort claims or liens; fifth, contract liens or liens arising out of maritime contracts; and then anything else.

If a preferred ship mortgage is involved, the rankings change as follows: first, expenses of going to court; second, preferred maritime liens (seaman's claims for wages, maintenance, and cure; salvage claims; and torts); third, preferred ship mortgages; and last, other maritime liens.

Once the ranking is established, claims within the same ranking or classification are determined by the date of incidence. The later ones take priority over the earlier ones by what is called the *inverse order rule.*

Implied maritime liens can arise from many maritime situations. A seaman working aboard a boat has a lien for his wages. A maritime *tort*, caused by someone's negligence while the boat is being operated, also gives rise to a lien. Even a salvage claim is secured by an implied maritime lien.

Unlike liens ashore, maritime liens do not need to be filed at a courthouse. Hence, they are sometimes called secret liens. Also, the person to whom the money is owed need not secure possession of the boat. Another unique element is that a maritime lien *attaches* to the vessel, or covers the vessel, and the owner is not personally liable for the debt.

This aspect is particularly important for chartered vessels, because a charterer can easily incur a lien without the owner's knowledge or permission. The boat can be sued just as if it were an individual.

According to the Federal Maritime Lien Act, anyone furnishing *necessaries* to a boat automatically acquires a maritime lien. Although the right existed before the federal law was enacted, the Maritime Lien Act helped people who work aboard or supplied vessels by stating the law clearly. Contrary to what its name implies, a preferred ship mortgage is usually ranked behind all but liens for necessaries.

The law says:

> any person furnishing repairs, supplies, towage, use of dry dock or marine railway, or other necessaries . . . to any vessel . . . upon the order of the owner . . . or of a person authorized by the owner . . . shall have a maritime lien on the vessel.

Some necessaries such as fuel and supplies are fairly clear, but other so-called necessaries depend on your point of view. Determining what is truly necessary has led to extensive litigation. Cruise ship brochures and advertising materials have been called necessary supplies by the courts, but so has liquor for the crew of a fishing boat and containers for a freighter.

Other cases have found taxi fares incurred in the delivery of supplies to a boat, clothing for crewmembers, and winter storage charges to be necessaries.

In order for the supplier to be protected by the Federal Maritime Lien Act, the supplies must be delivered to the boat, to its dock, or to another convenient place, and they must be used on the vessel. The supplier must have relied on the vessel's credit, meaning that if the supplier required the vessel's owner to sign a promissory note, then the supplier cannot assert a maritime lien. Also, supplies must have been ordered by someone with the authority to place the order, usually the owner, master, or a specially designated manager.

### Chartering and Liens

If a charter group rents your boat for a week, they could run up a huge fuel bill that might not come due to your account for weeks. By the time you find out about it, they've returned your boat, you've returned their deposit, and they've flown the coop.

Chartering creates special problems when a charterer incurs liens while on a cruise without express permission from the owner. As a result, many charter parties or charter agreements contain a prohibition against liens incurred by the charterer. Problems arise when the provisioner is unaware of the prohibition and supplies the necessaries, under the assumption that he or she can secure a maritime lien.

Prior to 1971, suppliers were obligated to determine if the incursion of a maritime lien was prohibited on individual chartered boats, because if such a prohibition existed, they couldn't create a lien against that boat. The law protected charter-vessel owners from unscrupulous renters.

In 1971, the law was changed, and the protection previously afforded boatowners was transferred instead to the suppliers. Today, a supplier is under no obligation to check for the prohibition clause in the charter party's agreement but need only rely on the representations of the charterer. If your charterer represents to the supplier that there is no prohibition—even though there is—the supplier can attach a lien to your boat.

Maritime liens cover, or attach, the vessel and all equipment that is associated with it or necessary to run it, even though the equipment may be owned by someone else.

### Enforcement of Federal Maritime Liens

A maritime lien can be enforced only in a federal court sitting in its admiralty capacity. In order for the lien holder to collect, he or she must file a complaint in federal court that describes the claim and the vessel. After the lien holder pays a deposit (to cover the marshal's fee) and a filing fee, the court clerk issues a warrant for the arrest of the vessel, just like the warrant for the arrest of an individual. Another unique aspect of maritime law is that it allows personification of the boat. Because of the transitory nature of commerce by boat, admiralty law has provided for actions by and against the vessel itself. That is why you will often hear of a vessel being "arrested" in admiralty cases and why, when admiralty cases are reported, they often carry the names of the vessels, rather than the names of the owners.

After the warrant is issued but before the boat is actually taken by the U.S. Marshal, the owner can secure a bond to avoid the seizure. However, if no owner appears to pay the lien or stop the seizure, the vessel seizure and possible sale must be advertised in a newspaper. If still no one appears, the court can order the vessel sold and the proceeds of the sale paid to the lien holder.

If the owner appears and contests the lien, the court holds a trial. The owner can post a bond at any time prior to the trial to secure the vessel's release. If the owner wins, the case and lien are dismissed. If the owner loses, he or she must pay the lien or the vessel will be sold to cover the cost of the lien and the expenses incurred by the U.S. Marshal.

Liens may be extinguished either by the passage of time, by a court proceeding to collect on the lien, or by the loss or destruction of the vessel. They may also be waived by the holder.

Unlike on land where the first claim filed is the first to be paid, a maritime lien is ranked by the type of claim and in accordance with a rule referred to as *last on, first off.* The last person to supply necessaries to a boat will be the first paid—among other claims for necessaries. This rule is usually limited to a given voyage of a vessel or to a calendar year, in order to simplify the process and to protect previous lien holders. In other words, suppliers of necessaries for a particular voyage will be ranked equally. For vessels on shorter voyages, some courts have developed shorter time limits.

The last on, first off rule becomes particularly important when the amount of the claims exceeds the value of the vessel. First to be paid are the expenses incurred in legal proceedings, including court costs and expenses for the care and operation of the vessel while in the custody of the U.S. Marshal. Second are seamen's claims for wages, followed by salvage claims, tort claims, and contract claims for necessaries—in that order. Boatyard bills are considered necessaries.

Obviously, if the higher-ranking liens amount to more than the value of the vessel, liens at the end of the list will not be paid. If your boatyard claims a federal maritime lien against your boat, and others are seeking money from you or from liens against the boat, the boatyard lien will be near the bottom of the list.

## State Liens

Liens against boats can also be created under state law. Prior to the Federal Ship Mortgage Act of 1920, some states passed lien laws in an effort to protect maritime suppliers in the vessel's home port, who were then unprotected by federal law. After the 1920 act was passed, liens arising from state law were ranked below any federal liens.

As a boatowner, you must be as vigilant for state liens as for federal ones—although locating them should be a little easier. Even though a boatyard or other supplier can claim a federal maritime lien or a state lien, someone doing work on your boat is more likely to file a state lien than a federal one, because it generally is cheaper to foreclose on a state lien in state court than on a federal lien in federal court.

The only real advantage of state liens to the prospective boatowner is that in order to be effective, most must be filed with a county courthouse or with some other agency a state may have designated for filing liens. You can therefore check your local filing authority to see if any liens have been filed against a boat before you buy it. If none show up on the records, you can be fairly sure that there are no state liens—at least in that jurisdiction.

You can also hunt for hidden maritime liens by asking local suppliers, yards and mechanics. Most tradesmen will be glad to tell you if they've done work on a particular boat and if they are still owed money. And at the cash register of most chandleries, you can see the long list of boats that the supplier has liens against.

If a state lien is foreclosed in state court, any federal liens are not affected. If both state and federal liens are filed against a boat, each must be foreclosed in its respective court. Federal liens always have priority over state liens, and state vessel liens statutes are preempted by federal maritime law.

There is no real difference between a state lien and a federal lien except for where they must be foreclosed. A boatyard or supplier has a choice of claiming either a state or federal lien for work done or supplies furnished. It is more likely however that a documented vessel will carry federal liens, while a state registered or titled boat will have state liens. You should check for both types of liens before buying a boat.

By the same token, if you are financing the purchase of a new or used boat that is too small to be documented and therefore does not qualify for a preferred ship mortgage, your lender probably will file a lien with the local courthouse to protect itself against default.

# 10
# Salvage

| | ✣ | |

The Good Samaritan who voluntarily helps get someone's car out of a ditch is legally entitled to a reward of sincere thanks from the owner, but nothing more. However, in the maritime world, a similar act of assistance can lead to very different results—ranging from valuable remuneration to charges of looting.

Due to the federal budget crunch, the U.S. Coast Guard performs far fewer acts of assistance than it used to. Boaters who were accustomed to the Coast Guard's free assistance have been shocked when their nonemergency requests were turned over to private assistance firms who charged for their seagoing services. Today, boaters are being exposed to the world of marine salvage more frequently. And for the uninitiated, it can be a strange and complicated world.

## Historical
## Basis of Salvage

The law of marine salvage can be traced back to the Byzantine Empire, when public policy encouraged people to save ships and the people on them, and to return salvaged property to its rightful owners. This policy was developed to discourage greedy salvors from appropriating wrecked or stranded ships or their cargoes and abandoning survivors. The solution was to develop a system of rewards for people who rescued sailors and saved maritime property.

The need to foster this benevolent attitude internationally was recognized in the Salvage Convention of 1910, which was adopted by an international panel in Brussels and approved by the United States in 1913. The U.S. government adopted its own federal statute, the Salvage Act of 1912, which conformed with the Salvage Convention and was supplemented to meet new salvage circumstances.

Later the U.S. adopted the Standby Act, which requires the master of any vessel involved in a maritime accident to stand by the other vessel until no further assistance is necessary, if he or she can do so without endangering passengers, crewmembers, or the vessel.

## Salvage Defined

Salvage is a voluntary effort that is at least partially successful in saving a vessel or other craft from loss or destruction on the high seas or navigable waters.

The first criterion for a salvage claim is that it involved a maritime situation that placed people or vessels in peril from which destruction, damage, or death may result. Typically, a boat's engine has quit and the boat is about to be blown onto a lee shore, or one boat helps free another that has run aground.

Raising a sunken ship and extinguishing a fire aboard a passenger liner are the kinds of dramatic actions that require tremendous bravery and brighten the annals of maritime history, but everyday acts of assistance also qualify as salvage. Radioing the position of a vessel in distress so others can come to its aid will qualify. Using your radio to guide a vessel out of an ice floe or away from a dangerous reef also qualifies as salvage. Even the mere act of standing by may entitle you to a portion of a salvage reward. The point is that the vessel was in peril and that your voluntary act contributed to her rescue.

Volunteerism is important. People who are required to provide rescue services are not usually entitled to accept financial rewards of salvage, because their services are not "voluntary." The Coast Guard or the master, crewmembers and passengers of the salvaged ship usually aren't compensated, and neither are public employees whose jobs require them to perform such services. There are exceptions, however.

Professional salvors are entitled to a reward as long as their presence is voluntary. Sheer avarice may be the motivation, but that doesn't disqualify professional salvors from claiming the lucre. It is important to have a clear understanding of how much the salvage will cost you. If you don't have a contract and you can't reach a later agreement with the salvor, the court determines the award. (See the discussion of pure versus contract salvage below under "Types of Salvage.")

If you do agree on an amount prior to the salvage but have "buyer's remorse" after the rescue and then decide not to pay, the salvor can sue you for breach of contract in state and federal court. If a judge then grants a monetary reward to the salvor or someone who participated in the rescue, you'll have to pay that amount.

The second criterion of a salvage claim is that the rescue effort was successful—either in whole or in part. An attempt that ends in failure will not qualify for payment, no matter how heroic it was.

Finally, as with all matters of maritime law, the rescue must have taken place either upon the high seas or on navigable waters.

Assuming all of these criteria are met, admiralty courts will provide a monetary reward to people who participated in a substantial way to the rescue effort, and you will have to pay it. We'll examine these criteria in detail later.

## What Salvage Is Not

A popular misconception is that, if a boat washes up on a beach, it is fair game; anyone may help himself to parts or equipment. Boating magazines have carried stories of boats that were stripped by scavengers who believed that some salvage law gave them the right to cart off anything they wished.

The dividing line between salvage and looting may be thin but it is quite clear. If the salvor receives a clear indication that the wreck has been abandoned forever by its owner, then it becomes a salvage operation. In the absence of such an indication, the act becomes scavenging and looting, which are illegal.

If your boat gets beached and you must go somewhere for help, leave someone standing guard. Or call local authorities to ask for help guarding your boat.

There is a difference, too, between salvage and towage. Not surprisingly, in many lawsuits between the rescued and the rescuer, the rescuer claims the act was salvage, warranting the greater reward, but the rescued claims that the act was merely towage, which is to be paid for at the standard towage rates—a far lower reward.

Each case turns on its own facts, but the courts will generally look at the situation in which the rescued vessel found itself immediately prior to salvage/towage. If the vessel was unable to navigate or reach port unaided, or if it was abandoned even though not in imminent danger, then the courts will call it salvage.

A classic case illustrating this difference between salvage and towing involved the oil barge *Bolikow*. In November 1920, the *Bolikow* was being towed from Tampico, in Mexico, to Galveston, Texas, by the steam tug *Barryton*. The *Barryton* ran low on coal and anchored the *Bolikow* out of the shipping channel about four miles off the Texas coast. When the *Barryton* didn't return as expected, the crew of the *Bolikow* put out a call for help, and the towboat *George C. Geer* arrived. The skipper of the *George C. Geer* demanded $20,000 for towing the *Bolikow* into Galveston. The skipper of the *Bolikow* refused to pay. The skipper of the *George C. Geer* then lowered his demand to $15,000 and threatened to leave. The skipper of the *Bolikow* agreed. *The George C. Geer* then towed the *Bolikow* into Galveston without incident.

In a later lawsuit to collect the $15,000, the court ruled that the action of the *George C. Geer* might have qualified as salvage, but its huge demand was nothing short of extortion, so the court awarded the towboat only the going rate for towing, which was substantially less than $15,000.

## Types of Salvage

There are three basic types of salvage: (a) contract salvage, (b) quasi-contract salvage, and (c) life salvage, but the differences between them may at times be blurred. Treasure salvage does not qualify as salvage in the legal sense, but it will be discussed later in this chapter.

Contract salvage refers to the services of a salvage company that are contracted for after a maritime misfortune has occurred. The contract may be written or oral, but must involve maritime property. The agreement may provide for payment on an hourly or daily basis whether the operation is successful or not. However, many contract-salvage agreements may include a *no cure, no pay* provision that entitles the salvor to payment only if he or she is successful. Because the salvor is taking a greater risk in no cure, no pay agreements, the financial rewards are generally higher than in the normal contract-salvage situation. See Appendix D for an example of a salvage contract.

Quasi-contract salvage, often called *pure salvage* by admiralty lawyers, generally arises from emergency situations during which a vessel is in imminent peril. The number of potential rescuers is low, and their risks are high. In these cases, the law will imply a contract between the rescuer and the rescued. Lawsuits that follow quasi-contract salvage operations usually dispute the amount of the reward and who should share in it.

Life salvage means the saving of human life in a maritime setting. Ironically, saving a human life without saving maritime property does not entitle the rescuer to a reward, but saving a life in connection with the salvage of a vessel or other maritime property does entitle the rescuer to a share of the reward.

## Property
## Subject to Salvage

Salvage must involve maritime property, although there is no clear definition of what is salvageable and what is not. Clearly, any vessel is subject to salvage whether on the high seas or navigable waters or under them. Property washed ashore after a maritime disaster can be contested as salvage, as can any cargo, equipment, tackle, and furnishings associated with the saved vessel that can be picked out of the water or are washed ashore.

The distinction seems to be that anything that washes ashore from a salvaged boat is also considered part of the salvage, but, if maritime property simply washes ashore, source unknown, it may or may not be ruled as salvage.

Some types of structures while they are on or under the high seas or navigable waters are not subject to salvage, according to the courts. Dry docks and offshore drilling platforms are not subject to salvage, because they are considered extensions of the land. However, one court has been known to reverse another court's decision in this matter, as in many other cases of marine salvage.

Less typical types of property are also subject to salvage. The rationale used by the courts in these situations is that the reward to the salvor comes from the proceeds of the sale of the salvaged property. If the property cannot be sold, the salvor cannot be rewarded. As a result, mail and other objects that don't carry any intrinsic value are not subject to salvage. The same rationale has been used to justify the fact that saving another's life does not entitle the rescuer to a reward.

Some unique cases have allowed salvage of *nonmaritime* property, including sea planes that have crashed on navigable waters, drifting fish traps, floating logs that have broken away from log booms, and even the money found on a corpse recovered from New York Harbor.

One morning at sunrise, a 50-foot fishing boat nearly collided with a large object floating just under the surface in the entrance to San Diego Bay. To prevent other boats from striking the hazard, the fisherman craned onboard what turned out to be a 4 feet x 12 feet x 4 feet stainless-steel salad bar carrying a Navy serial number. He immediately radioed the Coast Guard of his actions and, when he returned to shore that night, contacted the Navy. He was told that the salad bar had slipped off the deck of a carrier that had recently departed the port, and that the Navy offered no contest over his salvage rights. In fact, the Navy was grateful that its flotsam didn't cause an accident. The fisherman's morning catch was worth $1,000 in scrap-metal value.

No salvage may be made without the consent of the owner of the vessel or property, except in the case of derelicts. When it is clear that the property or vessel has been abandoned, a salvor may carry out salvage operations and take the salvaged property to any safe port of choice.

### Who Can Be a Salvor?

Since the legal definition of salvage requires that the act of salvage be voluntary, no one who is required to render assistance can qualify as a salvor. Because the master and crewmembers of a ship are required to assist in saving their ship, they do not qualify as salvors of that ship. Passengers are generally disqualified for this same reason. However, the same master, crewmembers, and passengers might qualify as salvors of another vessel.

There are exceptions. In the 1860s, the *Great Eastern*, a sail-assisted steamer about the size of the *Queen Mary*, regularly sailed between Liverpool and New York. During one of her voyages, her rudder was damaged, leaving her without steerage. She drifted in the Atlantic in heavy seas for several days while her crew tried to repair the rudder.

As the chief engineer was loosening a nut that held the rudder in place, Towle, a passenger and civil engineer, realized that doing so would cause the rudder to fall into the sea. Towle and the steamer's master discussed Towle's plan to jury-rig a rudder, and the master consented. By using chains wrapped around the rudder shaft, the *Great Eastern* was safely brought to port several days later. Towle was given salvage rights based upon his extraordinary efforts.

Because the Coast Guard engages in salvage operations as a normal course of duty, it is not recognized as a volunteer and is therefore not entitled to salvage rewards. However, the Coast Guard has received awards in some cases.

The most notable case involved a fire aboard the 571-foot *Amoco Virginia* in the Houston Ship Canal that began on Sunday, November 8, 1959. During the transfer of cargo—some six million gallons of gasoline and heating oil—fire broke out either near or aboard the ship. The efforts to extinguish the blaze, which threatened the entire port, involved fire departments from the city of Houston and 18 other municipalities as well as the Coast Guard. When all supplies of flame-retardant foam were exhausted in the Houston area, an airlift of more than half a million pounds of foam was launched by the Navy and Air Force from Ellington Air Force Base. The airlift involved almost 400 Air Force and Navy personnel and 42 military vehicles.

The Coast Guard made a claim for salvage of $89,676.60, for the cost of the foam and the expenses incurred by the Navy and Air Force in airlifting it to Houston. This particular claim was upheld.

In one case, the Coast Guard was allowed to make a salvage claim against itself. On January 28, 1960, the 57-foot purse seiner *Barbara Lee* was making for Westport, Washington, in light rain and fog, with winds between 25 and 30 knots. The Grays Harbor Bar is known as the roughest and most dangerous bar crossing on the West Coast, and the strong ebb current made it even more difficult.

The *Barbara Lee* safely crossed the bar just ahead of the 52-foot Coast Guard vessel *Invincible*, but the *Invincible* did not live up to her name this fateful day. About 600 feet off the jetty, the *Invincible* took a wave that rolled her on her beam ends. Her engine stalled when water entered through her exhaust stack, and her radio was also knocked out.

The *Barbara Lee*, seeing the *Invincible* in trouble, radioed the Coast Guard at nearby Westport. The Coast Guard dispatched three more vessels, a 36-foot motor lifeboat from inside Grays Harbor, the *McClane* from Aberdeen, and the *Yocona* from Astoria, some miles to the south. The Coast Guard also directed the *Barbara Lee* to try to tow the *Invincible* into the harbor.

The *Barbara Lee* went back out over the bar and, during the second of two attempts to tow the *Invincible*, was capsized by a large wave. Two of her three crewmembers were lost. The *Invincible* drifted over the bar and was able to anchor. The 36-footer arrived and put a tow line on the *Invincible*, her anchor line was cut and the 36-footer was hit by a wave causing her to stall with both vessels now adrift. Finally, the *McClane* arrived and towed the *Invincible* to safety.

In the lawsuit that followed, the federal court held that the Coast Guard, though saving its own vessel, was entitled to a small portion of the total award for the salvage of the *Invincible*. The major portion went to the *Barbara Lee's* skipper, crews' estates, and owner—in recognition of the heroic efforts and loss of her crew.

Other professional rescuers, such as harbor firemen, are not entitled to salvage rights when acting in the normal course of their duties. When working outside their assigned duties, however, they will be entitled to rewards.

On September 15, 1901, the towboat *R. B. Little* and a barge named *Josephus* were en route from Providence to Philadelphia. The barge was anchored in Newport's outer harbor by the tug because of rough seas. Around midnight, a fire broke out aboard the *Josephus* and her crew abandoned ship. The *R. B. Little*, which had moored at a dock in Newport, came out but found its equipment inadequate to fight the fire. Another tug, the *Sisson*, also came to the assistance of the *Josephus*, but with a crew made up of bystanders—including the chief engineer of the Newport Fire Department and the night editor of the *Newport Herald*.

In later litigation, the chief engineer was able to receive a part of the salvage award, because his normal duties with the Newport Fire Department did not include fighting fires.

Pleasure boaters who are members of the Coast Guard Auxiliary may engage in salvage operations, buoyed by the knowledge that they too may be rewarded. On March 16, 1960, the derelict schooner *Brindicate* was discovered off the southern coast of Puerto Rico by two fishermen, Suarez and Valentin.

They went to the Club Nautico in Aguerro Harbor to advise the police of the find. Apparently, the conversation with the police was overheard by Girod, a member of the Coast Guard Auxiliary and owner of a 23-foot cabin cruiser. A dentist, Dr. Dominguez, and one of his patients, Mr. Williams, also got wind of the find and, along with Girod, set out to secure the *Brindicate*.

In litigation between Suarez and Valentin on the one hand and Girod, Dr. Dominguez, and Williams on the other, Girod was allowed to share in the reward in spite of the fact that he was a member of the Coast Guard Auxiliary.

Unlike the Coast Guard, the Navy and other military branches have no obligation to act in emergency situations. As a result, when the Navy chooses to get involved in a salvage operation, as it often does, it generally is rewarded.

In cases involving multiple salvors, the courts often have to sort out what exactly happened, who did what, and the action's relative contribution to the rescue effort. Most importantly, the courts usually decide who will get a monetary reward for their effort.

## Salvage Awards

Of course, this whole exercise is for one reason only—money. We would all like to believe that most rescue efforts are purely humanitarian, but this is not the case.

A large majority of cases in admiralty courts are about salvage, and those cases almost universally concern the size of the check that the res-cuers will receive. The natural dynamic of the situation poses the salvor, who will try to embellish the value of the vessel saved and the moral worth of his efforts, against the owner, who will claim damages and negligence on the part of the salvor and seek to diminish the value of the property saved. As the risk of property loss decreases, the likelihood that a salvage claim will be rejected increases.

All admiralty awards in the U.S. are based on the Supreme Court case of the British ship *Blackwall*. The *Blackwall* was lying at anchor in San Francisco Harbor on August 24, 1869. She was fully loaded with wheat and preparing to depart when, at about 0300 hours, fire was discovered aboard her. The tug *Goliah* was enlisted to help, and two fire engines were brought aboard. The *Goliah* then tied to the *Blackwall*, and the fire was extin-guished.

In deciding the *Blackwall* case, the Supreme Court set out the elements that are now considered in giving salvage awards. They include:

- the labor extended by the salvors in their efforts;
- the skill, energy, and swiftness with which the salvors act;
- the value of the property employed by the salvors;
- the degree of danger to which that property is exposed;
- the risk incurred by the salvors;
- the value of the property saved;
- the degree of danger from which the property is saved.

The Court decided that the value of the *Blackwall* and her cargo was $100,000, and the value of the *Goliah* was $50,000. The master and owner of the *Goliah* were ultimately awarded $5,000 for salvage services.

Each case is measured against this yardstick, and awards vary widely. Only rarely will the award exceed one-half the value of the property saved.

While no court decision has come right out and said so, pleasure-boat owners experience a double standard when salvage awards are concerned. A review of awards shows that with few exceptions, pleasure boaters are awarded less in their claims to salvage rights than are commercial opera-tors who have participated in a rescue mission.

A partial explanation may be found in the fact that small-boat owners are involved in fewer such cases. But even discounting that fact, there still seems to be an unspoken bias against awarding a pleasure boater monetary rewards on a par with professional salvors.

There is a lesson to be learned. Going into admiralty court is a very expensive proposition. Unless the stakes are exceedingly high, any fantasies about a pot of gold at the end of a rescue mission should be dismissed.

If you do seek a salvage award, you should immediately seek an attorney specializing in admiralty matters and, particularly, salvage matters. Ask what fees the attorney expects and what pay-off. No lawyer can ethically guarantee what you'll recover, so any representation should be taken with a large grain of salt. These particular legal waters can be full of shoals.

## Treasure Salvage

Although referred to as salvage and romanticized by recent finds, treasure salvage is not salvage in the legal sense. Treasure salvage involves the *law of finds*, the law of the sea (which is different from admiralty law), sovereign immunity (whether you can sue a governmental body), and a plethora of state and federal statutes concerning abandoned property.

Treasure salvage also involves the natural conflict between the archaeologists, with their desire to preserve historic finds in their natural settings, or at least in a museum, and the salvors, with their desire to profit.

The underlying theory is: If maritime property is well and truly abandoned, anyone coming upon it may claim it as his own. Many of the operations involve recovery of artifacts of significant historical as well as pecuniary value, such as Mel Fisher's company Treasure Salvors, Inc. and the Spanish galleon *Nuestra Señora de Atocha*.

Treasure salvage involves determining who is entitled to the treasures. State and federal agencies and individuals can make claims, but it's a high-stakes game. Many lawyers have undoubtedly retired aboard their new yachts after representing the various interests involved in treasure salvage.

In its efforts to resolve such conflicts, the federal government has passed the Antiquities Act, the Archaeological Resources Protection Act, the Outer Continental Shelf Lands Act, and the Abandoned Shipwreck Act.

These efforts don't seem to have been successful, in light of recent litigation surrounding the SS *Central America*, which went down on September 12, 1857 off Charleston. Claims on the three tons of gold supposedly aboard came from no less than nine insurance companies, Columbia University, and an order of Catholic monks. In an appeal, the U.S. Supreme Court ruled that salvage law did apply and that the salvors could not take all but would still get an award in a new trial.

## Practical
## Advice About Salvage

It has been the policy of the Coast Guard for some time not to compete with privately owned commercial towing and salvage operations. Now, on receiving a call, the Coast Guard will attempt to determine the nature of the situation. It will also try to determine the vessel's ability to anchor, what speed and direction of current are present, what the expected weather and sea conditions are, whether darkness is approaching, and the condition of the people on board. If the Coast Guard foresees no threat to life, and if a qualified commercial operation is available, the call will be given a low priority.

The Coast Guard will then contact a commercial operation to assist the vessel and monitor the situation. If none is available or if darkness is imminent, the Coast Guard may contact local law-enforcement officials or may respond itself. If the Coast Guard does respond, the vessel will be towed to the nearest available mooring.

If you get into a problem that doesn't involve a risk of loss of life, you're probably going to have to pay the towboat operator just as you pay the towtruck operator on land—unless a fellow boater happens by.

Here are some practical tips to keep in mind. Rather than merely accepting a tow, which might be taken as acceptance of a formal agreement, talk about what the charge will be, if anything. You're less likely to find yourself fighting a salvage claim if you reached an understanding beforehand. The courts will recognize some standards of fairness. As with the *Bolikow*, they usually recognize extortion when they see it.

The tower is required to use reasonable care in his or her actions. If he jerks so hard he pulls the bitts out of your foredeck or crushes your bulwarks, the tower should be responsible for the damage. But, remember, these commercial towers are not licensed. They are unregulated and they are not required to carry insurance.

If you can't picture attempting to negotiate an agreement on the deck of your bobbing, disabled boat, one alternative is to investigate a membership in a vessel-assistance program. For an annual fee, one of these membership organizations will provide limited towing service with its own vessels or will reimburse you for expenses you incur if one of its boats isn't available—just as an auto club would.

Finally, if you find yourself in a position to help another boater, any thoughts of making a pile of money should be immediately dismissed. Asserting a salvage claim is not an easy process, and the costs will almost certainly exceed what you might hope to recover. In fact, it might help the situation if you indicate that you are there just as a good Samaritan and not as a salvor.

Being a good Samaritan may not pay much, but the satisfaction will certainly outweigh any money you might get. Besides, the next time, it may be you asking the other boater for help.

Also, be careful when helping another boater so that you don't inadvertently find yourself also needing to be rescued. Get a line to the stranded boat as safely as possible, making sure you have sufficient water under your keel. When trying to refloat a grounded boat, be aware that most recreational vessels are not designed to work as tugboats. If something gives way unexpectedly, severe damage and injury can result.

When towing, be sure the bitts or cleats can withstand the strain. If towing a trailerable boat, use its bow eye. Attach the towing rope to your boat as far forward as possible so the added pull doesn't hamper your boat's maneuverability. Start slowly and proceed cautiously. Don't let the tow rope tangle in your prop.

# 11
# Liability

| | ❖ | |

According to the latest figures from the National Transportation Safety Board (NTSB), the number of people who died in boating accidents dropped more than 40 percent between 1971 and 1991, down from 1582 to 924. Unfortunately, three-fourths of all those boating fatalities could have been prevented if the victims had been wearing PFDs. Alcohol is involved in two-thirds of all drownings and half of all boating accidents. Most boating fatalities involved vessels of less than 16 feet in length.

If these statistics aren't sobering enough, consider that about 350,000 boaters are injured annually, and that the number of lawsuits filed each year in state and federal courts is approaching 20 million. As a boater, you have a 1-in-10 chance of getting sued.

What these statistics can't measure is the personal and emotional toll of litigation. While insurance may protect you from financial destruction in a lawsuit, a protracted court battle is still expensive, time-consuming, and emotionally exhausting.

## Rules of the
## Road and Liability

Rules for driving a car on land are said to have come from the navigation rules for vessels which were written to prevent accidents at sea. The

*International Rules of the Road* were adopted by the U.S. and incorporated into federal law after an international conference in 1889. These rules were updated in 1972 and incorporated into the *International Regulations for Preventing Collisions at Sea,* or COLREGS.

In 1980, to conform with the COLREGS, three additional sets of rules governing inland waters and rivers (Inland rules for navigation on waters of the United States not on the high seas; Western rivers rules; and Great Lakes rules) were combined and updated, and, for the first time, combined with the international rules under one title, *Navigation Rules,* commonly known as *Rules of the Road.* The Coast Guard's *Pilot Rules* also amplifies these rules.

Recreational boaters who are geographically limited to inland waters need only obey the combined U.S. Inland Navigation Rules, but if they have access to the ocean, they must also know and obey the COLREGS. Once they cross the demarcation line, which is clearly indicated on charts, they have technically left inland waters and have entered international waters. This is particularly important to trailer boaters who may launch their boats in inland lakes just as easily as in harbors leading to the ocean.

Today, the most frequent cause of marine accidents is violation of the Rules of the Road.

After an accident, determining whether the parties were adhering to the Rules of the Road is one of the main criteria courts use to assess liability. Specifically, the courts will determine (a) whether the people involved were acting as prudent seamen would act, (b) whether any of the participants were in violation of any written statute or regulation governing the operation of the boat or boats, and (c) whether the parties were following recognized customs or usages—over and above statutes or regulations—for boats in the area.

The Rules of the Road are not mere guidelines; they are laws and regulations that must be followed. The real reason to know and follow the Rules of the Road is not just to keep you from being fined, it is to prevent collision and associated injury, loss of life, and damage to property. And with respect to your liability as a boatowner or operator, they are extremely important. You can expect to pay substantially more than a mere fine if you violate these rules.

Every powered vessel at least 39 feet long must legally carry a copy of *Navigation Rules* on board, and smaller boats would be wise to do so. This government publication is printed by various publishers under both names, *Navigation Rules* and *Rules of the Road*. It is sold in marine chandlers and nautical bookstores for under $10.

## Boating
## Safety and Accidents

In the U.S., more people die from accidents in fishing boats than in any other type of boat. Fishing boat accidents can range from the simple to the bizarre, from slipping on a fish to being hit in the eye with a fellow fisherman's lead sinker, but several factors routinely contribute to serious accidents: overloading, insufficient safety gear, and sudden bad weather. You can best protect yourself from liability by complying with all regulations, especially those for PFDs and posted weight limits. Use common sense and be prepared if the weather turns ugly.

Hidden hazards can play a significant role in boating accidents. Currents, unseen boats, logs, and submerged rocks are common culprits. Overloading is another significant cause of accidents, particularly in boats less than 16 feet long. Most boats carry a metal plate put on by the manufacturer specifying the boat's maximum capacity, both in numbers of people and total weight. Maximum capacities are determined after extensive testing, and the plates are required by the Coast Guard on all monohulled powerboats (outboard, inboard, or sterndrive) of less than 20 feet in length and built after November 1, 1972. On outboard-powered boats, the plate also specifies maximum horsepower. Boatowners must abide by these capacity ratings as a matter of good seamanship as well as legal common sense. The capacity plates protect the boat's builder from liability, so if you exceed the stated capacity of your boat and then have an accident, you're probably on your own. The builder's attorney will point to the plate and its stated load limits when trying to prove that you were at fault.

Drugs and alcohol are becoming as big a cause of boating fatalities as they are in auto accidents. Almost every state has laws that prohibit operating a boat while under the influence of drugs or alcohol. Enforcement is particularly difficult, because, in contrast with an automobile driver, a drunken recreational boater has no boating license to lose for his or her offense. But captains and crews of sportfishing charter boats and other commercial boats are subject to random drug and alcohol testing, and each year many lose their Coast Guard licenses for this reason.

Drugs and alcohol tend to slow reaction time, reduce vision, exaggerate physical conditions such as fatigue, and reduce inhibitions that would normally keep us from doing reckless things. While recreational boaters do not face license suspension, a citation for boating while intoxicated (BWI) can cause your insurance rates to skyrocket. It can also have a significant effect on your liability in a suit against you by one of your passengers or his or her heirs.

If you have an accident due to drunken boating in a state that has a law prohibiting boat operation while under the influence of drugs or alcohol, then any operation while under the influence is *negligence per se.* Negligence per se is usually defined as conduct that will be considered negligence without argument or proof merely because it is a violation of a state statute or municipal ordinance. If not negligence per se, a jury can still find negligence, probably gross negligence. In this case, you're not only likely to be held liable for any damages or injuries, you could also be criminally prosecuted.

Waterskiing is subject to regulation in most states. In Washington state and most other states, every boat towing a skier must have an operator and an observer whose job is to watch the skier continuously. The observer must display a flag immediately after the skier falls. The flag must be at least 12 inches square, bright red or brilliant orange, and on a pole not less than 24 inches long. It must be held up so it's visible from all directions. The skier must wear an adequate and effective Coast Guard–approved PFD (type I, II, or III) or a wet suit with personal flotation approved by the Coast Guard. In Washington and most states it is illegal to water ski from one hour after sunset to sunrise, and the operator of the tow boat must be at least 14 years of age.

A violation that causes an accident can result not only in criminal charges, including fines and imprisonment, but civil liability for monetary damages. If the victim can prove that you violated a state law, your liability will increase, and the victim—or his or her heirs—will have a much better chance of collecting money from you.

*Negligence* is generally defined as failure to do something a reasonable person would do, following the generally recognized care which governs everyone's conduct, or doing something the reasonable and prudent person would not do. The law has traditionally used the *reasonable man* test to determine what is negligent and what is not. Would a reasonable person have acted the way the person charged with negligent behavior acted? A jury usually determines what is reasonable and what is not.

The law recognizes three degrees of care that must be taken in particular circumstances: slight, ordinary, or extraordinary. Classifications of negligence—such as slight, ordinary, and gross—relate to the degree of care that may be required in certain special circumstances. So slight negligence is defined as an absence of that degree of care that a person of extraordinary prudence would use in a particular situation. Ordinary negligence is an absence of care that an ordinary person would use. Gross negligence is an intentional failure to act the way an ordinary person would act with reckless disregard for the consequences of his or her actions. Gross negligence presumes a willful and wanton attitude. Negligence per se, as mentioned earlier, usually arises when one has broken some law. If a jury finds any form of negligence, the plaintiff will be awarded damages.

Weather plays a more significant role in boating than in almost any other recreational activity; consequently, it also plays a considerable role in boating accidents and fatalities. Be aware of the weather and forecasts. As skipper of your boat, you are responsible—and liable—for its safe operation, no matter what the weather conditions. If a jury finds that a "reasonable" skipper would not have set out with indications of bad weather, you will be held liable.

If your boat is caught in bad weather, swamped, and two guests drown while you and the others are rescued, a jury may find that a reasonable skipper would have acted otherwise. But if you can show that you acted prudently and exercised ordinary care, you are not likely to be found liable.

Operating at night requires an extra degree of care and vigilance. In one tragic incident, a boat traveling at night and at high speed struck a lighted navigational marker, causing serious injuries to the owner and his passenger. It took almost an hour for the local authorities and others who heard the crash to locate the victims in the dark, and both were seriously injured. Though the operator claimed that the marker was unlighted and he'd had only two or three beers earlier in the day, intoxicants were found in what was left of the boat and in the water at the marker. Evidence showed the marker was lighted. The operator was convicted of negligent operation of a boat.

Darkness makes potential hazards harder—if not impossible—to see, and your rescue will be more difficult and take longer to accomplish in the dark.

A spoonful of gasoline allowed to evaporate in your boat's bilge has the explosive power of a stick of dynamite. Seasoned boaters rank fire aboard a boat as one of the most feared of all accidents. Once a fire starts—fed by flammable resins and plastics used in modern boatbuilding—it engulfs faster and burns hotter than almost any fire commonly seen on land. Keep the required firefighting equipment on your boat updated and follow proper procedures. If you fail to have firefighting equipment in working order, you can be held liable for injury due to fire.

Asphyxiation from carbon monoxide is an all-too-common cause of death on boats. You should regularly check engine and generator exhaust connections as well as heating equipment to make sure that carbon monoxide cannot leak into the cabin areas. Provide adequate ventilation when sleeping aboard your boat.

In one instance, an experienced yacht captain and his crewmember had just begun motoring a new yacht from Mazatlan to California, but a Mexican Navy boat found the yacht running in circles well offshore. When the Navy sailors were able to get aboard, they found one U.S. seaman slumped over the wheel and the other lying in his bunk. Both had died of asphyxiation, presumably from a faulty exhaust system.

What are your obligations when someone falls overboard? The skipper's obligation is to do everything a reasonable person would do in trying to rescue the person who has fallen overboard. Failing to do so may equate to negligence and result in criminal liability. The lengths to which a skipper must go depend on the circumstances.

An 1864 case involved a sailor accidentally falling overboard from the rigging of a ship from a height of 110 feet into the sea. The captain did not stop the ship, lower boats, or make any attempt at rescue. Later, in trial, much attention was paid to the manner in which the sailor fell, whether or not he hit the boat first, what the sea conditions were at the time, the difficulty of stopping the ship, and other factors. The judge told the jury that it was the duty of the skipper to do everything possible—when a seaman falls overboard and is not killed by the fall—to perform a rescue no matter what the expense or delay. Perhaps the jurors felt from testimony that the sailor was dead when he entered the water and that rescue would have been fruitless, because they acquitted the ship's captain.

Almost 100 years later in another case, the tanker *Bulkcrude* lost a crewman while sailing along the Florida Keys at night. After the discovery of the disappearance of the crewman, a search was made. When the crewman failed to turn up, the ship radioed the Coast Guard but continued on its course. It was determined later that when *Bulkcrude* notified the Coast Guard, it was 100 miles beyond the point where the crewman was last seen. The weather was calm but there was no moon. An appeals court reversed a lower court that had ruled the captain not to be negligent; the appeals court held that the ship had an obligation to use every reasonable means necessary to rescue a crewman who fell overboard.

The owner/operator of a vessel (recreational or commercial) is subject to fines for negligent action or failure to act, according to federal statues. One case involved a speedboat collision in the dark on Lake St. Clair. When one passenger died, the owner of the boat was found guilty of violation of federal law. It was determined that the passenger probably died as the result of being struck by another boat that had come to the rescue and not as a result of the accident itself, but the boat's owner was found to have been operating while under the influence of alcohol, without lights at night, at excessive speeds, and on the wrong side of the channel.

What constitutes negligence? As with many legal terms, negligence can be viewed from several standpoints. Strikingly similar negligence cases have been decided differently. A great deal depends on the judge and jury.

Boatowners have been found liable for injuries because, for example:

- their boats hit wakes from other boats;
- they entrusted control of the boat to someone who was intoxicated;
- they allowed defective conditions to exist on board;
- they set out on a trip despite bad weather.

Also, overloading, speeding, permitting guests to ride in unsafe positions, failing to control the boat or warn a guest of an impending maneuver, hitting things, not having proper lights, and failing to warn guests of dangerous conditions have spelled negligence and liability for boatowners.

What if the captain is not the owner of a vessel involved in an accident? That situation might raise different questions of liability following an accident. One of the primary goals of the Limitation of Liability Act is to protect boatowners. Since it's not likely the owner of a large commercial vessel acts as its captain, the act protects owners from liability for circumstances that occur out of their presence or beyond their control.

Since a captain's responsibility is for the operation of the vessel, he or she can face both criminal and civil liability if he or she does not act reasonably and an accident injures people or property. Of course, the owner is responsible for hiring adequately trained and experienced crew, seeing that the vessel is adequately maintained and equipped, and exercising reasonable management of the vessel's affairs. If not, the owner could then be liable.

Know and follow all boating laws and be safety minded. You cannot eliminate all potential for liability in a civil lawsuit, but common sense and a careful observance of the spirit and letter of the boating regulations will get you 99 percent of the way there.

## Seaman Status

The term *seamen* generally refers to people working aboard vessels for pay—thought to be quite different from recreational boaters. Yet passengers aboard recreational boats have been deemed "seamen" in some court cases. If a passenger is found to be a seaman, he or she has certain rights and benefits that arise from ancient sea law, including the right to *maintenance and cure*—a kind of workmen's compensation for mariners.

Seaman status also affords one protection in U.S. admiralty courts, which are considered to be some of the most liberal in this country. Seaman status has been characterized as a cradle-to-grave welfare state; it offers payment of wages, subsistence, medical care, comfort and safety aboard ship, and protection from all manner of crooks and thieves. The protections may encourage people who are injured in marine-related incidents to have themselves declared seamen. Within the recreational boating world, the issue of seaman protections arises most often among racing crews. The case of George Pennell aboard the *Meridian* is a good example, and it is discussed later in this section under the Jones Act.

### Maintenance and Cure

The concept of *maintenance and cure* had its beginnings in ancient sea codes that date back at least as far as medieval times. The concept has been recognized in the U.S. since 1823. The term applies to the rights granted to seamen when they become ill or are injured while in the service of their ship. Their rights usually include medical care, food, and lodging until fit to return to work, and wages to the end of the voyage, even if the seaman doesn't work.

Maintenance and cure is required no matter who is at fault, and the cause—whether by someone's negligence or not—is irrelevant. A crewmember who falls ill as a result of something unrelated to work is still entitled to maintenance and cure. The sole exception is willful misconduct on the part of the seaman—intentionally doing something that is likely to result in serious injury, or with reckless disregard for its consequences.

Payment of maintenance and cure must continue until the seaman is cured, or until he or she reaches the point of maximum medical recovery, if permanently disabled. All medical costs, as well as food and lodging of the kind and quality received aboard ship, must be paid. As of 1993, the per diem rates for maintenance and cure run from $8 to $30. A claim for maintenance and cure can be made for an injury that happens on land, as long as it occurred while the seaman was working for the ship.

*Contributory negligence* is defined as negligence on the part of the victim that contributes to the accident. Though a ruling of contributory negligence tends to reduce the amount a victim may recover for damages, under maritime law, it does not allow for the denial of maintenance and cure.

### The Jones Act

The Jones Act, passed in 1920, granted seamen the right to sue the owners of a vessel for personal injuries caused by the owners' negligence.

Under the Jones Act, a seaman—or his or her heirs—could sue for damages such as pain and suffering, loss of income, and other types of generally recognized damages above and beyond what a seaman would get under maintenance and cure.

The Jones Act adopted the benefits system already given to railroad workers under the existing Federal Employers' Liability Act (FELA). Specifically, injuries must be suffered while working on a ship or result from unsafe conditions aboard ship. Today, cases brought to court under the Jones Act generally involve injuries suffered by crewmembers aboard fishing vessels. Crews on yacht deliveries, yacht charters, and harbor excursions are also covered by the Jones Act. If the seaman is killed, his or her heirs may sue for damages on the seaman's behalf under the provisions of a variety of different acts, including the Jones Act, the Death on the High Seas Act, and the Outer Continental Shelf Lands Act. Where and by whom the deceased was employed, where the accident happened, and whether the defendant was the employer of the deceased all determine what type of suit can be filed, which court can hear the suit, and what damages can be sought.

Working conditions have generally improved since the Jones Act took effect, but seamen or their heirs have recovered damages for some surprising events: falling through rotted decks, delays in calling a doctor to treat a medical condition, assaults from fellow seamen, dog bites, and falling off docks in a drunken stupor and drowning, to name just a few. A recreational boater need not worry about the Jones Act under ordinary circumstances, but it may come into play when serious injuries, death, or the prospect of large damage awards enter the picture. Even then, your worries should be less if you have good insurance coverage.

### Unseaworthy Boats

Historically and under general maritime law, boat owners or operators have a duty—to seamen, owners of goods carried on board, and other maritime workers not covered by the Longshoremen's and Harbor Workers' Compensation Act—to ensure that the vessel is *seaworthy*. A seaworthy vessel is defined as one that is fit for its intended purpose.

This duty is different from that owed to guests or passengers on your boat. The owner or operator of a vessel that is determined unseaworthy in a court of law is liable for damages, no matter what the seaman may have done to cause the injury. This is known as *strict liability*. While it isn't likely that a 16-footer would have a paid crewmember, there are situations in which the seaworthiness of even small boats can be called into question. Many of the larger recreational boats hire part-time or full-time skippers, and many luxury yachts have full staffs when underway.

Seaworthiness became an issue for recreational boaters through a 1963 federal case in Florida. In early 1961, prior to the beginning of the Miami-Nassau Race, George Pennell became an unpaid member of the crew of *Meridian*, a 52-foot, two-masted auxiliary yacht. During the race, Pennell was struck on the head by a spinning winch handle and permanently injured.

In the lawsuit that followed, the court held that even though Pennell was unpaid, he was still a seaman as defined by the Jones Act. The court also found that *Meridian* was unseaworthy and that the vessel's unseaworthy condition caused Pennell's injury; and therefore the owners of the boat were liable for damages to Pennell in the amount of $43,000—the value of *Meridian*. The owners had petitioned to limit liability, which we'll look at later in this chapter.

Thus, if your boat is unseaworthy, you are liable for any injuries or deaths that occur.

Long ago, seaworthiness simply meant that the vessel had a sound hull, and that the gear on board was free of defects. In recent years, however, courts have extended the meaning. Even a spot of oil on a deck has been held to constitute an unseaworthy condition.

## Guests Versus Passengers for Hire

As a boatowner, you have a legal obligation to ensure that your guests come to no harm. This simple-sounding caveat contains a world of complexity. What does and does not violate your obligation?

What about the distinction between guests and passengers for hire?

Some Coast Guard officers contend that any contribution makes a guest a passenger for hire, but the courts have not agreed and it is the courts that ultimately decide negligence. It is highly unlikely that if you take people out on your boat and they happen to bring along snacks and beverages that you will be found to be carrying passengers for hire—and therefore held to the higher standard of care than if they merely were guests.

Carried to its logical conclusion, if you are found carrying passengers for hire, then you must be in the charter business and you would also be required to be licensed as a charter operation. Who doesn't take friends out on the boat for a day or weekend and allow them to bring food along? Are we all then in the charter business?

A paying passenger is entitled to *extraordinary care*, which essentially means that the slightest failure or omission on your part leading to a passenger injury could render you liable in the eyes of the court. A guest, on the other hand, is entitled to *reasonable care* while aboard your boat, meaning the degree of care that an ordinarily prudent person would provide under the same or similar circumstances.

Reasonable care is a subjective standard that might include advising all passengers as they come aboard where the PFDs are located if not in plain view or warning them not to stand up while the boat is underway. It might include not taking the boat out if the weather is bad or coming back early if bad weather threatens. Reasonable care includes anything a reasonable boat operator would probably do to prevent injury to himself or a passenger aboard his boat.

Reckless or dangerous operation of your boat can obviously render you liable, but so can failing to give proper instructions, such as, "Here's how the fire extinguishers work." Simply stated, you must act in a reasonable manner so your guests don't hurt themselves.

Develop a routine for welcoming guests aboard your boat. Point out the PFDs and demonstrate how to don one. Point out all the fire extinguishers and run through the drill on using one. Warn your guests about any activities that may be dangerous on board, such as, "Be sure to use both hands on the ladder rail when you climb up to the fly bridge." Mention any locations where they could get hurt, such as "Look out for this head-knocker; I hit it every time."

### Licensees Versus Guests

Historically, the law classified the people who might come upon your property as trespassers, licensees, or guests. Although you may not willfully harm a trespasser, he or she is owed nothing if harmed while aboard your boat. A *licensee*, on the other hand, is not a true guest but is on board at your request; for example, someone who has come to varnish your teak. Historically, your duty to a licensee was to warn him or her of any dangerous conditions that you might know about. If a hatch was missing on the foredeck, you were obligated to warn the varnisher not to fall in.

In a 1959 U.S. Supreme Court case, the court held that the historical distinction between a licensee and a guest was incompatible with maritime law. Since that decision was handed down, anyone who comes aboard your boat—except a trespasser— must receive reasonable care. Whether or not you were negligent when a guest or licensee was injured is a question decided by a jury or a judge.

Reasonable care is more rigorous than the traditional duty owed to a licensee, which was merely to warn him or her of dangerous conditions that you knew about. Understanding and fulfilling your legal obligations to guests and licensees is the best way to keep them safe, and it's the safest way to protect yourself.

## Injuries to Workers

Boatowners should be concerned about possible injuries to people who work on their boats. Under current law, workers are considered licensees, but their injuries are covered by the Federal Longshoremen's and Harbor Workers' Compensation Act (FLHWCA), with the exceptions listed below. The federal act was passed by Congress in 1927 to create a federal no-fault compensation system for land-based maritime workers.

It is funded by contributions from employers in maritime industries and covers longshoremen, shipbuilders, repairmen, and other maritime-industry workers who do not qualify as seamen. A 1984 amendment disqualified clerical and office employees of maritime industries; employees and suppliers of clubs, camps, museums, marinas, or recreational, restaurant, and retail operations; employees in the aquaculture industry; *and people who build and repair recreational vessels under 65 feet in length.*

Claims filed under the FLHWCA are processed through the federal Department of Labor. If those injured don't qualify as seamen and don't fall under the protection of the Jones Act, then their injuries might be covered either by the FLHWCA or—more likely—their employer's workers' compensation insurance. This insurance is regulated by state workers' compensation acts, and the employer pays the cost of coverage. If self-employed, workers sometimes carry their own workers' compensation insurance.

Claims under the FLHWCA and state-regulated workers' compensation programs are processed without regard to fault, so even if the boatowner was at fault, injured workers often opt to process claims through the FLHWCA or their workers' compensation coverage rather than sue a negligent boatowner, because they are guaranteed a settlement and don't necessarily have to go to court or hire a lawyer. They can choose to sue you instead if you were at fault, however, and you should carry insurance that protects you from such a suit. If an injury was not your fault and the worker is not protected under the Jones Act or the FLHWCA, and is not self-insured, he or she must pay the bill.

Recreational boatowners can minimize the chances of being sued by an injured worker by providing a safe working environment onboard: no fumes building up in your bilge, no leaky winter cover, no rotten steps in your ladders, and no dangling electrical wires.

## Limitation of Liability

If all of this talk about possible liability has you giving second thoughts to buying a boat or taking guests aboard, here is the good news. In certain cases, *limitation of liability* allows pleasure-boat owners to limit their liability to the value of their boat following an accident. This provision is unique to maritime law.

While this may appeal to someone facing a lawsuit for alleged negligence, the doctrine has created much controversy—particularly for those who represent the victims of alleged negligence.

### *Origins of Limitation of Liability*

Medieval sea codes introduced the concept of limitation of liability to encourage seagoing commerce and to protect owners of ships from the vagaries of marine ventures. These codes were adopted prior to the development of insurance.

To encourage investment in American ships and their use in foreign commerce and to put American shipping on an equal footing with that of England, France, and Germany, Congress passed the Limitation of Shipowners' Liability Act in 1851. It established the principles of limitation of liability that we still use today.

The doctrine basically states that when an accident occurs, the owners of the vessel may, in some situations, be liable for damages only up to the value of the vessel following the accident. In this specific situation, the vessel is either sold or the owner can put up money equal to its value. This amount serves as a fund for payment of damages to the injured.

Remember George Pennell (see page 153), the unpaid crewmember on the *Meridian*? Pennell received $43,000 because that was *Meridian's* value at the time of his injury. Her owners petitioned for limitation of liability after the accident.

### Applying the Limitation of Liability Law to Recreational Boats

In a precedent-setting 1990 U.S. Supreme Court case, Sisson versus Ruby, involving a fire aboard a recreational boat that damaged a Michigan marina and several other recreational boats docked at the marina, the court ruled that the suit could be heard in federal admiralty court.

No one was aboard *Ultorian* at the time of the fire, and its origin is unclear, although it seemed to have started in an onboard laundry compartment. When *Ultorian's* owner tried to get the court to limit liability, the lower-court judge ruled that noncommercial vessels did not qualify for protection under the federal limit of liability provisions. The owner appealed the decision, but the appeals court turned him down for the same reason. Following appeal to the U.S. Supreme Court, however, the higher court ruled that the case could be heard in admiralty court because the circumstances of the incident fulfilled the two criteria for admiralty jurisdiction: (1) the vessel's storage and maintenance at a marina constituted traditional maritime activity, and (2) the marina was located on a navigable waterway (See Chapter 2 for more on admiralty jurisdiction and its relevance for recreational boaters.)

It's important to note that the court did not decide whether the

*Ultorian's* owner had a right to sue for limitation of liability (this was not at issue), only that he had the right to bring the case into admiralty court.

### How to File for Limitation of Liability

The requirements for limiting your liability are few, but the process is complex—though not beyond the scope of an interested recreational boatowner. I don't recommend a layman trying to do this without a lawyer.

Let's say a guest fell down your slippery (possible negligence) companionway steps, permanently injured his spine (injury and damages), and is now suing you for every penny you're worth. If you did know or should have known about the negligent condition that resulted in the accident, forget about limiting your liability.

But let's say you did not know and could not have known. First, you must file a complaint or petition in the appropriate federal district court in its capacity as an admiralty court. This must be done within six months of receipt of written notification that claims are being filed against you by your guest or by someone whose property was damaged.

Next, you must either turn over your boat to the court or deposit with the court—along with the complaint—a sum equal to the value of your boat at that moment, even if it's at the bottom of the bay. If you're successful in limiting liability, the court will pay the claims on a pro-rata basis out of the fund.

Once these documents have been filed, the court will issue an injunction stopping all legal proceedings against you, at least with respect to the incident surrounding the claims. The court will then set a time limit for all claims arising out of the incident to be filed with the court.

The basis for limitation of liability makes sense, especially from the viewpoint of commercial owners. Their normal business practice is to contractually pass over all operational responsibility for their vessels to charterers. If a recreational boatowner had knowledge that could have prevented an accident, or if he or she committed a negligent act such as failing to follow Rules of the Road, then limitation of liability cannot and should not apply.

Much of the criticism leveled at the limitation of liability law comes from situations in which the fund—based on the value of the vessel after the incident—is unreasonably low considering the damages suffered by the people injured. This is particularly true when the boat sinks or is destroyed in the accident, leaving nothing to fund the damages. It is important to remember that victims have no recourse if a court decides that this doctrine applies.

Changing a legal doctrine is a long and gradual process often taking years to accomplish. Several attempts to remedy this situation have been unsuccessful.

# 12

# Insurance

| | ✧ | |

## Why Insurance?

Boat insurance has two basic parts. The first, called hull coverage, includes repair or replacement of your boat if it's damaged or destroyed as the result of some misfortune. The second, called protection and indemnity coverage, protects you and your assets from liability in the event you are sued by someone who is injured while on your boat or in an accident that is your fault.

Unfortunately, the tendency for many boatowners is to buy the least expensive policy they can find without researching what they are getting. Many boatowners don't bother with insurance at all. Many cruisers believe that their money would be better spent on a storm anchor and long-range radio than on insurance.

But time and effort spent now in selecting insurance for your boat could save you big dollars in the future.

## Types of Insurance Policies

Two types of policies are generally offered to boaters today. The differences between the two seem minimal at first glance, but a closer look reveals significant differences.

The first type, called a *boat policy*, is generally offered by the established insurance giants, such as Aetna, Allstate, Prudential, State Farm and others, that offer full lines of coverage for homes, autos, and boats as well as life insurance. The second type, called a *yacht policy*, is sold through agents who specialize in insuring boats. This coverage originates with specialized insurance companies, such as Lloyd's of London.

You may live in a part of the country where yacht policies are not available, or you may own a boat that makes it difficult or impossible to secure a yacht policy. (Many carriers will only insure boats 26 feet long or longer.) If so, a boat policy may be your only option. You may get coverage in the form of a rider on your homeowner policy or a separate policy from your car insurance company. In those cases, be sure you have adequate liability coverage, and discuss with your insurance agent the basis for payment in the event of loss. Many boatowners have had satisfactory results from boat policies.

The most important difference between a boat policy and a yacht policy is the amount the company will pay if your boat is damaged or destroyed. The so-called hull coverage portion of a yacht policy is usually based on an agreed or stated value—say $50,000—set at the time the policy is issued. In the event of a total loss, the amount of the check from the insurance company will be $50,000.

That is not the case with a boat policy. For a total loss covered by a boat policy, the amount of the check will be the depreciated value of the boat at the time of the loss, which can be substantially less than the stated or agreed value.

If you already have insurance coverage on your boat but don't remember what type of policy it is, you can look at the section of your policy papers dealing with how losses will be paid. It might be titled "Losses We Cover" or "Method and Amount of Settlement." If it talks about depreciation or contains some other type of limiting language such as:

"Actual Cash Value. There may be a deduction for depreciation . . ."
*or*
"Actual cash value to be established at the time of loss, with due regard for depreciation . . ."

*or*

". . . repair or replace with material of like kind and quality . . . "
then you have a *boat policy*, and you will not be paid the full stated value
of the boat.

Boat policies tend to cost less than yacht policies, because—if for no
other reason—you will be paid less in the event of a total loss. Your savings
in premiums may not be significant if you compare what you're getting
when you choose the yacht policy. Of course, you can get as many different
prices for insurance coverage as the number of company representatives
you contact.

While it may be convenient and quite possibly less expensive to have
your boat coverage with the same company that insures your car and
house, you should strongly consider dealing with an agency that specializes
in yacht insurance. As seasoned boatowners know all too well, boats
require special knowledge, and insuring a boat is a prime example. Your
neighborhood agent may not be familiar with all the nuances of a yacht
policy, even if he or she can offer you one.

## What's Covered?

One of the good things about boat insurance today is that policies are
generally written in plain English rather than in legalese, so they're relatively easy to understand. Instead of:

Touching the adventures and perils which we, the Assurers, are con-
tented to bear, and do take upon us, they are of the seas, men-of-war,
fire, enemies, pirates, rovers, assailing thieves, jettisons, letters of mart
and countermart, reprisals, takings at sea, arrests, restraints and
detainments of all kings, princes, and people, of what nation, condition or quality soever, barratry of the Master and Mariners, and of all
other like perils, losses and misfortunes, that have or shall come to the
hurt, detriment or damage of said yacht or any part thereof.

you are more likely to find:

We will pay for direct physical loss or damage to the covered yacht and
its equipment against all risks from any external cause except those
which are excluded.

Most policies are *all risk* policies, which means that if a type of loss is not specifically excluded, it will be covered. What if your boat is stored in a yard that is uninsured, and the boat is damaged during a fire there? If the loss isn't specifically excluded by your policy, it will be covered.

Exclusions vary from company to company however. You should take care in talking to your agent and reading the policy to understand exactly what is excluded from coverage.

The standard exclusions may include:

• intentional loss by you or someone else with your consent;
• loss caused by lack of proper maintenance, wear and tear, gradual deterioration, corrosion, dampness, borers or marine life, electrolysis, osmosis, or blistering;
• loss caused by electricity, except for lightning, unless there is a fire and then only for the fire damage;
• defects in the design or manufacture of the boat;
• loss caused by ice or freezing;
• loss due to the mysterious disappearance of equipment or personal effects;
• theft of the boat by someone you have lent it to;
• illegal use of the boat;
• loss resulting from war, civil war, insurrection, rebellion, or revolution;
• loss from radioactive contamination.

Insurance companies base their premiums on what their underwriters tell them about the average losses to be expected for a particular type of boat, used in a particular way, in a particular area. As a result, the premiums you pay are based upon what you have told your agent regarding your boat's use.

If the company discovers that you've misrepresented anything on your application, it can cancel your policy. If you take your boat out of the cruising area specified in your policy—or if you use it in a manner not covered by the policy—and you have an accident, you're on your own.

Avoid the problem by telling your agent if you plan to sail the Vic-Maui or TransPac to Hawaii, or that you might like to cruise the Caribbean. Your agent can rewrite your coverage to include your plans. Of course there may be additional requirements, but we'll discuss them later in this chapter.

By far the most important coverage is that which protects you from liability if you are sued—similar to the liability coverage on your car.

With a yacht policy, the *P&I* or protection and indemnity portion of the policy will protect you and your family and guests—not a paid captain or crew—from bodily injury and from damage caused by you, your family, and guests. Running into another boat, ramming a dock, and other such accidents are covered. It will also pay for the removal of the wreckage if the removal is required by law.

If you need separate coverage for a paid captain and crew, you should arrange for it with your broker.

Maximum limits set by the yacht policy may range from $25,000 to $500,000, with $300,000 being fairly standard, but if you seek a higher limit, expect higher premiums. The policy will include medical coverage for everyone (except hired captain and crew) in the range of $1,000 to $5,000. It also covers injuries to mechanics, repairmen, and similar workers on your boat, under the Federal Longshoremen's and Harbor Workers' Compensation Act (FLHWCA) or state regulated workers' compensation insurance policies taken out by employers and self-employed workers.

The FLHWCA, which is described in more detail in Chapter 11, constitutes a type of workers' compensation for marine workers who are injured while working on your boat, regardless of whether you are at fault or not. The act specifically excludes workers on recreational boats under 65 feet in length. In order for coverage to apply, the work must be done on navigable waters or adjoining piers, wharves, dry docks, terminals, building ways, marine railways, or other adjoining areas usually used for working on vessels.

So if someone works on your boat while it is on a trailer in your backyard, and if he or she falls off the boat and is injured, the accident won't be covered by the FLHWCA. It would have to be covered by the individual's workers' compensation insurance, if the worker has such insurance, or your liability insurance.

P&I coverage means that the insurance company is bound to pay the jury award against you or any settlement that might be reached up to the limits set in the policy. However, if the judgment exceeds the policy limits, then you will be liable for the balance. It's a good idea to ask your insurance broker about increasing the liability limits to a higher level if you can still comfortably pay the premiums.

P&I coverage is important from the legal standpoint, too, because the insurance company is bound to provide a lawyer to defend you in court if you are sued, assuming you were operating your boat in a manner and location covered by your policy.

Most yacht policies also cover damage and injuries resulting from an accident involving an uninsured boater. This is something like auto insurance protection from uninsured motorists. As long as the accident was the other guy's fault, your policy will pay for any bodily injury, although it may carry a maximum, such as $25,000. Any damage to your boat will be covered under your hull coverage, but only after you pay the deductible.

Your policy should also cover you and your family members from liability when you are operating someone else's boat with their permission, but some policies don't offer this coverage. It won't usually cover damage to the boat itself, since that should be covered under the other owner's policy. If the other owner has no insurance on his boat, don't operate it. You could be sued in order for him to recover his damages.

Most policies also cover the tender under both hull coverage and P&I liability, so long as it is under 15 feet in length and has a rated speed of less than 25 miles per hour.

## Navigational
## Limits: How Far Can We Go?

Insurance policies for boats are usually written to cover normal activities within specific geographic areas. For example, the standard pleasure-cruising area for Puget Sound is " . . . navigable waters of Puget Sound and its tributaries, not more than 50 miles beyond Cape Flattery, and the inside waters of British Columbia not North of 51 degrees north latitude . . ." In Southern California they are " . . . Pacific coastal waters and tributaries not north of Point Conception, California, nor south of Rio Santo Tomas, Mexico . . . ." East Coast limits are generally from Eastport, Maine, to Cedar Keys, Florida. You can get a rider covering the Bahamas for an additional premium.

Seasonal limitations are common in some parts of the country. Policies issued for boats in the Northeast may require a haulout for five months out of the year, due to severe winter storms. If you plan on having your boat in Mexico during hurricane season, you may be required to remain in certain harbors that are considered safe from hurricanes.

If you take your boat out of its specified cruising area or don't haul it when required to do so, you will be completely uninsured during that time, and your insurer could in some cases cancel your policy altogether.

## Cruising Outside
## Your Navigational Limits

If you are considering visiting the popular but foreign cruising grounds of Baja California, the Gulf Islands, the Bahamas, or other regions outside the navigational limits of your policy, you'll need to ask your insurer for a *rider* or trip policy for the voyage. And you can expect to jump some hurdles before you get it.

Your insurer will want to know how many people will be on board and exactly what their boating experience is. Many companies require a minimum number of crewmembers, depending on the size of your boat and where exactly you want to cruise and for how long.

As the skipper, your ability and experience are most important, so you may have to provide a resume that details your previous cruising experience, what types of boats you've owned or operated, your age and your health status. For hazardous regions, you might even be required to have someone on board who has cruised in that area before. Often, you'll be required to have two crewmembers who know celestial navigation and who can operate all your radios and navigational gear.

An extensive *trip survey* of the boat may be required, one that is over and above the general survey. If so, the following items will be checked:

- long- and short-range communication radios;
- heavy-duty anchoring system;
- navigation equipment;
- adequate charts for that region;
- firefighting equipment;

• safety equipment, including a life raft large enough for the entire crew and an EPIRB;
• medical equipment and manuals;
• tools and adequate spares for the engine;
• service and operating manuals for all equipment;
• bilge pumps.

Your boat and its systems will be inspected to make sure its general condition is adequate for the cruise, including your hull, decks, engine, rigging, sails, storm sails, cockpit drains and scuppers, ports and windows, batteries, fuel tanks and fuel-transfer system, navigational equipment, communication equipment, and ground tackle. Many surveyors also interview the skippers to be sure they know what they're doing.

You can expect to pay higher premiums to offset the perceived increased risks, but once you meet all the requirements, your new policy will cover you throughout your extended cruising grounds.

## Going Around the World

If you are dreaming of making a circumnavigation or cruising to a location for which insurers don't generally give trip policies or riders, you should first investigate the special insurance problems this creates. As a general rule, the cost of the coverage—if you can get it—will be out of the reach of most cruising families.

Bluewater sailing is not the stock in trade at the office of your friendly local insurance agent. Lloyd's of London is the only carrier that will write such coverage. The hoops to be jumped through are numerous and expensive. Insurance brokers who specialize in yacht policies are usually able to get a quote for coverage provided by Lloyd's, if they have an established relationship with a London broker familiar with Lloyd's. Securing a policy with Lloyd's will take some time due to the communications involved and to the way Lloyd's does business, so plan ahead. Payments of claims will also be much slower because of the distances involved.

Expect to face an even more rigorous examination than if you were merely going on an extended cruise. Because of the international nature of such coverage, the policy will be much different from the standard yacht policy. It will probably be a *named peril* rather than an *all risk* policy. Named perils are those named in the policy. Any perils not named aren't covered.

Your departure date for sailing around the world will probably have to wait until your boat is paid for. Bankers require coverage at least equal to the amount that is still owed them. The coverage is in the form of an endorsement referred to as a 438BFU.

If you're heading for the South Seas and decide to cancel your existing policy, your bank will be informed of the cancellation, because it is named as an *additional insured* in the policy. Your bank will request or demand that you get coverage. If you don't, they will get it for you. Nobody's going to let you sail blithely off into the sunset while they're left holding the bag—whether it's an unsecured debt or a risky insurance liability.

## What Affects
## the Size of Premiums?

After shopping around, you'll be surprised at the variations in the cost of yacht insurance. Many factors determine each company's rates, including their experience in insuring boats, the perceived risks involved, and the judgment of the broker and underwriters working for the company.

Simple geographic differences result in different insurance rates. In spite of the fact that you can sail and cruise year-round along the West Coast, rates there tend to be lower than those along the East Coast. Rates with some companies are lower in Puget Sound than they are in California, because most of the sailing and cruising in the Pacific Northwest is done on sheltered waters. Rates are generally higher for the Gulf of Mexico and the east coast of Florida than they are for Chesapeake Bay, the Great Lakes and the Pacific Coast—due to the increased likelihood of hurricanes.

Having more than just the minimum amount of safety and navigational equipment on board can help keep your premiums down. Your insurer will want to know about your VHF radio, RDF, single-sideband, depthsounder, vapor detector, satnav or Loran or GPS receiver, radar, Halon system, bilge alarms, automatic bilge pumps, lighted marine compass, and burglar-alarm systems. The more safety and navigation equipment you have, the lower the rates are likely to be, even though these discounts are minimal. On the other hand, the more toys and theft-prone items you have, the higher will be your premiums. Jet skis are a favorite toy—and a favorite with thieves, too.

More significant discounts may be given by insurance companies if you and your crewmembers are in their desirable age range, have plenty of practical experience, and own a diesel-powered boat—as opposed to a gasoline-powered boat. A sailboat is usually cheaper to insure than a powerboat of similar value, because sailboats move slower and therefore have a lower loss ratio.

Also, completing a piloting or seamanship course offered by the U.S. Power Squadron or the Coast Guard Auxiliary goes a long way toward reducing your premiums. If you're an active member of the United States Coast Guard Auxiliary or the United States Power Squadron, that will help even more.

Any losses paid by an insurance company in your behalf in the last three to five years will most certainly not help. A bad boating record, like a bad driving record, can cost you up to 25 percent on your premiums, or at least the loss of a preferred rate.

As with car insurance, the higher your deductible the lower your premiums. Be sure you're comfortable with the amount of the deductible, because, in event of an accident, you will have to shell out that much before your insurer begins paying off.

## Special Situations

Because insurance companies base their premiums on what their underwriters tell them, any unique situations that don't fit the norm tend to create problems for insurance companies. Not all companies are alike in this respect. Some are even worse.

Living aboard your boat is one of those unique situations. Some of the full-service giants that have little experience insuring larger boats may refuse to insure a boat on which you live. On the other hand, companies that specialize in recreational boat insurance will often give liveaboards a reduced rate. Their theory is that bad things are less likely to happen if someone is aboard most of the time.

The newest wrinkle in liveaboard coverage is a policy similar to a homeowner's policy but designed specifically for liveaboards. It covers the boat as any other yacht policy would, but it also covers all personal possessions on board and in storage at other locations, and it provides personal liability coverage for things that may happen to you off the boat. Because of the increased coverage, you can expect to pay a little more than for the normal yacht policy, but knowing that all of your possessions are covered should make it worth the added cost.

Older boats, particularly older wooden boats, are considered unique not only by lovers of fine craftsmanship but also by insurance companies. Older wooden boats often cost more to insure because they supposedly cost more to repair. Some companies won't insure boats that are older than 15 or 20 years. You may have to get a survey performed before a regular carrier will insure it, and you may need a dry-dock survey every couple of years or so. At your expense, of course.

If you're having trouble finding insurance for your old wooden boat, ask people who belong to vintage-yacht groups and wooden-boat clubs. Most of them maintain group insurance coverage through their memberships.

Most insurance companies have a problem with gasoline-powered boats, particularly gasoline inboards, because of increased fire risk. Some insurers will not come near a gas boat with a barge pole. Others will simply charge a higher premium. Many insurance companies accomplish the same thing by giving discounts for diesel-powered boats.

Chartering causes special problems for almost every insurer. Most prohibit you from chartering your boat, even on an occasional basis, without requiring some qualification procedures for determining the experience level of the charterers who would operate your boat. Some insurers will require that the charterer have a captain on board, someone who has been qualified with that insurer. If you charge people even once, your insurance company will consider it a commercial operation.

If you are considering bareboat charter on a regular basis as part of a business, special coverage is required. It will be dependent on what procedures you establish for qualifying the charterers, and even then only certain companies will write such coverage. If you place your boat in service with a regular charter operation, most of them carry group policies covering their fleets. Be prepared to pay significantly higher rates whenever chartering is involved.

Sailboats aren't thought of as unique situations, but when you plan to race, a unique-situation flag pops up in your insurer's mind. And your insurance rates can go up, along with that flag. Accidents that occur during a race are not covered unless racing is specifically covered by your policy. Some companies will cover the mast and rigging only for an additional charge. Sails are not often covered under any circumstance.

If you're financing the purchase of your boat, your lender will require a *loss payable clause* on your insurance policy. The clause stipulates that, if the boat is destroyed or damaged, the bank will be paid first—and in the amount still owed on the loan. This protects the bank from losses.

Be very careful not to allow your coverage to lapse. If it does, the bank has the right to get its own insurance on your boat and charge you for it. Their coverage can cost as much as 10 times what you would otherwise pay. Some banks are not sympathetic to your wallet when it comes to insuring property covered by their loans. Avoiding the increased premiums is difficult.

Insurance companies are rated just as some companies are, and some lenders require that you carry insurance only with specifically rated insurance companies.

Most marinas require you to carry at least liability or P&I coverage before they let you moor your boat in their facility. The idea is to protect themselves in case something bad happens while you're tied up there.

## Homeowner's Coverage

Your homeowner's policy might cover certain personal items that you take on the boat, while some boat policies don't cover personal items or set a rather low maximum for what they will pay for the loss. If you have a loss that isn't covered by your boat policy, check to see if it's covered by your homeowner's insurance.

If you are a liveaboard and have no homeowner's policy, you should see about increasing your boat policy's coverage for the personal items you carry on your boat.

## How to
## Find an Insurance Agent

Developing a good working relationship with a competent insurance broker can be very important. That association can be worth a lot if bad things happens, because you'll want your agent on your side.

Finding the best insurance coverage and agent is just like finding the best deal on a boat—you've got to shop around. Word of mouth recommendations from friends with boats are your best sources. One of the best places to comparison shop is at boat shows.

Many yacht brokers offer insurance services, and yacht-insurance specialists are listed in boating-service directories and in most large-city Yellow Pages. When you talk to the various agents, be sure you are giving each the same basic information, so you can compare their prices.

Certain groups such as the Boat Owners' Association of the United States (BOAT/U.S.) or Recreational Boaters of America offer vessel insurance. These groups, as well as others, provide their own insurance programs at competitive rates, although if you don't live near one of their offices, you can't just run downtown to talk with their agent. Claims service may therefore be more difficult.

Your decision on coverage should be based not only on the cost of the policy but more importantly on the service you get from your agent and the type of coverage you're buying. Just about anybody can write boat insurance, so find out from the agent about whether this is a boat policy or a yacht policy.

An experienced agent should be able to answer any questions you have about coverage. If a prospective agent can't answer a few fairly simple questions and will have to check on them, you should move on. It's likely that agent doesn't deal with boats very often. There is nothing wrong with shopping around and getting quotes from a number of companies. Just be sure you are comparing apples with apples.

## Making a Claim

On that unhappy day when you have to make a claim on your boat insurance, it's important to remember that photos and accurate records can help speed the process of repair and get you back on the water.

Your policy will tell you what to do. The first thing is to protect the boat from any further loss. If the engines, motors, electrical equipment, or electronics have been submerged in salt water, they should be thoroughly flushed out with fresh water, dried quickly, and oiled. Your insurance company will not allow you to abandon your boat or equipment without its prior written approval.

You should notify your broker, agent, or the insurance company directly. If your boat or other insured item was stolen, the local police should be notified, and you should secure a copy of their police report. If you live in a part of the county where the Coast Guard has a presence, and if anyone was injured, the Coast Guard should be notified, and you should try to get a copy of its report as well.

Be sure to get the names and addresses of any people involved in the accident and of any witnesses, so your insurance company can contact them later. It's also a good idea to get pictures of any damage as soon as possible, even if the insurer says it is going to send someone out to look at the boat.

You'll be expected to cooperate with the insurance company by providing a signed, detailed statement of what happened and by providing all bills, invoices, and time sheets needed to substantiate your claim. You'll have to make the boat available for inspection by a surveyor hired by the insurance company and may even have to testify in court later, if the accident wasn't your fault and the insurance company goes after the other guy.

Don't authorize any repairs until told you can do so. In the U.S., you may be asked to get a number of quotes from different yards, or a surveyor hired by the company may oversee the work.

If you're outside the U.S. and you're the only one capable of doing the work, although your policy will normally not cover your own labor or personal expenses, it's a good idea to keep time sheets of hours worked—in the hope that some of your expenses might be covered.

If your boat is written off as a total loss, you'll have to sign over the title, registration, or documentation to the insurance company. After all, if they pay you for the boat, they are in effect buying it.

# 13

# Chartering
# Your Boat

| | ✥ | |

Boatowners who are familiar with the chartering business have called it a "golden goose" of opportunity, because the golden eggs that it rewards them with are an income and tax benefits. While enjoying the profits, they can also reap satisfaction from helping other people enjoy the water.

Chartering your boat is not difficult to do, and it can become an interesting part- or full-time business. This chapter will help you decide if chartering is for you. Although getting into chartering can be an adventure, it should be handled like what it is—a business—so you won't have problems with the IRS.

## Historical Commercial
## Chartering Arrangements

Admiralty law has historically recognized three charter arrangements almost always involving cargo vessels—*voyage, time,* and *demise* or *bareboat charters.*

In a voyage charter, the charterer hires a ship for a single voyage. The ship's owner retains control of the ship, his master and crew operate it, and the route and destination are generally established beforehand. The owner's best interest is in completing the trip as quickly as possible, so he or she can get on to the next charter. A voyage charter is like hiring a taxi to take you to a specified destination.

In a time charter, the charterer hires the ship for a specified length of time. While the ship's owner still provides and retains control of the master and crew, the charterer determines the ports, the cargo, and the general operation of the ship. This type of charter compares to hiring a car and driver for an afternoon to tour the city; the passenger decides where to go and how long to stay at any given attraction.

Under demise or bareboat charters, the charterer becomes, in effect, the owner of the boat, also for an agreed length of time. If he or she employs the owner's master and crew, then technically it is a demise charter, but if the charterer hires his or her own master and crew, then it is a bareboat charter. These are both generally compared to renting a car from Avis or Hertz; the charterer has complete control of the operation of the boat, along with the legal and financial responsibility for it.

No matter which kind of charter arrangement is used, it should be in writing—although oral agreements are recognized by the courts. And all parties to the contract accept serious legal obligations under admiralty law.

Historically, the contract representing the charter agreement was called the *charter party*. During medieval times, the agreement was written in duplicate, side by side on a piece of paper. It was then torn in half, and one half was given to the owner of the ship, the other half to the charterer. The theory was that only those two pieces would fit together because of the irregular pattern of the tear. When the pieces were put back together, they could be compared, thus assuring both parties that the other party couldn't change the contract. The Latin term for the torn paper was *carta partita*, hence "charter party."

All three of the above arrangements are used extensively in shipping today. The voyage charter is typically used for shipping bulk cargoes of raw materials such as logs, iron ore, or grains. An extensive worldwide network of brokers and ship owners' representatives is dedicated to tracking and procuring suitable vessels.

Once the ship is found, the negotiations are carried out and an agreement is signed. Certain standardized agreements have evolved within each "trade" to save time and money. A grain shipment might be covered by the standard Austral, which is a form developed by the Chamber of Shipping Australian Grain Charter of 1928. Or perhaps the ship owner and the charterer might use the Baltimore Berth Grain Charter Party (Form C). A cargo of rice might be shipped under the Burma Rice Charter Party.

## Types of Recreational Chartering

In recreational boating, the primary charter arrangement is the demise or bareboat charter. The basic one- or two-week yacht charter in the Caribbean or San Juan Islands is the type most people are familiar with, although larger yachts might be time chartered with their captains and crews. Most of the boats in charter fleets are owned by people other than the charter operators. Individual boatowners have placed them into service with the charter operators.

If you are thinking of placing your boat into such a group, most charter operators will be happy to send you information. Of course, some fleets comprise only boats designed for the charter company's operations, such as dive boats fitted with special swim steps, compressors, and scuba-tank holders. These charter companies can't accept unsuitable boats.

Other charter companies are interested only in certain brands of boats such as Beneteaus or Grand Banks trawlers. If you don't already own one of the brands such a charter group is looking for, you should consider its value in chartering before you buy your next boat, and contact the charter organization before you purchase.

Other charter companies will be happy to consider just about any type of boat so long as it is:

• fairly new;
• in good condition;
• laid out well below decks for comfortable dining;
• laid out on deck for easy operation;
• well equipped.

In some parts of the country, chartering is seasonal. For example, the prime charter season in the San Juan Islands runs from around the first of

June to the middle of September. The advantage to this type of chartering is that you can make a good deal of money during a short period of time. Your boat is in charter for only a part of the year, leaving it available for maintenance or for your own use during part of the rest of the year—subject, of course, to restrictions that may be imposed by your taxing authorities. ⌣

The primary disadvantage to seasonal chartering is that your boat is occupied during the prime boating season. The only way you can use it is to take it out of charter for a week or so—and thus forgo the income.

*Time-share chartering* is growing in popularity in year-round boating regions of the world. A time-share charter operates something like a vacation condo; you can contract with a time-share operator who will then line up four or five charterers, each of whom pays a monthly fee for use of your boat for a certain number of days during each month or quarter.

The major advantage to this type of charter arrangement is that, once the charterers are lined up, you can expect a fairly constant inflow of money year-round. The major disadvantage is that your boat is in charter year-round.

To get involved, contact a reputable charter or time-share operation or talk to boat brokers. Whether you are doing it yourself with your own boat or putting in with a large charter fleet, you should seek competent legal and accounting help from professionals who are experienced in this area. See Appendix E for a sample charter agreement.

There are other charter arrangements as well, and each can provide income from your boat. If short-term charter is more to your liking, you have several options. Some new boat dealers will offer to charter back a boat they just sold to you. They will use it for a period of time as a demonstrator model to show prospective buyers.

Depending on your skills and your boat's capabilities, you might want to use your boat to teach boating skills to others. Charter boats are used for many purposes, including sportfishing, sport diving, harbor excursions, weddings, even business seminars afloat. Next time you watch a colorful movie or documentary about an exotic island or underwater reef habitat, think about the owners who chartered their boats to those researchers and film makers.

## The Economics
## of Chartering

Let's assume that you're thinking of buying that new 30-foot sailboat and the dealer is asking $50,000 for the pleasure of sailing it away. You go to your friendly local banker and learn that he is willing to lend you 75 percent of the boat's purchase price. That means you have to come up with $12,500. You've been frugal and saved carefully for this day, so you just happen to have about $15,000 just sitting there in your savings account, gathering more dust than interest.

Your banker also tells you that since it's a new boat, he's willing to carry the loan at 10 percent interest for 10 years, and that the payments will be $495.57 a month. You've paid off all your credit cards and decided that you can drive the old car for a while longer, so your budget can handle the payments.

But, wait. Where are you going to moor the new boat? Assuming you've found a decent marina that still has a slip open, you will have to pay between $3 and $12 per foot per month to park it. Let's assume that you've found a real deal at a fairly nice marina not far from where you live, and they will let you have the slip for $7 per foot. That's another $210 a month. You are now looking at a monthly outgo of $705.57. Add another $150 a month for maintenance and you're at $855.57.

Your banker, who isn't looking quite so friendly now, also mentions that the boat will have to be insured so that the bank can recover its money if anything bad should happen. You call a marine insurance agent, and he tells you that full coverage of the boat and all the equipment will run about $600 per year—or another $50 a month. Your dream is now going to cost you about $905.57 per month. You swallow hard, take another look at your budget, and decide that you can still afford the dream.

You go back to the dealer and talk again about buying the boat, and he mentions that you shouldn't forget that in addition to the purchase price, there will also be sales tax and registration or documentation fees, all of which have to be paid before you can sail off into the sunset. They can cost you another $2,500.

You notice also that there are no sheets or towels, and that you'll have to furnish the galley with cookware, tableware, silverware, and counter appliances, not to mention food. Add in another $1,500 to $2,000.

The dealer mentions that before you can go cruising in safety, you really need to add a heavier anchor and chain set, buy a dinghy, have chocks or davits installed and buy a complete set of boat tools. And you had your heart set on that new GPS. You go home and decide that maybe boat ownership isn't all it's cracked up to be.

Buying and owning a boat is an expensive proposition. The first year of ownership in our example—with down payment, sales tax, registration, documentation, payments on the loan, moorage, insurance and maintenance—will run more than $26,000. Each subsequent year it will cost almost $11,000.

At the end of five years you will have paid almost $70,000 for your $50,000 boat, including $15,558 in interest, $14,176 in principal, $12,600 for moorage, $3,000 for insurance premiums, and $9,000 for maintenance, assuming no major work had to be done. You will still owe the bank $23,324. If you decide to sell the boat that year, and your boat broker finds a buyer willing to pay $35,000 for it, after the broker's commission and paying off the bank, you end up with $8,176. On an average monthly basis, after recovering part of your costs through the sale of the boat, your dream boat will have cost you about $1,030 a month, or $12,365 a year. That's a lot of money for a toy you only use on weekends.

Maybe there's a better way.

You go back to the dealer and say, "Joe, I just can't swing the 30-footer. Maybe I should look at something smaller."

Joe happens to mention that he knows of a local charter company interested in including in its charter fleet a boat just like the one you're trying to buy. If you buy the boat, they will guarantee at least 10 weeks of charter this coming summer, and it appears likely that the boat will charter for 12 weeks. The charter rate per week is $1,000.

After checking further, you find that the charter company takes a 30 percent commission on gross income, and you keep the rest. That's $8,400 coming to you for 12 weeks of charter. Now instead of $26,000 the first year and $11,000 a year after that, the boat may cost you only $17,600 the first year and only $2,600 each year after that.

In fact, depending upon the number of charters you can get in a year, the size of your down payment, and the type of boat you're considering—and taking into account the tax benefits you can claim on your personal tax return, such as depreciation and other expenses—it's possible to eliminate having to pay out anything after the first year and even to make a little money to set aside.

Your broker is quick to point out that some people have taken it a step further by rolling the profit from their chartering into a series of boats, finally ending up with one that is free and clear of debt.

You say to yourself, "Hmmm. This sounds like a pretty good deal. But if it's such a good deal, why isn't everyone doing it?"

A lot of people are. If you look at the annual chartering issues of any of the national boating magazines, you'll see that the fleets those companies offer are, as a general rule, owned by other people.

So, what's the catch? Many people don't do it because:

• they don't know anything about it;
• they can't stand the idea of someone else living on their boat;
• they're simply not willing to live with the limitations imposed by the IRS or other tax authorities on their use of their own boat during the time it's not in charter.

## Taxes and Chartering

Some of the tax rules that apply to owning rental property also apply to chartering or time-share. After all, you're renting your boat to someone else. But instead of letting people (tenants) live in your house or apartment for months or years, you're letting people (charterers or clients) rent your boat for days or weeks.

As with rental property, many expenses associated with chartering are deductible on your income-tax return, including depreciation, moorage, interest, insurance, and other operating expenses. Sounds terrific, but there are some hurdles to overcome. You can't simply declare your boat a charter boat and then not charter it out.

As they did with vacation condominiums, the IRS has imposed restrictions on the amount of time that an owner can use his or her own boat and still claim it as a business. At present, an owner is allowed a minimum of 15 days per year of personal usage up to a maximum of 10 percent of the number of days that the boat is actually in charter.

If you want to use your own boat for four hours on Friday and four hours on Saturday, the IRS is likely to look at each specific day of use, so those eight hours would count as two days.

In other words, no matter how much charter time the boat has, the owner is allowed to use the boat strictly for personal use at least 15 days each year. And it works out that if the boat is chartered for more than 150 days in a year, the owner gets one additional day of personal use for each 10 additional days that the boat is in charter. So if the boat is chartered for 180 days in a year, the owner can use it for 18 days. Two hundred days of charter reward the owner with 20 days of personal use.

Why the limitation? If you are going to be in business and claiming the inherent tax deductions, then the IRS expects you to generate an income and eventually make a profit. The IRS doesn't mind if you occasionally play aboard your business property, so long as you don't make a habit of it. Hence, their rules. The IRS frowns on people who try to turn their hobbies into business deductions while still keeping them as hobbies. So, for the time being, recognize that if you are going to operate a charter business, the IRS will impose restrictions on your use of your boat, and on the use of losses from your charter business to offset active income from other sources. For more on this subject, see Chapter 3.

Remember, the IRS could look at your official "ship's log book" to verify the number of charter days and personal-use days.

Depending on where you live or keep your boat, your state or local tax authorities may also have something to say about your use of the boat when it's not in charter. For example, in Washington and some other states, if a boat is purchased specifically for charter, no sales tax is collected at the time of purchase, because sales tax will be collected on the income generated by the boat. In Washington state, where the sales tax is presently 7.9 percent, the savings can be significant.

The catch in Washington is that the Department of Revenue does not recognize any time for personal use of the boat! Despite the IRS's allowance, even one day of personal use requires the owner to pay sales tax to the Department of Revenue, based on the value of the boat as of the day of personal use. However, no law says you can't take the boat out periodically to check the sails and run the engine—and have a little fun while you're at it.

Check with your own state's tax authorities to determine if you can use your own charter boat and how often.

## Placing Your Boat in a Charter Operation

The easiest way to get into chartering or time-share is to contact a local operation and get information on how things work. If they use other people's boats, they probably already have a mailer-packet of information explaining the services they offer, the types of boats they are looking for, the rates they charge, and their percentage.

The charter operator may offer your boat either *crewed* or *bareboat* without affecting your tax deductions, but you can expect your insurance rates to go up—often doubling your annual premium. In most fleets, while the operator handles maintenance and repairs, you are responsible for securing and paying for your insurance. The bright side is that some fleet operators can arrange for a group or fleet rate for the boats they handle. Be sure to ask the manager any other questions you might have.

If you're still interested, and if they're interested, they will probably ask you to sign a contract committing your boat to their fleet. You may have to deliver your boat to a moorage close to their operation.

Once your boat is in their fleet, they should handle all aspects of the operation, such as arranging the charters, provisioning, hiring crew, collecting money, taking care of maintenance and repairs, and everything else that goes into chartering, except paying the insurance premiums. Then, they will deduct all their expenses, take a percentage of the profit, and send you a monthly statement and check for the balance.

Beware of fly-by-night charter operators. Good ones that have been in business for a while and have established a good reputation should be willing to give you the names of some of their boatowners. Ask those owners what their experience has been with that operator.

Although you don't want to look for trouble where there is none, problems can arise with charter operators, including:

- failing to fully account for all charter income;
- failing to make needed repairs;
- charging you for repairs not made;
- charging you for replacement of equipment that was lost through the fault of charterers.

You should also be clear on where your boat is on the operator's list of available yachts, so you avoid misunderstandings about whether they are steering charter prospects to other boats instead of yours.

## Doing It Yourself

If you have that entrepreneurial spirit and are looking for something rewarding to do with your spare time, you might consider setting up your own charter service with your boat. Many people have and are making a living doing it. If you see yourself as a one-person operation—sending grateful groups of landlubbers out for a day on your boat on the bay or perhaps taking them out yourself—here are some important considerations to investigate.

Get as much professional advice as possible about writing your business plan, setting up your books, and marketing your charter business—for starters. Fees for professional advice are legitimate expenses in most businesses. It's much cheaper to pay an attorney and an accountant for a few hours of guidance than it is to pay them to get you out of hot water later.

Select an accountant and a lawyer who have plenty of recent experience setting up small yacht-charter businesses like the one you envision. Chapter 1 in this book can help you select a lawyer. If you can't find professional advisors with this exact experience, at least get someone who regularly helps people set up and run small businesses.

Your accounting advisor will help you decide what type of bookkeeping system will be best for you and your charter boat. When all that money—you hope—starts rolling in, or when the bills start piling up, you need to know how to account for it. Recent changes in the tax laws mean that the way you keep some accounts has also changed. The IRS will require you to keep adequate records, even during your start-up.

Your legal advisor will help you decide what kind of a business structure is best for you, such as sole proprietorship, a partnership, or a corporation. Each type has differences in taxing and liability exposure. He or she can tell you of the rules and licensing requirements specific to your yacht-charter business.

It's a good idea to put together a business plan, even for a small business. Some community organizations offer low-cost or free advice on business plans and all aspects of small-business start-ups. The Small Business Administration has many helpful volunteers, professionals, and handy pamphlets. Some of these groups even put on workshops and seminars to help people who are just getting started in new businesses.

And many books can offer guidance and support in this area. For example:

*Small-Time Operator* by Bernard Kamoroff. Published by Bell Spring Publishing, it covers just about everything you need to know to start and operate a small business—from financing the start-up to licenses and permits to bookkeeping and taxes.

Another is *Growing a Business* by Paul Hawken. A companion volume to a PBS series by the same name, the book provides a unique perspective on starting and "growing" a business.

You will probably need some form of business license. Contact your municipal, county, and state licensing authorities to determine what other licenses you may need before you begin chartering.

Your state and local governments may require you to collect taxes from the people chartering your boat, and you may have to pay state income tax as well. Your accountant or lawyer should guide you in setting these up.

Call your insurance person to see about changing your boat's insurance to cover chartering. You may want to go back and read the chapter on insurance, which offers specific information about chartering.

Now, where are all those clients who want to charter your boat? How come your phone's not ringing yet? Money and time invested for advice from a marketing consultant could be well spent. Of the many possible marketing strategies, not all are appropriate for a yacht-charter business, and not all are tailored for you, your boat, your location, etc. You do need to get the word out, but would brochures and signs be right, and where do you need to advertise? Someone with expertise in marketing the charter of boats like yours should be able to help you develop a marketing plan.

If all of this sounds a little overwhelming, remember, you're starting a business, even if it's as glamorous as a yacht-charter business. A large but unglamorous part of any business is filling out forms for various agencies.

If you are going to charter only your own boat and not handle other people's boats, too, then you should be able to run the office portion out of your home. If and when you enlarge, you may face restrictions. Some localities limit the types of businesses that may be operated from a residence.

One advantage to running the office part of your yacht-charter business out of your home is that you may be able to claim deductions on your income tax for a home office. Ask your lawyer about the current laws in your community.

## Chartering
## and the Coast Guard

No matter which type of charter operation you intend to run, you can expect to have an ongoing relationship with the Coast Guard. It makes a very important distinction between bareboat chartering and crewed chartering, which it considers to be a commercial operation.

If your business is limited to bareboat or time-share chartering, then you do not drive the boat, your clients do. If that is the case, your boat needs to pass only the Coast Guard's courtesy inspections for safety and have the required equipment aboard during occasional boardings. Even if you're not on board, you are responsible to see that all the required equipment is. See the chapter on Rules and Regulations for the complete list of requirements.

### Commercial Chartering

As mentioned, the Coast Guard makes a big distinction between bareboat chartering and a commercial or crewed operation. Bareboat is not considered commercial operation in the eyes of the Coast Guard. Carrying passengers for hire is.

A *passenger for hire* is defined as anyone who is not (1) the owner or his representative, (2) the operator of the boat, (3) a member of the crew, or (4) a guest who is aboard the boat exclusively for pleasure and has not contributed any compensation, monetary or otherwise.

The Coast Guard definition of a passenger for hire is broad enough to include almost any situation people might think of creating to avoid licensing. In each of the following situations, the Coast Guard has ruled that the particular person is a passenger for hire:

- when one of your guests brings a gift of food or drink to be used on the trip;
- when one of your guests takes you ashore for dinner;
- when one of your guests helps pay for the fuel or other provisions used on the trip;
- when your guests have agreed in advance to share in the expenses of the trip.

Nearly any passenger could be considered a passenger for hire, and the number of paying passengers on board at any one time determines what the Coast Guard demands of the person running the boat and the vessel itself.

If the boat is never going to carry more than six passengers, you or the person running the boat must obtain the Coast Guard's entry level skipper's license called the OUPV (Operator of Uninspected Passenger Vessel).

Even though the boat is considered an *uninspected vessel*, it must meet the safety and operation requirements spelled out in the Code of Federal Regulations. 46 CFR, Subchapter C, parts 24, 25, and 26 cover boats carrying fewer than six passengers. These rules regard safety equipment such as life jackets and fire extinguishers. Compliance with uninspected vessel regulations is assured by healthy fines paid by the boatowner if a routine boarding finds the vessel to be "not in compliance."

To begin the licensing process that will allow you to operate an uninspected passenger vessel—even if it's your own boat—you should submit an application to the nearest Officer in Charge, Marine Inspection of the Coast Guard. To be issued a license, you must be over 18 years old, verify at least one year's experience in operating boats, pass a physical exam and a drug test. The stiffest requirement may be to pass an extensive exam that covers the Rules of the Road, piloting, firefighting, lifesaving, coastal navigation, first aid, seamanship, and boat handling. Once you pass, your OUPV license will be valid for five years.

If you ever carry more than six passengers for hire, or if your boat displaces more than 100 gross tons, then you or the person running the boat must obtain the next higher license, the Master's license. And your boat will have to qualify as an *inspected vessel* as described below.

The Master's license requires verification of additional boathandling experience and, in some cases, experience working as a mate. To prepare for the Coast Guard's licensing exam, you could study for it on your own, take a home-study course, or you could attend a license-preparation school. You can find such courses and schools advertised in most boating magazines. The test is not easy. Of the 10,000 people who take it each year, only 60 percent pass. If you fail it the first time, you can take it again.

### Inspected Vessels

Any passenger-carrying boat that weighs more than 100 gross tons or, regardless of tonnage, ever carries more than six passengers will be asked to pass muster as an inspected vessel. Keep in mind that courtesy inspections and boarding inspections are not what is meant by inspected vessel status.

Unlike standard pleasure boats or the uninspected vessels described above, these vessels must be inspected to determine if they comply with the many safety criteria spelled out in 46 CFR, Subchapter T, parts 175 through 187, which list the requirements for such vessels under 100 tons. This subchapter deals with construction methods and materials, arrangement of architecture, lifesaving and firefighting equipment, installation of propulsion and electrical systems, and vessel control.

If your passenger-carrying vessel happens to be more than 100 gross tons, its inspection requirements are listed in 46 CFR, Subchapter H, parts 70 through 89. Because larger vessels are expected to carry more passengers for longer distances, their safety standards are accordingly more stringent.

Even on inspected vessels under 100 tons, the certification inspectors look at everything from the size of the deck hatches and companionway openings to the elegance of the wiring installations and the helmsman's view over the bow. Many of the requirements for an inspected vessel are not common on recreational vessels, such as collision bulkheads, bilge piping, and heavy-duty fire pumps. Some equipment commonly found on recreational vessels, such as propane cooking stoves, is prohibited on inspected vessels.

An inspected vessel certificate is good for three years, when the boat will need to be inspected again.

Converting a yacht to an inspected vessel can be a daunting process requiring the service of an experienced naval architect, but the Coast Guard stands ready to work with you. No matter how much time and money you invest in modifications, not every yacht can be turned into an inspected vessel.

The Coast Guard recommends that you start by getting two publications: from nautical bookstores, federal bookstores, or law libraries you'll need a copy of 46 CFR, Parts 166 through 199, which cover conversion; and from your nearest Coast Guard MSO you can pick up a "Conversion Check-off List" or similar hand-out they've prepared for this project.

Before any work is begun on the conversion of an existing boat or on a new one, an Application for Inspection (form CG-3752) must be submitted to the Officer in Charge, Marine Inspection (OCMI) of the Coast Guard district nearest to where the work will be done.

You then need to file your construction or conversion plans. They need not be formal blueprints; neat, clean line drawings showing all the required information are acceptable. Once the Coast Guard has reviewed your plans, they will either approve them or return them to you for modification and revision. The approval and conversion processes can be complex, especially if the boat will operate in a district other than where the conversion or construction is being performed. Different districts have different requirements. Just be sure to go to the Coast Guard before you start the work, not after.

Once your plans are approved, you may begin the work but must stick to the plans. Depending on the extent of the work called for, the MSO inspectors may make intermediate inspections as your conversion proceeds. When you are ready for the final inspection, MSO officers will come aboard to pass or fail your boat. If it fails, they will tell you why, and after further work you can try again. Although the Coast Guard's advice and inspection are free, the modifications can be very expensive.

The easier method is to buy a boat—new or used—that already carries an inspection certificate. You can also buy or build a boat that is a sistership of a boat that has been inspected and certified, as long as no disqualifying modifications have been made. This makes the process faster and less expensive, but it doesn't eliminate the certification requirement.

Because Coast Guard offices in different regions may interpret the regulations differently, you should be careful when buying a certified boat in one area if you intend to move it to another Coast Guard region. Careful planning can save time, money, and frustration in getting your boat inspected.

## Legal Obligations Involved in Chartering

As the owner of the boat, your primary legal responsibility is to provide a boat that is seaworthy, or in the words of most charter contracts, "tight, staunch, strong, and in every way fitted for the service." That doesn't mean that it must be fitted for an around-the-world cruise if it's only intended to cruise on Puget Sound or Chesapeake Bay. It must be ready for the use that is expected of it by the charterer and must meet all Coast Guard requirements.

On the other hand, the charterer's obligation is to pay the rent or charter fee and return the boat in the same good condition in which he or she received it, except for any reasonable wear and tear.

Many disputes question whether a boat is seaworthy, and even more disputes involve whether some damage is due to normal wear and tear or the charterer's sin of commission or omission when he or she had possession of the boat. To partially eliminate the problem, many charter companies have a diver check the bottom of the boat each time it comes in from a charter.

Although insurance isn't required as a legal matter, both you, as the boat's owner, and the person chartering it should carry insurance coverage so that if something happens while he or she is chartering, the charterer's insurance will pay for repairs, not yours. Although your policy covers damage not covered by the charterer's policy, it is more for protection from liability in case the charterer does serious damage and you are sued as the owner of the boat.

### Drugs and Chartering

One other important matter needs discussion—drug seizures and forfeiture. Most drug laws include strict provisions calling for the forfeiture of property used in the transportation of drugs. The government's zero tolerance policies have resulted in seizures of vessels found to be carrying minor amounts of illegal drugs for personal use by passengers. You can't stress enough to your charter clients that no illegal drugs should be aboard the boat. This is also true when you are just out for an afternoon cruise. The results can be devastating. For more information, see Chapter 2 and the section covering search and seizure.

For example, in Puerto Rico the Pearson Yacht Leasing Company leased a $20,000 boat to two local residents. A couple of months after the lease was executed, a marijuana cigarette was discovered aboard the boat by police. The boat was seized under Puerto Rico's Controlled Substance Act and later forfeited to the government of Puerto Rico. Pearson knew nothing of the seizure until it tried to repossess the boat for nonpayment of the lease. It sued to get the boat back. Despite an appeal to the U.S. Supreme Court, the forfeiture was upheld, and Pearson lost the boat.

As a result of this case and others like it, you or your charter company have the responsibility of making sure that the people who charter your boat do not use it for drug-related activities. You, as an innocent owner, can lose your boat and be left with no recourse except against the charterer, who may already be in jail or "wanted" as a smuggler. Meanwhile, your dream boat could be sold at public auction by the U.S. Marshal's office.

Since you are the person who stands to lose so much, it is up to you to ensure that no illegal drugs are ever brought aboard your boat.

# Appendix A

## SALES AGREEMENT

THIS AGREEMENT made this ___ day of _____,
199__, between _____,
whose address is _____,
City of _____, State of _____,
referred to as **SELLER**, and _____,whose
address is _____, City of
_____, State of _____, referred
to as **BUYER.**

WITNESSETH:

SELLER is the owner of the vessel described below and, subject to the
provisions of this Agreement, desires to sell such vessel to BUYER, and

BUYER, in accordance with the provisions of this Agreement, desires
to purchase such vessel from the SELLER.

IN CONSIDERATION of the above recitals and the following
covenants and conditions, the parties agree as follows:

1. **DESCRIPTION OF VESSEL.** SELLER sells, and BUYER purchases,
the \<type of vessel\>, \<name\>, an \<undocumented/documented\> vessel
together with such vessel's equipment as set forth on the Personal Property
List attached hereto and made a part hereof as Exhibit "A", and all other
necessary equipment on such vessel presently berthed at \<marina or
port\>. The vessel bears the following HIN # _____ and/or
documentation # _____.

2. **TERMS OF SALE.** The total purchase price of the vessel is

_____ Dollars ($). SELLER acknowledges receipt of a deposit of _____ Dollars ($), and BUYER promises to pay the balance, together with _____ percent (%) interest per annum, before <date>. SELLER promises to execute a bill of sale for transfer of title in the vessel and deposit it in escrow with _____, City of _____, State of _____, to be delivered to the BUYER on payment in full.

**3. CONDITION OF VESSEL—SURVEY.** This contract is made subject to an acceptable survey to be made by _____, a marine surveyor chosen by BUYER, to be completed within _____ days of the effective date of this Agreement. If the findings of the survey indicate that the vessel is not seaworthy and otherwise in good condition, then this contract will be renegotiated or terminated at the BUYER's option, and SELLER will return the above-stated deposit made under this Agreement if the Agreement is terminated. Failure of BUYER to give notice to SELLER of an unsatisfactory survey prior to the date of transfer of possession as set forth in Paragraph 4 shall create the presumption that a satisfactory survey was completed.

**4. TRANSFER OF POSSESSION.** Subject to the condition of Paragraph 3, relating to an acceptable survey of the vessel, BUYER will take possession of the vessel, and assume all risk of damage to and loss of the vessel, on <date>.

**5. PROTECTION OF SELLER'S INTEREST.** BUYER shall purchase and maintain marine insurance on the vessel from an insurance company acceptable to the SELLER in the following amounts:

a. Hull insurance on a declared value of _____ Dollars ($); and

b. Protection and indemnity in the amount of _____ _____ Dollars ($).

All policies shall contain a loss-payable clause acceptable to SELLER, naming SELLER as loss-payee, and the policies shall be held by SELLER as security for this contract, and in event of repossession of the vessel, as SELLER's sole property. BUYER shall not use the vessel and shall not permit it to be used in any way prohibited by or not covered by such insurance.

BUYER shall not remove the vessel beyond <geographical limits> without the prior written permission of SELLER.

**6. RESTRICTION OF MARITIME LIENS.** BUYER shall not permit any lien or charge having priority to or preference over the title of SELLER in the vessel to continue beyond _____ days after the charge becomes due and payable, and shall pay or cause to be discharged or make adequate provision for the satisfaction or discharge of all lawful claims or demands that might have precedence over the title of SELLER as a lien or charge on the vessel. BUYER shall carry a properly certified copy of this Agreement with the vessel's papers and shall take such other appropriate steps as SELLER may from time to time direct as will give notice to the public that BUYER has no right, power, or authority to suffer or permit to be imposed on or against the vessel any liens or claims that might be deemed superior to or a charge against the interest of SELLER in the vessel.

**7. WARRANTY.** SELLER expressly warrants that the vessel is not encumbered by any mortgage, bond, or maritime lien, except the following:_____. All liens set out above shall be paid by SELLER upon transfer of title to BUYER. Except as so provided, the vessel is sold as is and where is, SELLER making no guarantee, warranty, or representation, express or implied, as to the kind, size, quality, description, or condition of the vessel, or its fitness for any use or purpose.

**8. NO WAIVER.** The failure of either party to this Agreement to insist on the performance of any of the terms and conditions of this Agreement, or the waiver of any breach of any of the terms and conditions of this Agreement, shall not be construed and remain in full force and effect as if no such forbearance of waiver had occurred.

**9. DISPUTE RESOLUTION.** In the event of a disagreement that cannot be settled through direct discussions, the parties agree to first attempt resolution of the dispute through mediation by and through the American Arbitration Association. Any controversy or dispute not settled through mediation shall be settled by arbitration. Such arbitration shall be effected by an arbitrator selected as hereinafter provided and shall be conducted in accordance with the rules existing at the date thereof of the American Arbitration Association. The dispute shall be submitted to an arbitrator who shall be selected by the American Arbitration Association and who shall have had at least ten (10) years' experience in a marine-related business. The meetings of the arbitrator shall be held at such place or places as may be selected by the arbitrator. Judgment may be entered or any award rendered by the arbitrator in any state court having jurisdiction. Each party shall bear equally the costs of the fees and expenses of the arbitrator.

**10. BINDING EFFECT.** This Agreement shall be binding upon the heirs, executors, administrators, successors, and assigns of the parties hereto.

**11. GOVERNING LAW.** It is agreed that this Agreement shall be governed by, construed, and enforced in accordance with the laws of the State of _____.

**12. ATTORNEY FEES.** In the event any arbitration or legal action is filed in relation to this Agreement, the unsuccessful party in the arbitration or legal action shall pay to the successful party, in addition to all the sums that either party may be called on to pay, a reasonable sum for the successful party's attorney fees.

**13. EFFECT OF PARTIAL INVALIDITY.** The invalidity of any portion of this Agreement shall not be deemed to affect validity of any other provision.

**14. ENTIRE AGREEMENT.** This Agreement constitutes the entire agreement of the parties and supersedes all prior agreements and understandings, written or oral. This Agreement may be amended only in writing executed by both parties.

**IN WITNESS WHEREOF,** the parties hereto have set their hands to this Agreement the day and year first above written.

SELLER:

_____

BUYER:

_____

_____

STATE OF _____ )

          ) ss.

COUNTY OF _____ )

On this day personally appeared before me _____ to me known to be the person, described in and who executed the within and foregoing instrument as SELLER, and acknowledged that he/she/they signed the same as his/her/their free and voluntary act and deed, for the uses and purposes therein mentioned.

GIVEN under my hand and official seal this _____ day of _____, 199__.


_____
Notary Public in and for the State
of _____ residing at _____.
My appointment expires:_____

STATE OF _____)
                                        ) ss.
COUNTY OF _____)

On this day personally appeared before me _____ to me known to be the person(s) described in and who executed the within and foregoing instrument as BUYER, and acknowledged that he/she/they signed the same as his/her/their free and voluntary act and deed for the uses and purposes therein mentioned.

GIVEN under my hand and official seal this _____ day of _____, 199__.


_____
Notary Public in and for the State
of_____, residing at _____.
My appointment expires:_____

# Appendix B

## PLEASURE BOAT
## CONSTRUCTION AGREEMENT

THIS AGREEMENT made the _____ day of _____,
199__, between _____, hereinafter referred to as
BUILDER, and _____, hereinafter referred to as
OWNER.

WITNESSETH:

WHEREAS, BUILDER has a plant and facilities designed to construct, and is in the business of designing and constructing custom-
designed and custom-built boats, and

WHEREAS, OWNER has obtained custom-designed plans for the
construction of a boat and desires to contract with BUILDER to construct a boat in accordance with such plans, and

WHEREAS, BUILDER desires to contract with OWNER to construct
a boat for OWNER.

NOW, THEREFORE, in consideration of the above recitals and the
following mutual covenants and agreements, the parties agree as follows:

1. SCOPE OF WORK. BUILDER, in accordance with the terms and
conditions of this Agreement, shall construct, at its plant located at
_____, a boat according to the design and specifica-
tions set forth in Exhibit "A," which is attached hereto and made a part of
this Agreement.

2. ADDITIONAL INFORMATION. BUILDER shall provide any
naval architectural and marine engineering services in addition to the
information set forth in the specifications and drawings referred to

above, that are necessary for the construction of the boat.

3. COOPERATION. It is understood and agreed that any problems arising during the construction of the boat can best be resolved by maintenance of close liaison among BUILDER, OWNER, and architect, and that the parties will make every effort to avoid and resolve any problems and disputes by maintaining such close liaison between and among OWNER, BUILDER, and architect.

4. COMPENSATION. Select one:

_____ OWNER shall pay BUILDER for the construction of the boat, in full compensation, a fixed price of

_____ Dollars ($_____), which is not subject to adjustment for escalations and which is otherwise subject to adjustment only by mutual agreement in writing between OWNER and BUILDER.

_____ OWNER will pay the cost of all materials necessary to build the boat pursuant to the design and specifications set forth in Exhibit "A" and actually used in the construction, and will pay the wages of all craftsmen and other workers for actual time spent on the job and will pay BUILDER _____ percent (___%) of the cost of the materials, labor, and other expenditures necessary for the completion of the work such as workers' compensation. In consideration of this _____ percent (___%), BUILDER agrees to execute close supervision over the work at all times and will devote whatever time necessary to ensure that the boat is built to the design and specifications. BUILDER will pay all materials bills, wages, and invoices, paying therefore the actual cost of such material less any and all discounts. Payment shall be made as follows:

5. PAYMENTS. Payment of the contract price shall be made by the OWNER to the order of the BUILDER in accordance with the following schedule:

a. One-third of the contract price, in the amount of _____ Dollars ($_____) upon signing this Agreement, receipt of which is hereby acknowledged;

b. One-third of the contract price upon notice to the OWNER of "turnover" in the amount of _____ Dollars

($_____), as adjusted by any change orders executed by the parties prior to the date of "turnover." "Turnover" is the time when final finish work on the boat begins. BUILDER will notify OWNER not less than seven (7) days prior to the turnover date and will furnish to OWNER a statement or invoice stating the amount which is then due and payable;

c. The unpaid balance of the contract price as adjusted for any executed but unpaid change orders, plus applicable sales tax, is due and payable in full upon delivery of the finished boat to OWNER at the BUILDER's yard.

d. The OWNER agrees to pay interest on any unpaid portion of such payments at a rate _____ ( ) percentage points more than the "prime rate" quoted by <name, location of bank>, from time to time, from the time such payments become due through the date the amount owed plus interest is fully paid. This rate of interest will be "fully floating," in that the rate will be adjusted at the same times the bank announces changes in its "prime rate". If the OWNER fails, neglects, or refuses to make any of the payments provided for in this Agreement within 30 days after they are due, the BUILDER may stop work under this Agreement and declare this Agreement terminated. Upon termination, the BUILDER may retain as its own property the boat and all material, supplies, equipment, and components then identified with this Agreement together with all payments made by the OWNER as liquidated damages for OWNER's breach of this Agreement. OWNER and BUILDER agree that the value of the liquidated damages described above constitutes a reasonable estimate of the damages which the BUILDER would likely incur under the circumstances which would entitle BUILDER to recover them.

**6. COMPLETION AND DELIVERY.** Delivery shall be made within _____ ( ) months from the date of this Agreement. Any delay in delivery will be excused if caused by Acts of God, *force majuere*; strikes or labor disputes; weather or other natural phenomenon; vandalism, arrest, seizure, or attachment of property; injunctions; shortages or unavailability of labor, materials, or equipment; time necessary to implement Change Orders; default, miscarriage, or interference by the OWNER or other causes of like or similar nature. In the event of delay, delivery of the boat as above stated shall be postponed for a period of time corresponding to the length of time the BUILDER determines it is delayed because of the above specified causes. On completion of the boat in accordance with all requirements of this Agreement, delivery shall be made free of liens of any kind, in the water, ready for use at the BUILDER's yard.

7. INSPECTION. All work in process at BUILDER's yard shall be subject to inspection by OWNER and architect, and BUILDER shall grant OWNER and architect access to BUILDER's premises for such inspection at all reasonable times.

8. WARRANTIES. BUILDER warrants the boat against defects in material or workmanship, but makes no warranties, express or implied, unless the word "guarantee" is used. WARRANTIES OF MERCHANTABILITY OR OF FITNESS FOR A PARTICULAR PURPOSE OR ARISING FROM A COURSE OF DEALING OR USAGE OF TRADE ARE SPECIFICALLY EXCLUDED. Any affirmation of fact, description of goods, or sample or model referred to in this Agreement, whether or not the same relate to production or capability of the boat to perform, are not the basis of this Agreement, unless the word "guarantee" is used in connection therewith, in which case the affirmation, description, sample, or model shall be an express warranty. The liability of the BUILDER shall exist only if the boat has been subject to normal use for the purpose for which the boat was designed; has not been subject to misuse, negligence, or accident; and has not been repaired by persons other than BUILDER in any respect which in the judgment of the BUILDER affects the condition or operation of the boat. As to parts or components that are warranted free from defects in workmanship and/or materials by their manufacturers or others not parties to this Agreement, the OWNER agrees to accept such warranties, and the rights and responsibilities provided for thereunder, in place of any warranties of the BUILDER.

9. CHANGE ORDERS. Alterations to or extra work on the boat shall be authorized only by written Change Order. Change Orders will set forth in detail a precise description of the changes, alterations, additions, or deletions to be made. The Change Order will also state the amount of money, if any, to be paid in addition to, or credited against, the contract

price payable by the OWNER to the BUILDER. Any changes in the amount of money payable by the OWNER to the BUILDER provided for under any Change Order will be cumulative.

**10. INSURANCE AND RISK OF LOSS.** Once the boat is assigned a hull number by the BUILDER, it will be the OWNER's responsibility to insure the boat and all accessories, components, and equipment incorporated, or intended to be incorporated, in it against all insurable risks of physical loss, damage, or casualty. OWNER will bear all cost of said insurance. After assignment of a hull number, OWNER will bear all risk of loss to the boat, and all accessories, components, and equipment at and after the time the OWNER is required to provide insurance, whether or not OWNER acquires or maintains such insurance and whether or not any particular risk or peril that may cause loss, damage, or destruction of the boat or any such accessories, components, or equipment are, or may have been, a risk or peril covered by any such insurance. BUILDER will not be responsible, directly or indirectly, to the OWNER or to any party who may succeed to any rights, claims, or interests of the OWNER by assignment, subrogation, or otherwise, for any physical loss, damage, or casualty suffered by the OWNER, the boat or any accessories, components, or equipment, regardless of when it occurs and regardless of its cause. It is expressly understood and agreed that the Contract Price provided for herein has been established in part, in consideration of the terms, provisions, and legal effect of this paragraph.

**11. OWNER-FURNISHED MATERIAL.** OWNER shall furnish to BUILDER without cost, and with transportation charges paid, that material set forth in the specifications as being owner-furnished, for installation by BUILDER. Owner-furnished material shall be delivered to BUILDER in sufficient time to enable BUILDER to construct the boat in an orderly and efficient manner. BUILDER shall notify OWNER within _____ ( ) days of the date of this Agreement, when the owner-furnished material shall be needed.

**12. DISPUTE RESOLUTION.** In the event of a disagreement that cannot be settled through direct discussions, the parties agree to first attempt resolution of the dispute through mediation by and through the American Arbitration Association. Any controversy or dispute not settled through mediation shall be settled by arbitration. Such arbitration shall be effected by an arbitrator selected as hereinafter provided and shall be conducted in accordance with the rules existing at the date thereof of the American Arbitration Association. The dispute shall be submitted to an arbitrator who shall be selected by the American Arbitration Association and who shall have had at least ten (10) years' experience in the boat-building business. The meetings of the arbitrator shall be held at such place or places as may be selected by the arbitrator. Judgment may be entered or any award rendered by the arbitrator in any state court having jurisdiction. Each party shall bear equally the costs of the fees and expenses of the arbitrator.

13. NOTICES. Notices shall be either personally served or shall be sent certified mail, return receipt requested, and by first-class mail to BUILDER at:

_____

_____

and to OWNER at:

_____

_____

The parties will notify each other of any change of address in writing.

14. BINDING EFFECT. This Agreement shall be binding upon the heirs, executors, administrators, successors, and assigns of the parties hereto.

15. NO WAIVER. The failure of either party to this Agreement to insist on the performance of any of the terms and conditions of this Agreement, or the waiver of any breach of any of the terms and conditions of this Agreement, shall not be construed as thereafter waiving any such terms and conditions, but the terms and conditions shall continue and remain in full force and effect as if no such forbearance or waiver had occurred.

16. GOVERNING LAW. It is agreed that this Agreement shall be governed by, construed, and enforced in accordance with the laws of the State of _____.

17. ATTORNEY FEES. In the event any arbitration or legal action is filed in relation to this Agreement, the unsuccessful party in the arbitra-

tion or legal action shall pay to the successful party, in addition to all the sums that either party may be called on to pay, a reasonable sum for the successful party's attorney fees.

**18. EFFECT OF PARTIAL INVALIDITY.** The invalidity of any portion of this Agreement shall not be deemed to affect validity of any other provision.

**19. ENTIRE AGREEMENT.** The Agreement constitutes the entire agreement of the parties and supersedes all prior agreements and understandings, written or oral. This Agreement may be amended only in writing executed by both parties.

**IN WITNESS WHEREOF,** the parties hereto have set their hands to this Agreement the day and year first above written.

By _____

President

ATTEST:

_____
Secretary

OWNER:

STATE OF _____)

)ss.

COUNTY OF _____)

On this day personally appeared before me _____ to me known to be the President of _____, described in and who executed the within and foregoing instrument as BUILDER, and acknowledged that he/she/they signed the same as the free and voluntary act and deed of _____, for the uses and purposes therein mentioned.

GIVEN under my hand and official seal this _____ day of _____, 199__.

_____

Notary Public in and for the State
of _____, residing at_____.
My appointment expires:_____

STATE OF _____)
                   ) ss.
COUNTY OF _____)

On this day personally appeared before me _____ to me known to be the person(s) described in and who executed the within and foregoing instrument as OWNER, and acknowledged that he/she/they signed the same as his/her/their free and voluntary act and deed for the uses and purposes therein mentioned.

GIVEN under my hand and official seal this _____ day of _____, 199__.

_____

Notary Public in and for the State
of _____, residing at_____.
My appointment expires:_____

# Appendix C

## CO-OWNERSHIP
## AGREEMENT

THIS AGREEMENT entered into this ___ day of _____,
199__, between _____
and _____,
WITNESSETH:

WHEREAS, the parties to this Agreement are desirous of entering into co-ownership of a boat for the sole purpose of recreational activity, and

WHEREAS, the parties are desirous of setting forth their understanding and expectations concerning their respective obligations.

NOW, THEREFORE, in consideration of the mutual covenants and promises herein contained, the parties agree as follows:

1. TERMS. The word "party" or "parties" refers to the parties to this Agreement. The terms "vessel", "yacht," and "boat" refer to the watercraft that is the subject of this Agreement, and includes all equipment on the boat as of the date of this Agreement or whenever the boat is purchased, as well as any equipment that is purchased jointly by the parties as replacement of existing equipment or additional equipment. The term "equipment" includes all machinery, dinghies, gear, sails, tackle, rigging, trailers, cradles, furniture, utensils, and anything else purchased jointly by the parties and used in connection with the boat.

2. OWNERSHIP. Each of the parties to this Agreement shall hold an equal, undivided interest in a _____ <type of boat>, built in the year _____, bearing the name _____

_____ and the HID # _____,
and documented with the United States Coast Guard <and/or registered>
in the State of _____, and titled in the name of
_____, who shall hold title for the parties in
accordance with the terms of this Agreement.

3. STATUS OF PARTIES. It is specifically understood and agreed
between the parties that this Agreement extends only, and is limited to, the
rights and obligations under this Agreement, and nothing herein shall be
construed to constitute either party the agent or general partner of the
other, nor in any manner to limit the parties in the carrying on of their
respective businesses or activities other than the activities included within
the scope of this Agreement.

4. LIEN PROHIBITION. Except where specifically permitted by this
Agreement or with the unanimous consent of the parties, neither party
shall permit or cause the transfer, pledge, assignment, or hypothecation of
any interest in the vessel. Neither party shall allow any lien to attach to the
vessel. Any party violating this provision shall reimburse the other parties
for any losses they may suffer as the result of the lien or obligation, including attorney fees, costs, and expenses and shall immediately take steps to
cause the lien or other obligation to be satisfied and released.

5. INSURANCE. The parties shall at all times maintain insurance on
the vessel as follows:

    a. Hull insurance covering the vessel in the amount of
_____ Dollars ($_____), with a deductible of
_____ Dollars ($_____);

    b. Protection and indemnity insurance, with liability limits in
the amount of _____ Dollars ($_____);

    c. Medical payments coverage of not less than _____
Dollars ($_____) per person.

The policies shall name all parties to this Agreement as insured and
shall specify _____ as its navigational
limits with coverage in effect during all time that the boat is in use. No
party shall make use of the vessel unless full coverage is in effect, nor shall
the vessel be removed from the cruising area specified in the insurance
coverage without policy coverage being extended. In the event of a loss,

proceeds shall first be used to repair or replace the vessel, and in the case of a total loss, proceeds shall be distributed to the parties as their interests in this Agreement shall appear.

6. UNINSURED DAMAGES. If the vessel suffers damage for which the parties are not fully indemnified, their liability shall be as follows:

a. Damages due to wear and tear, hidden defects, unavoidable accidents, and through joint negligence of the parties shall be shared by the parties jointly in proportion to their ownership interests.

b. For damages resulting from the negligence of a party, that party shall be liable for all or any part of damages not covered by insurance or not paid by insurance.

c. A party shall be liable for all damages resulting from the unauthorized use of the vessel or from permitting a third party to use the vessel in violation of this Agreement, including, but not limited to, damages to the vessel, loss of use, costs associated with the damages, as well as all other damages permitted by law or this Agreement.

7. UNAUTHORIZED USE. The vessel shall not be used nor shall a party authorize its use when it is uninsured, during the layup period, outside the navigational limits specified in the insurance policy, or in any manner prohibited or excluded by the insurance policy.

In the event of unauthorized use, the innocent party may terminate this Agreement and proceed as set forth in the paragraph concerning voluntary sale. In addition, the party involved in the unauthorized use shall be liable to the innocent party for all damages and costs associated with or arising out of the unauthorized use.

8. BERTH. The vessel shall be moored at _____ _____, until another moorage is agreed to with the unanimous consent of the parties.

9. EQUIPMENT. All equipment contained on the attached Equipment List and made a part hereof as Exhibit "A," as well as any equipment purchased jointly by the parties to this Agreement and used in conjunction with the vessel shall be considered a part of the vessel, and shall be permanently stowed aboard the vessel. All items purchased for replacement of the equipment as so defined shall be charged jointly to the parties.

10. MAINTENANCE. The vessel shall be maintained at all times in a

clean and working condition in compliance with then-current Coast Guard regulations. Any work to be done shall either be done by a yard mutually agreed to by the parties or shall be maintained by the parties. Each party, while using the vessel, shall be responsible for the maintenance and cleanliness of the vessel and shall return the vessel to her mooring in a clean and working condition with water and fuel tanks full.

11. USE SCHEDULE. In January of each year, the parties shall decide the use of the boat for the ensuing year. The schedule shall be divided equally among the parties on the basis of weekdays and weekends except that each party may schedule _____ (___) continuous weeks of use of the vessel.

12. RULES. The parties agree to abide by the Rules, a copy of which is annexed hereto as Exhibit B, as well as any additional rules that may be adopted by the unanimous consent of the parties following the adoption of this Agreement.

13. SHIP'S LOG. Each party agrees to maintain the Log on board the vessel including engine running times, maintenance and repair items, and any significant matter affecting the other party's or parties' use of the vessel.

14. GUESTS AND CHARTERING. At no time shall any party carry any passenger-for-hire, nor shall a party authorize the chartering of the vessel to a third party. Parties are authorized to allow guests to participate as volunteer crewmembers, but may not authorize operation of the vessel by a third party. No party shall be hired as a master or crewmember either on a temporary or permanent basis without the unanimous consent of the parties, and then only when insurance coverage is first secured providing general liability coverage for paid crew, including maintenance and cure, Workers' Compensation (if required), Jones Act, and admiralty liability.

15. FINANCIAL MATTERS. The parties shall open a checking account in a bank mutually agreed to by the parties, which shall be used exclusively for the purpose of this Agreement. The parties shall select one of their number to make purchases, keep financial records, determine the need for assessments, and make required payments of all obligations incurred by the vessel. The parties shall periodically agree to the pay assessments as needed to meet the financial operations of the vessel, including all reasonable charges and costs.

**16. ASSESSMENTS.** The parties agree to pay all assessments within thirty (30) days of notification of the assessment. A party's use of the boat shall be suspended if an assessment is not paid within thirty (30) days and shall remain suspended until paid in full. If a party fails to pay an assessment for a period of ninety (90) days, the remaining party or parties may elect to sell the delinquent party's interest in the vessel or to buy the delinquent party's interest in the vessel at a price which they determine to be reasonable and so as to expedite the sale. This Agreement shall serve as a Power of Attorney empowering the nondelinquent party or parties to accomplish the things set out in this paragraph of this Agreement and to effectuate the sale of the vessel as herein set forth. The delinquent party agrees to execute all documents necessary and required to effectuate said sale if requested to do so by the remaining parties. The nondelinquent party or parties are hereby authorized to act as the delinquent party's or parties' attorney in fact to execute any and all required documents.

**17. RESTRICTION ON ASSIGNMENT OF INTEREST—RIGHT OF FIRST REFUSAL.**

a. Neither of the parties voluntarily shall sell, assign, hypothecate, or in any other manner transfer or assign his or her interest in the vessel without first offering his interest therein to the other party upon the same terms upon which such sale, assignment, hypothecation, or transfer is proposed. For the purposes hereof, the party proposing to sell, assign, hypothecate, or transfer all or a portion of his interest shall be referred to as the "selling party."

b. The selling party shall notify the other party in writing when he/she has received any bona-fide offer for sale, assignment, hypothecation, or other transfer of all or any part of his/her interest in the vessel that he/she proposes to accept. The notice shall set forth all of the terms of the offer. The other party shall have sixty (60) days within which to accept the offer by notice in writing.

c. If the other party accepts the offer, then the sale or other transfer shall be concluded by its terms. If the other party does not accept the offer, and does not wish to continue with this Agreement, then the vessel shall be sold pursuant to the provisions governing voluntary sale. If the nonselling party approves of the original offer, then the selling party shall have the right to proceed with the original offer.

d. No third party shall be allowed to participate in this Agreement except as provided in this paragraph or with the prior written consent of both parties.

e. No involuntary sale, assignment, hypothecation, or transfer of a joint venturer's interest herein shall be binding upon the other party and the happening of any such involuntary sale, transfer, assignment, or hypothecation without the consent of the other party shall constitute an event of default hereunder.

**18. DEATH OR DISABILITY.** Should either of the parties die, his/her estate shall give written notice of such death to the remaining party, and such notice shall commence the Purchase Procedure as of the date of such notice as to the deceased party's interests in this Agreement on the date of his/her death. Should either of the shareholders become permanently disabled, or be unable to use the boat for a period of one year, he/she shall give written notice of such disability to the remaining party, and such notice shall commence the Purchase Procedure as of the date of such notice as his interest in this Agreement. In the event that either of the parties becomes so disabled that he is not able to enjoy the active use of the vessel but said disabled party does not consider himself/herself to be permanently disabled as contemplated by the provisions of this Agreement, the remaining party may submit the questions of his/her disability to competent medical authority.

The "Purchase Procedure" shall be implemented and followed according to the procedures herein set forth after written notice of the implementation of the Purchase Procedure is given to the remaining party as required hereby. Such notice shall set forth the reasons that the Purchase Procedure is invoked, the price, terms, and conditions upon which the interest is to be purchased. If the price upon which the Purchased Share is to be purchased depends upon the completion of a survey, such notice shall state that fact and shall be supplemented with the survey data and the amount of the price when the survey is completed, and such notice shall be considered final and effective upon the delivery of such supplement.

Upon receipt of the notice of commencement of the Compulsory Purchase Procedure, the remaining party shall purchase all of the

Purchased Share for the Fair Market Value, and such purchase shall be completed within three (3) months after receiving such notice. Such purchase shall be on the terms set forth in the respective paragraph under which the Compulsory Purchase Procedure arises and shall be exercised by delivering to the selling party the appropriate down payment and promissory note.

**19. INDEMNIFICATION.** Each party shall be indemnified by the other and held harmless against and from all claims, demands, actions, and rights of action that shall or may arise by virtue of anything done or omitted to be done by the other (directly or through or by agents, employees, or other representatives) outside the scope of, or in breach of the terms of this Agreement, provided that the other shall be promptly notified of the existence of the claim, demand, action, or right of action, and shall be given reasonable opportunity to participate in the defense thereof, and further provided that failure to give such notice shall not affect the other's obligations hereunder, except to the extent of any actual prejudice to it resulting therefrom.

**20. TERMINATION.** This Agreement shall terminate upon the happening of any one of the following events:

a. The failure of a party to perform his or her obligations under this Agreement for a period of forty-five (45) days after notice of such failure by the other party.

b. The filing of either a voluntary or involuntary bankruptcy petition, or other action evidencing insolvency on the part of either party.

c. By mutual agreement of the parties.

Upon termination of the Agreement, all of the property and assets covered by this Agreement shall be liquidated as soon as possible and one-half of the net proceeds distributed to each party.

**21. DISPUTE RESOLUTION.** In the event of a disagreement that cannot be settled through direct discussions, the parties agree to first attempt resolution of the dispute through mediation by and through the American Arbitration Association. Any controversy or dispute not settled through mediation shall be settled by arbitration. Such arbitration shall be effected by an arbitrator selected as hereinafter provided and shall be conducted in accordance with the rules existing at the date thereof of the American Arbitration Association. The dispute shall be submitted to an arbitrator who shall be selected by the American Arbitration Association and who shall have had at least ten (10) years' experience in boating matters. The meetings of the arbitrator shall be held at such place or places as may be selected by the arbitrator. Judgment may be entered or any award rendered by the arbitrator in any state court having jurisdiction. Each joint venturer shall bear equally the costs of the fees and expenses of the arbitrator.

**22. WAIVER OF BREACH.** A party's waiver of a breach of any provision of this Agreement by any other party shall not operate or be construed as a waiver of any subsequent breach by the party. No waiver shall be valid unless in writing and signed by a party.

**23. ASSIGNMENT.** The parties acknowledge that this arrangement is unique and personal. Accordingly, no party may assign his rights or delegate his duties or obligations under this Agreement.

**24. SEVERABILITY.** Should any provision of this Agreement be or become invalid or unenforceable, the remaining provisions of this Agreement shall be and continue to be fully effective.

**25. ENTIRE AGREEMENT.** This Agreement contains the entire understanding of the parties. It may not be changed orally but only by an agreement in writing signed by the parties.

**26. GOVERNING LAWS.** This Agreement shall be deemed to have been made in the State of _____ and shall be construed according to the laws of the State of _____.

**IN WITNESS WHEREOF** the parties have executed this Agreement the day and year first above written.

# Appendix D

# SALVAGE
# AGREEMENT

On board the &lt;name of vessel&gt;
Dated _____, 19__

It is hereby agreed between Captain &lt;name of person signing on behalf of owners of property to be salvaged&gt; for and on behalf of the owners of the &lt;name of vessel to be salvaged&gt;, her cargo, and freight, and &lt;name of master of salvaging vessel&gt; signing for and on behalf of &lt;name of salvage contractor&gt; **or** &lt;name of salvage contractor&gt; hereinafter called CONTRACTOR.

    **1. AGREEMENT TO SALVAGE; NO CURE-NO PAY; COMPENSATION.** CONTRACTOR agrees to use his best efforts to salvage the &lt;name of vessel to be salvaged&gt; and her cargo and take them into &lt;destination&gt; or other place to be hereafter agreed on with the master, providing at his own risk all proper steam and other assistance and labor. The services shall be rendered and accepted as salvage services on the principal of "no cure-no pay" and CONTRACTOR's remuneration in the event of success shall be _____ Dollars (_____$), unless this sum shall afterward be objected to as hereinafter mentioned, in which case the remuneration for the services rendered shall be fixed by arbitration in _____ in the manner hereafter prescribed: _____. Any other differences arising out of this Agreement or the operations thereunder shall be referred to arbitration in the same way. In the event that the services referred to in this Agreement, or any part of such services, shall have been already rendered at the date of this Agreement by CONTRACTOR to the vessel or her cargo, it is agreed that the provisions of this Agreement shall, as changed according to the circumstances, apply to such services.

2. USE OF GEAR; LOSS OR DAMAGE DURING SALVAGE. CONTRACTOR may make reasonable use of the vessel's gear, anchors, chains, and other appurtenances during and for the purpose of the operations free of costs, but shall not unnecessarily damage, abandon, or sacrifice it or any other of the property.

3. COMPENSATION FOR PARTIAL SALVAGE. Notwithstanding anything stated above, should the operations be only partially successful without any negligence or want of ordinary skill and care on the part of CONTRACTOR or of any person employed by him in the operations, and any portion of the vessel's cargo or stores be salvaged by CONTRACTOR, he shall be entitled to reasonable remuneration not exceeding a sum equal to _____ percent (___%) of the estimated value of the property salvaged at _____ <site of salvage operation> or if the property salvaged shall be sold there, then not exceeding the same percentage of the net proceeds of such sale after deducting all expenses and customs, duties, or other amounts paid or incurred thereon; but he shall not be entitled to any further remuneration, reimbursement, or compensation whatsoever, and such reasonable remuneration shall be fixed in case of difference by arbitration in the manner hereinafter prescribed.

4. NOTICE FOR SECURITY; SECURITY IN ABSENCE OF NOTICE. CONTRACTOR shall immediately after termination of the services or sooner notify the _____ (Committee of Lloyd's, or as the case may be)*, of the amount for which he requires security to be given. Failing any such notification by him not later than _____ ( ) hours (exclusive of Sundays or legal holidays) after the termination of the services he shall be deemed to require security to be given for the sum named in Paragraph 1, or, if no sum be named in Paragraph 1, then for such sum as the Committee of Lloyd's in their discretion shall consider sufficient. Such security shall be given in such manner and form as the <insurance carrier> in its discretion may consider sufficient but the Committee of Lloyd's shall

*In this case, the boatowner's insurance company.

not be in any way responsible for the sufficiency (whether in amount or otherwise) of any security accepted by them or for the default or insolvency of any person, firm, or corporation giving the same.

**5. SALVOR'S LIEN.** Pending the completion of the security as provided above, CONTRACTOR shall have a maritime lien on the salvaged property for his remuneration. The salvaged property shall not without the consent in writing of CONTRACTOR, be removed from _____ or the place of safety to which the property is taken by CONTRACTOR on the completion of the salvage services until security has been given to the Committee of Lloyd's as provided above. CONTRACTOR agrees not to arrest or detain the salvaged property unless the security is not given within _____ ( ) days (exclusive of Sundays or other legal holidays) of the termination of the services (the Committee of Lloyd's not being responsible for the failure of the parties concerned to provide the required security within _____ ( ) days) or CONTRACTOR has reason to believe that the removal of the property salved is contemplated contrary to the above agreement. In the event of security not being provided as set out above, or in the event of any attempt being made to remove the salvaged property contrary to this Agreement, CONTRACTOR may take steps to enforce his lien. The arbitrator, arbitrators, or umpire (including the Committee of Lloyd's) appointed under Paragraphs 7 or 8 hereof, shall have power, at their discretion, to include in the amount awarded to CONTRACTOR the whole or such part of the expenses incurred by CONTRACTOR in enforcing his lien as they shall think fit.

**6. CALL FOR PAYMENT; RECEIPT OF SALVOR.** After the expiration of _____ ( ) days from the date of the completion of the security the Committee of Lloyd's shall call on the party or parties concerned to pay the amount thereof and in the event of nonpayment shall realize or enforce the security and pay over the amount thereof to CONTRACTOR unless they shall meanwhile have received written notice of objection and a claim for arbitration from any of the parties entitled and authorized to make such objection and claim or unless they shall themselves think fit to object and demand arbitration. The receipt of CONTRACTOR shall be a good discharge to the Committee of Lloyd's for any money so paid and they shall incur no responsibility to any of the parties concerned by making such payment and no objection or claim for arbitration shall be entertained or acted on unless received by the Committee of Lloyd's within the _____ ( ) days above mentioned.

7. ARBITRATION. In case of objection being made and arbitration demanded, the remuneration for the services shall be fixed by the Committee of Lloyd's as arbitrators or at their option by an arbitrator to be appointed by them unless they shall within _____ ( ) days from the date of this Agreement receive from CONTRACTOR a written or telegraphic notice appointing an arbitrator on his own behalf in which case such notice shall be communicated by them to the owners of the vessel and they shall within _____ ( ) days from the receipt thereof give a written notice to the Committee of Lloyd's appointing an arbitrator on behalf of all the parties interested in the salvaged property. If the owners shall fail to appoint an arbitrator as provided above, the Committee of Lloyd's shall appoint another arbitrator on behalf of all the parties interested in the salvaged property or they may, if they think fit, direct that CONTRACTOR's nominee shall act as sole arbitrator. Thereupon the arbitration shall be held in _____ by the arbitrators or arbitrator so appointed. If the arbitrators cannot agree they shall forthwith notify the Committee of Lloyd's who shall thereupon either themselves act as umpires or shall appoint some other person as umpire. Any award of the arbitrators or arbitrator or umpire shall (subject to appeal as provided in this Agreement) be final and binding on all the parties concerned and they or he shall have the power to obtain , call for, receive, and act on any such oral or documentary evidence or information (whether the same be strictly admissible as evidence or not) as they or he may think fit. They or he shall conduct the arbitration in such manner in all respect as they may think fit, shall maintain, reduce, or increase the sum, if any, named in Paragraph 1, and shall, if in their or his opinion the amount of the security demanded is excessive, have power in their or his absolute discretion to condemn CONTRACTOR in the whole or part of the expense of providing such security and to deduct the amount in which the CONTRACTOR is so condemned from the salvage remuneration. Unless the arbitrators or arbitrator or umpire shall otherwise direct, the parties shall be at liberty to adduce expert evidence on the arbitration. The arbitrators or arbitrator and the

umpire (including the Committee of Lloyd's if they act in either capacity) may charge such fees as they may think reasonable, and the Committee of Lloyd's may in any event charge a reasonable fee for their services in connection with the arbitration, and all such fees shall be treated as part of the costs of the arbitration and award and shall be paid by such of the parties as the award may direct. Interest at the rate of _____ percent (___%) per year from the expiration of _____ ( ) days (exclusive of Sundays or legal holidays) after the date of the publication of the award by the Committee of Lloyd's until the date of payment to the Committee of Lloyd's shall (subject to appeal as provided in this Agreement) be payable to CONTRACTOR on the amount of any sum awarded after deduction of any sums paid on account. Except as stated above, the statutory provisions as to arbitration in force in _____ shall apply. The arbitration is hereinafter in this Agreement referred to as the original arbitration , and the arbitrator or arbitrators or umpire thereat as the original arbitrator or the original arbitrators or the umpire and the award of such arbitrator or arbitrators or umpire is the original award.

   **8. APPEAL AND CROSS-APPEAL; HEARING AND DETERMINATION.** Any of the persons named under Paragraph 14, except the Committee of Lloyd's may appeal from the original award by giving written notice of appeal to the _____ within _____ ( ) days (exclusive of Sundays or legal holidays) from the publication by the Committee of Lloyd's of the original award. Any of the other persons named under Paragraph 14 (except the Committee of Lloyd's) may, without prejudice to their right of appeal under the first part of this clause, within _____ ( ) days (exclusive of Sundays or legal holidays) after receipt by them of notice of such appeal from the Committee of Lloyd's (such notice, if mailed, to be deemed to be received 3 days after it was mailed) give written notice of cross-appeal to the Committee of Lloyd's. As soon as practicable after receipt of such notice or notices, the Committee of Lloyd's shall themselves, alone or jointly with another person or other persons appointed by them (unless they be the objectors), hear and determine the appeal, or if they shall see fit to do so or if they be the objectors, they shall refer the appeal to the hearing and determination of a person or persons selected by them. Any award on appeal shall be final and binding on all the parties concerned. No evidence other than the documents put in on the original arbitration and the original arbitrator's, arbitrators', or umpire's notes, if any, of the proceedings, and oral evidence, if any, at the original arbitration, shall be used on the appeal unless the arbitrator or arbitrators on the appeal shall, in his or their discretion , call for other evidence. The arbitrator or arbitrators on the appeal may conduct the arbitration on appeal in such manner in all respects as he or they may think fit, and may maintain, increase, or reduce the sum awarded by the original award with the same power as is conferred by Paragraph 7 on the original arbitrator or arbitrators or umpire to condemn the CONTRACTOR in the whole or part of the expense of providing security and to deduct the amount disallowed from the salvage remuneration. Arbitrator or arbitrators shall also make such order as he or they may think fit as to the payment of interest (at the rate of _____ percent [___%] per year) on the sum awarded to CONTRACTOR. The arbitrator or arbitrators on appeal (including the Committee of Lloyd's if they act in that capacity) may direct in what manner the costs of the original arbitration and of the arbitration on appeal shall be borne and paid and may charge such fees as he or they may think reasonable and the Committee of Lloyd's may in any event charge a reasonable fee for their services in connection with the arbitration on appeal. All such fees shall be treated as part of the costs of the arbitration and award on appeal and shall be paid by such of the parties as the award on appeal shall direct. Except as stated above, the statutory provisions as to arbitration in force in _____ shall apply.

### 9. PAYMENT; ENFORCEMENT OF SECURITY.

(a) In case of arbitration, if no notice of appeal be received by the Committee of Lloyd's within _____ ( ) days after the publication by the Committee of the original award, the Committee shall call on the party or parties concerned to pay the amount awarded, and in the event of nonpayment shall realize or enforce the security and pay therefrom to CONTRACTOR (whose receipt shall be a good discharge of them) the amount awarded to him together with interest as provided above.

(b) If notice of appeal be received by the Committee of Lloyd's in accordance with the provisions of Paragraph 8 hereof, they shall, as soon as but not until the award on appeal has been published by them, call on the party or parties concerned to pay the amount awarded, and in the event of nonpayment shall realize or enforce the security and pay therefrom to CONTRACTOR (whose receipt shall be a good discharge to them) the amount awarded to him together with interest, if any, in such manner as shall comply with the provisions of the award on appeal.

(c) If the award on appeal provides that the costs of the original arbitration or of the arbitration on appeal or any part of such costs shall be borne by CONTRACTOR, such costs may be deducted from the amount awarded before payment is made to CONTRACTOR by the Committee of Lloyd's unless satisfactory security is provided by CONTRACTOR for the payment of such costs.

(d) Without prejudice to the provisions of Paragraph 4 hereof, the liability of the Committee of Lloyd's shall be limited in any event to the amount of security held by them.

10. PAYMENT OF ACTUAL EXPENSES. The Committee of Lloyd's may in their discretion, out of the security (which they may realize or enforce for that purpose), pay to CONTRACTOR on account, before the publication of the original award and/or the award on appeal, such sum as they may think reasonable on account of any out-of-pocket expenses incurred by him in connection with the services.

11. NO AUTHORITY OF MASTER TO PAY. The master or other person signing this Agreement on behalf of the property to be salvaged is not authorized to make or give, and CONTRACTOR shall not demand or take, any payment, draft, or order for or on account of the remuneration.

12. DETERMINATION OF CONTRIBUTION TO SECURITY OR AWARD. Any dispute between any of the parties interested in the property salved as to the proportions in which they are to provide the security or contribution to the sum awarded or as to any other such matters shall be referred to and determined by the Committee of Lloyd's or by some other person or persons appointed by the Committee whose decision shall be final and is to be complied with forthwith.

13. MASTER NOT PERSONALLY LIABLE. The master or other person signing this Agreement on behalf of the property to be salvaged enters

into this Agreement as agent for the vessel, her cargo, and freight, and the respective owners thereof, and binds each (but not the one for the other or himself personally) to the due performance thereof.

**14. PARTIES ENTITLED TO OBJECT.** Any of the following parties may object to the sum named in Paragraph 1 as excessive or insufficient, having regard to the services that proved to be necessary in performing the agreement or to the value of the salvaged property at the completion of the operations and may claim arbitration: (1) the owners of the ship; (2) such other persons collectively interested as owners and/or underwriters of any part not less than one-fourth of the estimated value of the salvaged property as the Committee of Lloyd's in their absolute discretion may by reason of the substantial character of their interest or otherwise authorize to object; (3) CONTRACTOR; (4) The Committee of Lloyd's. Any such objection and the original award on the arbitration following thereon shall (subject to appeal as provided in this Agreement) be binding not only on the objectors but on all concerned, provided always that the arbitrator or arbitrators or umpire may, in case of objection by some of the parties interested, order the costs to be paid by the objectors only, provided also that if the Committee of Lloyd's be objectors they shall not themselves act as arbitrators or umpires.

**15. APPEARANCE AT ARBITRATION.** If the parties to any such arbitration or any of them desire to be heard or to adduce evidence at the original arbitration they shall give notice to the effect to the Committee of Lloyd's and shall respectively nominate a person in the _____ to represent them for all the purposes of the arbitration. Failing such notice and nomination being given, the arbitrators or arbitrator or umpire may proceed as if the parties failing to give the same had renounced their right to be heard or adduce evidence.

**16. SINGING OF AWARD, NOTICE, AUTHORITY, ORDER, OR OTHER DOCUMENTS.** Any award, notice, authority, order, or other documents signed by the chairman of Lloyd's or a clerk to the Committee of Lloyd's on behalf of the Committee of Lloyd's or as the case may be shall be deemed to have been duly made or given by the Committee of Lloyd's and shall have the same force and effect in all respects as if it had been signed by every member of the Committee of Lloyd's.

**17. CURRENCY IN WHICH AWARD PAYABLE.** It is hereby further agreed that the security to be provided to the Committee of Lloyd's and the award shall be made in United States currency.

For and on behalf of CONTRACTOR

For and on behalf of the owners of the property to be salvaged

_____

_____

Signature

Signature

Adapated by permission from Lawyers Cooperative Publishing, a division of Thomson Legal Publishing, Inc.

# Appendix E

## CHARTER PARTY
## AGREEMENT

THIS CHARTER AGREEMENT, effective the ___ day of _____
_____, 199_, is between _____ of
<address>, City of _____, County of _____, State of
_____, referred to as OWNER, and
_____, of <address>, City of
_____, County of _____, State of
_____, referred to as CHARTERER.

WITNESSETH:

OWNER lets, and CHARTERER charters and takes for hire, the
<description of vessel>, <name of vessel>, registration No.
_____, referred to as the VESSEL, subject to the fol-
lowing terms, conditions, and agreements:

1. CONDITION OF DELIVERY. The VESSEL is a ___-year-old <sail-
boat or motoryacht>, valued at _____ Dollars
($_____), with a length overall of ___ feet, beam of ___ feet, mean
draft of ___ feet, ___ inches, with accommodations for ___ persons total; the
VESSEL is equipped with all safety equipment required by the United States
Coast Guard for such a vessel; the VESSEL was overhauled and inspected by
the OWNER on <date>, and at that time was found or made to be seaworthy and otherwise in good condition. Acceptance or use of the VESSEL by
CHARTERER will be deemed to be an acknowledgment that the VESSEL is
seaworthy, in good condition, and fit for CHARTERER's purposes.

CHARTERER, at the expense of CHARTERER, may obtain a survey of the VESSEL by a qualified marine surveyor prior to acceptance. If the report of this survey is that the VESSEL is not seaworthy and in good condition, then this Agreement shall terminate and OWNER shall reimburse CHARTERER for all of expenses incurred by CHARTERER in connection with this Agreement, including those of the survey.

CHARTERER acknowledges that the VESSEL is of a size, design, and capacity suitable for CHARTERER's use.

**2. TERM AND RENT.** The initial term of this Agreement is _____ months at a rate of _____ Dollars ($_____) per month payable in advance at the office of the OWNER at <address>, City of _____, County of _____, State of _____. Receipt of the first month's rent is acknowledged by OWNER. This Agreement shall continue for _____ ( ) months and thereafter on a month-to-month basis subject to termination by either party by written notice at least _____ ( ) days prior to the end of any month.

**3. SECURITY DEPOSIT.** OWNER acknowledges that CHARTERER has deposited with OWNER as security the sum of _____ Dollars ($_____), and CHARTERER agrees that this deposit shall be security for performance of CHARTERER's obligations under this Agreement. At OWNER's option, this sum may be applied to satisfy any obligation of CHARTERER that may be in default, but neither the making of this deposit nor its use by OWNER shall excuse CHARTERER from performance of any such obligation. Any portion of such deposit that has not been so applied by OWNER shall be returned to CHARTERER at the termination of this Agreement.

**4. LOCATION OF USE.** The VESSEL will be permanently berthed at <name of marina> in the City of _____, County of _____, State of _____. CHARTERER shall give OWNER ___ days' written notice of any change in permanent berthing of the VESSEL.

CHARTERER shall not remove the VESSEL from the following defined geographic area without the prior written permission of the OWNER.

**5. LIMITATION ON USE.** The VESSEL shall be used only for general pleasure cruising and recreation, and CHARTERER shall not carry passengers or cargo for hire <if appropriate add: and shall not race the VES-SEL, formally or informally>.

**6. LIABILITY FOR LOSS OR DAMAGE.** CHARTERER assumes all risk of loss of and damage to the VESSEL from any cause. In the event of loss or damage to the VESSEL, CHARTERER at the option of OWNER shall:

a. Place the VESSEL in good repair; or

b. Surrender the VESSEL to OWNER and pay the lowest of three shipyard repair estimates obtained by OWNER, whereupon this Agreement shall terminate; or

c. If the VESSEL is lost, pay OWNER in cash the value of the VESSEL as set forth in Paragraph 1, whereupon this Agreement shall terminate.

Obligations of CHARTERER established in this paragraph shall be abated to the extent of insurance payments received by OWNER.

**7. RETURN OF VESSEL.** On expiration or earlier termination of this Agreement, CHARTERER shall return the VESSEL to owner by delivering it to the harbor at which CHARTERER accepted it, or at such other location within ____ ( ) miles thereof as OWNER shall direct, free of all liens and encumbrances and in good repair, ordinary wear and tear resulting from proper use alone excepted.

**8. INSURANCE.** CHARTERER shall purchase from an insurance company favorable to OWNER, and thereafter maintain in full force and effect, insurance policies made payable to OWNER in the following amounts:

a. Standard yacht hull insurance providing full marine coverage in the amount of _____ Dollars ($_____).

b. Protection and indemnity insurance in the amount of _____ Dollars ($_____).

**9. INVENTORIES OF FUEL AND STORES.** The VESSEL shall be delivered to CHARTERER with fuel and potable water tanks topped off, and with the following provisions and stores:

CHARTERER shall return the VESSEL to OWNER at the expiration of this Agreement with the same stores and fuel on board, or pay OWNER for any shortages at retail prices.

**10. ALTERATIONS.** CHARTERER shall make no alterations in or to the VESSEL without the prior written permission of OWNER. Any such alterations permitted by OWNER shall be at the sole expense of CHARTERER and shall be the property of OWNER.

**11. DEFAULTS.** The difficulty of securing an OWNER's interest in a chartered vessel requires OWNER to reserve the right of summary repossession. Accordingly, CHARTERER agrees that any failure to pay rent as required by this Agreement within _____ ( ) days of the due date or any failure to perform in accordance with the terms and conditions of this Agreement shall constitute an immediate default, and OWNER shall have the right to seize the VESSEL wherever it may be found, summarily and without notice.

In the event of such default and consequent repossession by OWNER, this Agreement shall terminate after CHARTERER has paid all rent due and any other amounts payable pursuant to this Agreement.

**12. MARITIME LIENS.** CHARTERER shall not incur any maritime liens or other encumbrances on the VESSEL other than for salvage, and shall not remove or deface any notice that may be posted on the VESSEL by OWNER as evidence of OWNER's interest.

**13. INDEMNITY.** This Agreement is a demise charter, and OWNER maintains no control over CHARTERER's use of the VESSEL except as set forth in this Agreement. Therefore, CHARTERER shall indemnify and hold harmless OWNER from and against all claims, actions, proceedings, damages, and liabilities, arising from or connected with CHARTERER's possession, use, and return of the VESSEL.

**14. ASSIGNMENT.** CHARTERER shall not assign or sublet CHARTERER's interest in the VESSEL without the prior written consent of OWNER. Owner may assign OWNER's right to payments under this Agreement by written notice to CHARTERER.

**15. OPERATION OF VESSEL.** CHARTERER certifies that CHARTERER is at least ____ years old and that <he or she> understands fully, and is experienced in, the navigation of the class of vessel chartered and is experienced in the use of the equipment provided. CHARTERER further certifies that <he or she> will not operate the VESSEL while under the influence of alcohol or narcotics or permit any other person to operate it in such condition, and that CHARTERER will neither use it nor permit it to be used for any illegal purpose. CHARTERER FURTHER CERTIFIES THAT <HE OR SHE> WILL NOT POSSESS NOR ALLOW ANYONE ON BOARD TO POSSESS ANY ILLEGAL NARCOTICS OR DRUGS OF ANY KIND OR DESCRIPTION.

**16. LIMITATION OF WARRANTY.** OWNER has not made and does not make any representation, warranty, or covenant, express or implied, with respect to the condition, quality, durability, or suitability for CHARTERER's intended use of the VESSEL excepting only that the VESSEL was seaworthy and in good condition when last inspected on <date>. OWNER will not be liable to CHARTERER for any liability, loss, or damage caused or alleged to be caused directly or indirectly by the VESSEL, by any inadequacy of, or defect in, or any incident in connection with, the VESSEL.

**17. DISPUTE RESOLUTION.** In the event of a disagreement that cannot be settled through direct discussions, the parties agree to first attempt resolution of the dispute through mediation by and through the American Arbitration Association. Any controversy or dispute not settled through mediation shall be settled by arbitration. Such arbitration shall be effected by an arbitrator selected as hereinafter provided and shall be conducted in accordance with the rules existing at the date thereof of the American Arbitration Association. The dispute shall be submitted to an arbitrator who shall be selected by the American Arbitration Association and who shall have had at least ten (10) years' experience in the boat-building business. The meetings of the arbitrator shall be held at such place or places as may be selected by the arbitrator. Judgment may be entered or any award rendered by the arbitrator in any state court having jurisdiction. Each party shall bear equally the costs of the fees and expenses of the arbitrator.

**18. BINDING EFFECT.** This Agreement shall be binding upon the heirs, executors, administrators, successors, and assigns of the parties hereto.

**19. NO WAIVER.** The failure of either party to this Agreement to insist on the performance of any of the terms and conditions of this Agreement, or the waiver of any breach of any of the terms and conditions of this Agreement, shall not be construed as thereafter waiving any such terms and conditions, but the terms and conditions shall continue and remain in full force and effect as if no such forbearance or waiver had occurred.

20. GOVERNING LAW. It is agreed that this Agreement shall be governed by, construed, and enforced in accordance with the laws of the State of _____.

21. ATTORNEY FEES. In the event any arbitration or legal action is filed in relation to this Agreement, the unsuccessful party in the arbitration or legal action shall pay to the successful party, in addition to all the sums that either party may be called on to pay, a reasonable sum for the successful party's attorney fees.

22. EFFECT OF PARTIAL INVALIDITY. The invalidity of any portion of this Agreement shall not be deemed to affect validity of any other provision.

23. ENTIRE AGREEMENT. This Agreement constitutes the entire agreement of the parties and supersedes all prior agreements and understandings, written or oral. This Agreement may be amended only in writing executed by both parties.

IN WITNESS WHEREOF, the parties hereto have set their hands to this Agreement the day and year first above written.

OWNER:

_____

CHARTERER:

_____

STATE OF _____ )
                          ) ss.
COUNTY OF _____ )

On this day personally appeared before me _____ to me known to be the person, described in and who executed the within and foregoing instrument as OWNER, and acknowledged that he signed the same as his free and voluntary act and deed, for the uses and purposes therein mentioned.

GIVEN under my hand and official seal this _____ day of _____, 199__.

_____

Notary Public in and for the State
of _____, residing at _____.
My appointment expires:_____

STATE OF _____ )
                      ) ss.
COUNTY OF _____ )

On this day personally appeared before me _____ _____ to me known to be the person(s) described in and who executed the within and foregoing instrument as CHARTERER, and acknowledged that he/she/they signed the same as his/her/their free and voluntary act and deed for the uses and purposes therein mentioned.

GIVEN under my hand and official seal this _____ day of _____, 199__.

_____

Notary Public in and for the State
of _____, residing at _____.
My appointment expires: _____

Adapted with permission from Lawyers Cooperative Publishing, a division of Thomson Legal Publishing, Inc.

# Appendix F

# State and Coast Guard Offices

## State Agencies Responsible for Administration of Boat Numbering Laws

ALABAMA
Marine Police Division
Department of Conservation &
    Natural Resources
Folsom Administration Building
Montgomery, Alabama 36130

ALASKA
Boat Registration Office
P. O. Box 3-5000
Juneau, Alaska 99802

ARIZONA
Game and Fish Department
2221 West Greenway Road
Phoenix, Arizona 85023

ARKANSAS
Revenue Division
Department of Finance & Administration
P. O. Box 1272
Little Rock, Arkansas 72203

CALIFORNIA
Vessel Registration Section
Department of Motor Vehicles
P.O. Box 942869
Sacramento, California 94269-0001

COLORADO
Division of Parks & Outdoor Recreation
13787 S. Highway 80
Littleton, Colorado 80125

CONNECTICUT
Marine Vessel Section
Department of Motor Vehicles
60 State Street
Wethersfield, Connecticut 06109

DELAWARE
Division of Fish & Wildlife
Richardson & Robbins Building
P.O. Box 1401
Dover, Delaware 19903

FLORIDA
Department of Natural Resources
3900 Commonwealth Blvd.,Mail Stn. 660
Tallahassee, Florida 32399-3000

GEORGIA
Game & Fish—Law Enforcement
Department of Natural Resources
East Tower, Suite 1366
205 Butler St. SE
Atlanta, Georgia 30334

HAWAII
Harbors Division, Department of Transportation
79 S. Nimitz Highway
Honolulu, Hawaii 96813

IDAHO
Department of Parks & Recreation
2177 Warm Springs Avenue
Statehouse Mail
Boise, Idaho 83720

ILLINOIS
Department of Conservation
Lincoln Tower Plaza
524 S. Second Street
Springfield, Illinois 62701-1787

INDIANA
Law Enforcement Division
Department of Natural Resources
606 State Office Building
Indianapolis, Indiana 46204

IOWA
Department of Natural Resources
Wallace Building
Des Moines, Iowa 50319-0035

KANSAS
Department of Wildlife & Parks
Route 2, Box 54A
Pratt, Kansas 67124

KENTUCKY
Division of Water Patrol
Department for Natural Resources
107 Mero Street
Frankfurt, Kentucky 40601

LOUISIANA
Department of Wildlife & Fisheries
7389 Florida Boulevard, 3rd Floor
Baton Rouge, Louisiana 70895

MAINE
Department of Inland Fisheries & Wildlife
284 State Street, Station 41
Augusta, Maine 04333

MARYLAND
Licensing & Consumer Services
Department of Natural Resources
P.O. Box 1869
Annapolis, Maryland 21404-1869

MASSACHUSETTS
Division of Law Enforcement
Room 910, 9th Floor
100 Nashua Street
Boston, Massachusetts 02214

MICHIGAN
Bureau of Driver & Vehicle Records
Department of State
7064 Crowner Drive
Lansing, Michigan  48918

MINNESOTA
License Bureau
Department of Natural Resources
500 Lafayette Road, Box 26
St. Paul, Minnesota  55155-4026

MISSISSIPPI
Department of Wildlife, Fisheries & Parks
P.O. Box 451
Jackson, Mississippi 39205

MISSOURI
Marine Registration
Department of Revenue
P.O. Box 100
Jefferson City, Missouri 65102-0100

MONTANA
Registrar's Bureau
Motor Vehicle Division
Department of Justice
Deer Lodge, Montana 59722

NEBRASKA
Game & Parks Commission
2200 N. 33rd Street
P.O. Box 30370
Lincoln, Nebraska 68503-0370

NEVADA
Division of Law Enforcement
Department of Wildlife
1100 Valley Road
P.O. Box 10678
Reno, Nevada 89520-0022

NEW HAMPSHIRE
Marine Patrol
Division of Safety Services
Department of Safety
Hazen Drive
Concord, New Hampshire 03305

NEW JERSEY
Motorboat Numbering Section
Division of Motor Vehicles
25 S. Montgomery Street, 7th Floor
Trenton, New Jersey 08666

NEW MEXICO
Motor Vehicle Division
Taxation & Revenue Department
P.O. Box 1028
Santa Fe, New Mexico 87504-1028

NEW YORK
Department of Motor Vehicles
Swan Street Building
Empire State Plaza
Albany, New York 12228

NORTH CAROLINA
Boat Registration Section
Wildlife Resources Commission
512 N. Salisbury Street
Raleigh, North Carolina 27604-1118

NORTH DAKOTA
Game & Fish Department
100 N. Bismarck Expressway
Bismarck, North Dakota 58501-5095

OHIO
Division of Watercraft
Department of Natural Resources
1952 Belcher Drive, C-2
Columbus, Ohio 43224

OKLAHOMA
Tax Commission
409 N.E. 28th
Oklahoma City, Oklahoma 73105

OREGON
State Marine Board
3000 Market St., NE, Suite 505
Salem, Oregon 97310

PENNSYLVANIA
Boat Registration Division
Pennsylvania Fish Commission
P.O. Box 1852
Harrisburg, Pennsylvania 17105-1852

RHODE ISLAND
Office of Boat Registration & Licenses
Division of Boating Safety
Department of Environmental Management
22 Hayes Street
Providence, Rhode Island 02908-5000

SOUTH CAROLINA
Wildlife and Marine Resources Department
P.O. Box 167
Columbus, South Carolina 29202

SOUTH DAKOTA
Department of Revenue
Kneip Building, 3rd Floor
700 Governor's Drive
Pierre, South Dakota 57501

TENNESSEE
Wildlife Resources Agency
Ellington Agricultural Center
P.O. Box 40747
Nashville, Tennessee 37204

TEXAS
Parks & Wildlife Department
4200 Smith School Road
Austin, Texas 78744

UTAH
Motor Vehicle Division
1095 Motor Avenue
Salt Lake City, Utah 84116

VERMONT
Department of Motor Vehicles
120 State Street
Montpelier, Vermont 05603

VIRGINIA
Department of Game & Inland Fisheries
P.O. Box 11104
Richmond, Virginia 23230-1104

WASHINGTON
Division of Title & Registration
Department of Licensing
P.O. Box 9909
Olympia, Washington 98504

WEST VIRGINIA
Department of Motor Vehicles
Capitol Complex Building No. 3
1900 Kanawha Blvd. East
Charleston, West Virginia 25305

WISCONSIN
Bureau of Law Enforcement
Department of Natural Resources
P.O. Box 7924
Madison, Wisconsin 53707

WYOMING
Watercraft Safety
Game & Fish Department
5400 Bishop Blvd.
Cheyenne, Wyoming 82006

DISTRICT OF COLUMBIA
Harbor Patrol
Metropolitan Police Department
500 Water Street, S.W.
Washington, D.C. 20024

PUERTO RICO
Office of Commissioner of Navigation
Department of Natural Resources
P.O. Box 5887
Puerto de Tierra Station
San Juan, Puerto Rico 00906

VIRGIN ISLANDS
Department of Planning & Natural
    Resources
Nisky Center, Suite 231
St. Thomas, Virgin Islands 00802

## Coast Guard District Offices

Commander
1st Coast Guard District
408 Atlantic Avenue
Boston, Massachusetts 02210

Commander
2nd Coast Guard District
1430 Olive Street
St. Louis, Missouri 63103

Commander
5th Coast Guard District
431 Crawford Street
Portsmouth, Virginia 23705

Commander
7th Coast Guard District
Bricknell Plaza Building
909 S. E. 1st Avenue
Miami, Florida 33131

Commander
8th Coast Guard District
500 Camp Street
New Orleans, Louisiana 70130

Commander
9th Coast Guard District
1240 East 9th Street
Cleveland, Ohio 44199

Commander
11th Coast Guard District
400 Oceangate Blvd.
Long Beach, California 90882

Commander
13th Coast Guard District
915 2nd Avenue
Seattle, Washington 91874

Commander
14th Coast Guard District

300 Ala Moana Blvd.
Honolulu, Hawaii 96813

Commander
17th Coast Guard District
P.O. Box 3-5000
Juneau, Alaska 99801

## Coast Guard Documentation Offices

U.S. Coast Guard
Documentation Officer
447 Commercial Street
Boston, Massachusetts 02109

U.S. Coast Guard
Documentation Officer
601 Rockwell Avenue, Room 455
Cleveland, Ohio 44114

U.S. Coast Guard
Documentation Officer
433 Ala Moana Blvd., Room 1
Honolulu, Hawaii 96813

U.S. Coast Guard
Documentation Officer
7300 Wingate Street, Room 326
Houston, Texas 77011

U.S. Coast Guard
Documentation Officer
612 Willoughby Avenue
Juneau, Alaska 99801

U.S. Coast Guard
Documentation Officer
165 N. Pico Avenue
Long Beach, California 90802

U.S. Coast Guard
Documentation Officer
155 S. Miami Avenue
Miami, Florida 33130

U.S. Coast Guard
Documentation Officer
F. Edward Hebert Building
600 S. Maestri Pl.
New Orleans, Louisiana 70130

U.S. Coast Guard
Documentation Officer
Battery Park Building
New York, New York 10004

U.S. Coast Guard
Documentation Officer
Federal Building
200 Granby Mall
Norfolk, Virginia 23510

U.S. Coast Guard
Documentation Officer
U.S. Custom House, Room 805
Philadelphia, Pennsylvania 19106

U.S. Coast Guard
Documentation Officer
6767 N. Basin Avenue
Portland, Oregon 97217

U.S. Coast Guard
Documentation Officer
210 N. Tucker Blvd., Room 1128
St. Louis, Missouri 63101

U.S. Coast Guard
Documentation Officer
Bldg. 14, Room 128
Government Island
Alameda, California 94501

U.S. Coast Guard
Documentation Officer
1519 Alaskan Way, S., Building 1
Seattle, Washington 98134

# Coast Guard Marine Safety and Marine Inspection Offices and Detachments

USCG Marine Safety Detachment
CG Supt. Center
P.O. Box 5A
Kodiak, Alaska 99619-5000

USCG Marine Safety Detachment
Lloyd Center, Room 202
329 Harbor Drive
Sitka, Alaska 99835-7554

USCG Marine Safety Office
701 C Street, Box 17
Anchorage, Alaska 99513-0065

USCG Marine Safety Office
612 Willoughby Avenue
Juneau, Alaska 99801-1732

USCG Marine Safety Office
P.O. Box 486
Valdez, Alaska 99686-0486

USCG Marine Safety Detachment
402 Lee Street, Room 306
Decatur, Alabama 35601-1855

USCG Marine Safety Office
1900 1st National Bank Bldg., Box 2924
Mobile, Alabama 36652-2924

USCG Marine Safety Detachment
Bldg. 188, NAVWPNSTA
Concord, California 94520-0001

USCG Marine Safety Detachment
Cdr. Marianas Sect., Box 176
FPO San Francisco, California 96630

USCG Marine Safety Detachment
111 Harbor Way
Santa Barbara, California 93109-2315

USCG Marine Safety Office
Bldg. 14, Coast Guard Island
Alameda, California 94501-5100

USCG Marine Safety Office
165 N. Pico Avenue
Long Beach, California 90802-1096

USCG Marine Safety Office
2710 Harbor Drive, N.
San Diego, California 92101-1064

USCG Marine Inspection Detachment
Custom House, Room 6
150 Bank Street
New London, Connecticut 06320-6084

USCG Marine Safety Detachment
Federal Building, Room 204
301 Simonton Street
Key West, Florida 33040-6812

USCG Marine Safety Office
Justice Building
155 S. Miami Avenue
Miami, Florida 33130-1609

USCG Marine Safety Office
Talleyrand Avenue, Room 213
Jacksonville, Florida 32206-3497

USCG Marine Safety Office
155 Columbia Drive
Tampa, Florida 33606-3598

USCG Marine Safety Office
P.O. Box 8191
Savannah, Georgia 31402-8191

USCG Marine Safety Office
433 Ala Moana Blvd., Room 1
Honolulu, Hawaii 96813-4909

USCG Marine Safety Detachment
Federal Office Building, Room 332
131 E. 4th Street
Davenport, Iowa 52801-1513

USCG Marine Safety Detachment
Foot of Washington Street
East Peoria, Illinois 61611-2039

USCG Marine Safety Office
610 S. Canal Street
Chicago, Illinois 60607-4573

USCG Marine Safety Detachment
P.O. Box 3391
Evansville, Indiana 47732-3391

USCG Marine Safety Office
600 Federal Pl., Room 360
Louisville, Kentucky 40202-2230

USCG Marine Safety Office
P.O. Box 7509
Paducah, Kentucky 42002-7509

USCG Marine Safety Detachment
626 Main Street
Baton Rouge, Louisiana 70801-1999

USCG Marine Inspection Detachment
P.O. Box 989
Houma, Louisiana 70360-0989

USCG Marine Safety Detachment
Port of Lake Charles, 150 Marine
Lake Charles, Louisiana 70601-5612

USCG Marine Safety Office
Hebert Building
600 S. Maestri Pl.
New Orleans, Louisiana 70130-3476

USCG Marine Safety Office
P.O. Box 2374
Morgan City, Louisiana 70280-2374

USCG Marine Safety Detachment
Mary Dunn Road, Barnstable Airport
Hyannis, Massachusetts 02601-1995

USCG Marine Safety Office
447 Commercial Street
Boston, Massachusetts 02109-1086

USCG Marine Safety Office
U.S. Custom House
Baltimore, Maryland 21202-4022

USCG Marine Safety Detachment
871 Hammond Street
Bangor, Maine 04401-4303

USCG Marine Safety Office
P.O. Box 108
Portland, Maine 04112-0108

USCG Marine Inspection Office
Municipal Building
St. Ignace, Michigan 49781-1425

USCG Marine Safety Office
2660 E. Atwater Street
Detroit, Michigan 48207-4418

USCG Marine Safety Detachment
P.O. Box 65428
St. Paul, Minnesota 55165-0428

USCG Marine Safety Office
Canal Park
Duluth, Minnesota 55802-2352

USCG Marine Safety Office
P.O. Box D-17
St. Louis, Missouri 63188-0017

USCG Marine Safety Detachment
P.O. Box 882
Greenville, Mississippi 38701-0882

USCG Marine Safety Detachment
Maritime Building, Room 126
113 Arendell
Morehead City, North Carolina 28557-4248

USCG Marine Safety Office
272 N. Front Street, Suite 500
Wilmington, North Carolina 28401-3907

USCG Marine Inspection Office
Battery Park Building
New York, New York 10004-1466

USCG Marine Safety Detachment
P.O. Box 1886
Alexandria Bay, New York 13607-1086

USCG Marine Safety Office
Federal Building, Room 1111
111 W. Huron Street
Buffalo, New York 14202-2395

USCG Marine Safety Detachment
4335 River Road
Cincinnati, Ohio 45204-1094

USCG Marine Safety Detachment
P.O. Box 129
Marietta, Ohio 45750-0129

USCG Marine Safety Office
Federal Building, Room 101
234 Summit Street
Toledo, Ohio 43604-1590

USCG Marine Safety Office
1055 E. Ninth Street
Cleveland, Ohio 44104-1092

USCG Marine Safety Office
6767 N. Basin Avenue
Portland, Oregon 97217-3929

USCG Marine Inspection Office
801 Custom House
Philadelphia, Pennsylvania 19106-2974

USCG Marine Safety Office
700 Kossman Building
Forbes & Stanwix
Pittsburgh, Pennsylvania 15222-1371

USCG Marine Safety Detachment
P.O. Box 34, Playa Station
Port Ponce, Puerto Rico 00734-3034

USCG Marine Safety Office
P.O. Box S-3666
Old San Juan, Puerto Rico 00904-3666

USCG Marine Safety Office
John O'Pastore Federal Building
Providence, Rhode Island 02903-1790

USCG Marine Safety Office
P.O. Box 724
196 Tradd Street
Charleston, South Carolina 29401-1899

USCG Marine Safety Office
A-935 Court House Annex
110 9th Avenue, S.
Nashville, Tennessee 37203-3817

USCG Marine Safety Office
100 N. Main Street, Suite 1134
Memphis, Tennessee 38103-5014

USCG Marine Inspection Office
8876 Gulf Freeway, Suite 210
Houston, Texas 77017-6595

USCG Marine Safety Detachment
Box 2, Star Route
Brownsville, Texas 78521-9217

USCG Marine Safety Office
Federal Building
2875 75th Street & Highway 69
Port Arthur, Texas 77640-2099

USCG Marine Safety Office
Post Office Building, Room 301
601 Rosenberg
Galveston, Texas 77550-1705

USCG Marine Safety Office
P.O. Box 1621
Corpus Christi, Texas 78403-1621

USCG Marine Safety Office
Federal Building
200 Granby Mall
Norfolk, Virginia 23510-1888

USCG Marine Safety Detachment
P.O. Box 818
St. Thomas, Virgin Islands 00801-0818

USCG Marine Safety Detachment
P.O. Box 291
Anacortes, Washington 98221

USCG Marine Safety Office
1519 Alaskan Way, S., Building 1
Seattle, Washington 98134-1192

USCG Marine Inspection Office
360 Louisiana Street
Sturgeon Bay, Wisconsin 54235-2479

USCG Marine Safety Office
2420 S. Lincoln Memorial Drive
Milwaukee, Wisconsin 53207-1997

USCG Marine Safety Office
P.O. Box 2412
Huntington, West Virginia 25725-2412

# Index

If you enjoyed *Boatowner's Legal and Financial Advisor,* you may be interested in the following books from the International Marine library. Prices are subject to change.

### *Boating for Less: How to Save Money When Buying, Owning, and Selling Your Power or Sail Boat,* Second Edition
### Steve Henkel

An indispensable guide, whether you're a first-time buyer of a small boat or a boatowner trading up to a larger yacht.

"There is so much solid information in this book that it's difficult to imagine how anyone who studies it can fail to derive a return many times its modest cost."—*Sail*

Paperbound, 320 pages, 60 illustrations, $19.95. Item No. 028206-4.

### *Gently with the Tides: The Best of* Living Aboard
### Edited by Michael L. Frankel

Fueled by 18 years of letters and articles from *Living Aboard* journal and the results of hundreds of surveys, *Gently with the Tides* is a powerful testimonial to the lure of living aboard. It includes information about why people move aboard—and why some move back ashore, the "perfect" boat, galley, and provisioning hints, the law and liveaboard rights, and much more.

"A must for anyone seeking insights into the wonderful world of the liveaboard."—*Heartland Boating*

Paperbound, 240 pages, 22 illustrations, $14.95. Item No. 021895-1.